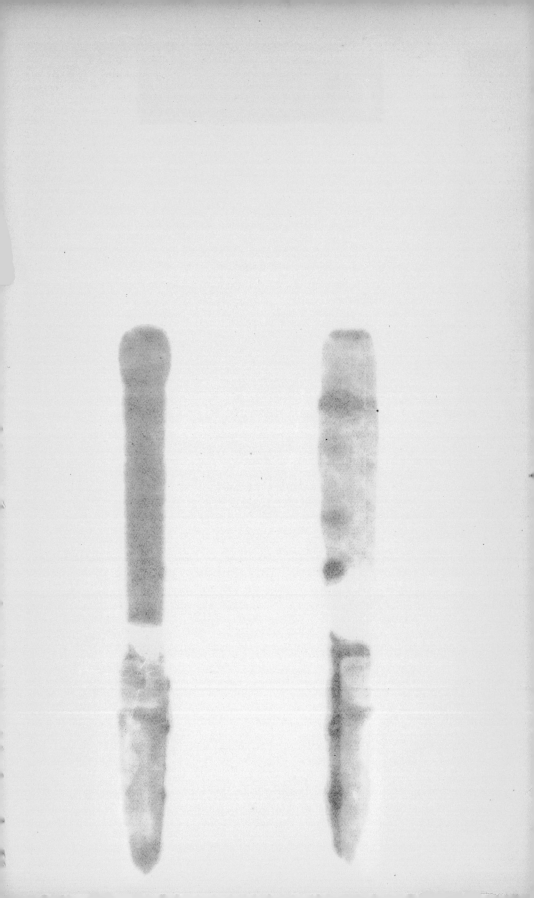

EIGHT YEARS WITH
WILSON'S CABINET

WOODROW WILSON

FROM THE WOOD ENGRAVING BY TIMOTHY COLE

AFTER THE PORTRAIT BY JOHN S. SARGENT

EIGHT YEARS WITH WILSON'S CABINET

1913 to 1920

With a Personal Estimate of the President

by
DAVID F. HOUSTON

In Two Volumes

VOLUME I

GARDEN CITY   NEW YORK
DOUBLEDAY, PAGE & COMPANY
1926

AUTHOR'S NOTE

The material in this work for the most part deals with the author's own experiences and gives his views on problems which were discussed in Cabinet meetings, or his treatment of events with which he had direct contact and of which he had personal knowledge. The record was made the day of the event, except that in respect to broad movements it was made at the end of an appropriate period, which accounts for the differences in tenses.

The record is a partial one only, for the author noted only the more novel or striking happenings falling under his direct observation or jurisdiction, and it is necessarily partial because he made no attempt except incidentally or occasionally even to indicate the views or to deal with the activities of other members of the Cabinet. He offers it, not as a complete or balanced account of the events, but as a contemporaneous record which may help to fill in the picture of eight important years and be of value to the historian.

CONTENTS

VOLUME I

CONTENTS

VOLUME I

LIST OF ILLUSTRATIONS

EIGHT YEARS WITH
WILSON'S CABINET

EIGHT YEARS WITH WILSON'S CABINET

CHAPTER I

EVENTS LEADING UP TO BALTIMORE CONVENTION

*Colonel House Suggests Cabinet Position—Vicarious Invitation
to Become Secretary of Agriculture*

IN THE spring of 1912, as the political parties began
to plan their programmes and strategy for the election
of that year, I was more than normally interested in
the political situation and its developments. I had
always been interested in public affairs and, since the beginning of my college days, had devoted myself to the
study of private and public law, American and compara-
tive government, history, and economics, and had specialized for three years in the Graduate School of Harvard in
government, taxation, banking, international payments,
budgets, and industrial history. Afterward I lectured on
these subjects for eight years in the University of Texas.
Then I became exclusively entangled in executive work
and was turned aside from my original purpose to practise law.

During my years of preparation, I was a close observer
of political developments. There was nothing, however,
in the ideals, practices, or leaders of either party which

commanded my admiration or aroused my enthusiasm till the nomination of Grover Cleveland by the Democrats, in 1884. I watched with great satisfaction the triumph of good government under his leadership in that year and, as good luck would have it, I cast my first vote for him in 1888. In a sense, I have been voting for him ever since.

I was not surprised at the defeat of Cleveland in 1888 or at his success in 1892. During the last campaign, I was at Harvard and had the very great advantage of witnessing the struggle in eastern Massachusetts. It was a stimulating, liberalizing, and reassuring experience to hear and to know such leaders and champions of real democracy as William Everett, Nathan Matthews, John E. Russell, William E. Russell, Richard Olney, and President Eliot. The last I recall particularly as a participant at a ratification meeting of Cleveland's nomination in Boston some time before the election. He was the last speaker where there were more able speakers than I had ever before seen or have since seen at any one time, and what he said made a lasting impression on me. He had, as he said, a message to young men, and it was in substance this: Democracy is a very difficult form of government. To be successful it must be based on an intelligent and thoughtful citizenship. But it is difficult for the masses to get all the necessary facts underlying public issues, and to digest and interpret them. It is of the first importance that they have frank, intelligent, patriotic, and, above all, courageous leaders to aid them, men who have an eye single to the public interest and who would scorn to mislead the people or to use government for private or personal ends. Grover Cleveland had demonstrated that he was such a leader, and young men should show their civic interest and patriotism by casting their first ballot for him. Above all, they should do their own thinking and be independent.

I shall never forget President Eliot as he stood that evening before the huge audience. I realized what it meant at that time for the President of Harvard to stand forward as the advocate of a Democratic candidate. There was an element of the spectacular in his appearance, and he was most impressive, as he, the leader of learning in America, as noble a figure, perhaps, as America has produced, took his position near the front of the platform, standing as straight as an Indian, with heels together, hands clasped in front, without a gesture, and in rich tones and effective, precise English made his appeal to an audience which listened so intently that one could almost have heard a pin drop.

When Cleveland was overwhelmingly elected, I had the feeling that, if the Democrats could and would adhere to his policies and discover and uphold leaders of his type, they would have an indefinite lease of power. But this was expecting too much; and it actually became clear, before the end of his Administration, not only that the expectation would not be realized, but that the Democrats would not have the wisdom to recognize a good thing when they had it, and to remain loyal to their leader and to sound causes. The reversal of attitude was tragic and dramatic, and finds its explanation, such as it is, in a situation which had rapidly come to a head but which, in part, was due to influences or forces of long standing.

The character of our currency, which had never been satisfactory and had been in debate since the very foundation of the Union, and which for years had been dealt with timidly and in a spirit of weak compromise by both parties up to Cleveland's Administration, had, because of declining prices after the panic of 1893, come acutely to the front. The "Light in the West" appeared and the West and South were blinded by it. William Jennings Bryan rose up as the champion of the free coinage of silver at sixteen to one. "The people shall not be crucified on a cross of gold," he cried. The masses in the South and West for a time lost their heads. They got a glitter in their eyes. They ceased to think and began to feel, and the principles and purposes of the Democratic party were obscured. The issues for which Cleveland stood and on which he was swept into power were forgotten. The people of the nation, after an interval sufficient for reflection and study, supported the cause of sound money, as they always have in a pinch; and the opponents of free silver triumphed.

The Republicans returned to power without the inspiration and high purposes which had called the party into existence, and resumed their former policies and practices. It was charged that the "Old Guard" had once more, and more firmly, resumed its control of the party and of the nation's affairs, and had become more conspicuously than ever an agency of "special interests," a tool for putting profits into the pockets of the rich. Reforms, it was asserted, should not be undertaken, because they might hurt business.

When Theodore Roosevelt succeeded to the Presidency after the death of McKinley, a new spirit was for a time infused into our national life and policies. Roosevelt was astute and aggressive. He knew the value of direct appeal to the people, and he lost no opportunity to address them over the heads of the bosses. There were few issues he did not touch upon; and he lectured from his high rostrum on everything from modified spelling and race suicide to international peace and the government of backward races. While his noise-making capacity was greater than his sense of direction, he succeeded in securing the enactment of a number of meritorious measures, and he effected improvements in the domestic and foreign services of the government. But his largest contribution was the awakening of great numbers of Republicans to a need of committing and holding their party to policies and practices more in the interest of the whole body of the people. This was a valuable contribution; but it was not obvious to some of the leaders of the party who continued in power when Roosevelt's second term expired and he made his pilgrimage abroad, leaving his friend, Judge Taft, to guide his party.

Everybody had a right to expect excellent things of Mr. Taft. He was known to be a lovable man, an upright and public-spirited citizen, and a good lawyer and judge. Roosevelt had said that Mr. Taft was the best man he knew for Chief Justice of the Supreme Court, and also for President of the United States. Apparently, he had made a good Secretary of War and a good administrator in the Philippines. It was not known how much power of leadership, sense of direction in politics, and initiative he had.

Mr. Taft was elected, and soon thereafter it began to be asserted and believed that not he but the "Old Guard" was the real leader and President; that it had learned nothing; and that it was once more playing its old game of making laws and administering them for special inter-

[5]

ests, or, as Roosevelt called them, "the corrupt interests," on the theory that if these interests were made to prosper, they, in turn, would pass some of the prosperity on to the masses—a theory which Cleveland savagely attacked in his fourth annual message of his first term, dated December 3, 1888, saying: "He mocks the people who proposes that government shall protect the rich and that they in turn will care for the labouring poor. Any intermediary between the people and their government, or the least delegation of the care and protection the government owes to the humblest citizen in the land, makes the boast of free institutions a glittering delusion and the pretended boon of American citizenship a shameless imposition."

The regular Republican party, under the leadership of the extreme conservatives, drifted toward defeat. Ignorant of the course of public sentiment, or ignoring it, it continued its efforts to hold its machine together through traffic in offices, and persisted in its policy of erecting higher and higher tariff barriers. It placed the Payne-Aldrich measure on the statute books, which carried rates to the highest point ever reached in our history; and this more than forty-three years after the Civil War; and Mr. Taft was unfortunate and misguided enough to inform the people in his Winona Speech that the measure was the best of its kind ever enacted and was a compliance with the demands of the people.

In 1912, Mr. Taft was renominated. Mr. Roosevelt immediately made a savage assault on him and the regular Republicans, charging that the nomination had been brought about by the manipulation of delegates, and that the rank and file of the party had been betrayed. He and his followers bolted and organized the Progressive party. With great show of emotion, the Progressives met in convention and nominated their idol for the Presidency; and there followed a campaign of great fury and noise. This, in substance, was the indictment: Both old parties are worse than useless. There is nothing good in them. Both are the playthings of professional politicians—mere time servers. They furnish only a nominal government. The real government is "the invisible government of the corrupt interests, by the corrupt interests, and for the corrupt interests." The Progressives only can save the nation. Their Moses will lead it into the Promised Land.

Clearly the chance of the Democratic party had come. Would they seize it? If they nominated a man of character, vision, and high purpose, if they could find and select a second Cleveland, they would win; if they could not or would not, then Roosevelt would run away with the election; for it was clear that independent men of all parties were tired of the old gangs and their futilities.

More and more the best element of the Democratic party was turning its gaze in the direction of New Jersey and its high-minded and courageous Governor, Woodrow Wilson; but the old leaders of the party, thinking that the split in the Republican ranks made Democratic victory certain, were clamorous for one of their own kind who would play the game. Champ Clark, a typical Missouri politician, was their man. They no more were aware of the drift of public thought than were their fellow Republican professionals.

When the Democratic Convention assembled in Baltimore, the issue was Woodrow Wilson. It was Wilson versus the bosses—the enlightened element of the party against the machine. It was Wilson against Champ

[7]

Clark—or, if neither, perhaps Bryan. Bryan had not stopped running; and while it was his sharp challenge to the bosses and his opposition which made Wilson's nomination inevitable, it is by no means certain that he intended or expected such an outcome.

During the interesting struggle in this Convention, I was in northern Michigan, anxiously watching the course of things, but with no thought of any bearing it might have on my fortunes, and no desire to become involved actively in political life. I had begun to see a great deal of one of the finest citizens of St. Louis, a Democrat of the Cleveland type, Rolla Wells. In our frequent contacts, we constantly discussed the situation and particularly the developments in Baltimore. We were of the same mind. Finally, when the Convention adjourned over Sunday, Mr. Wells came to my house in Wequetonsing and said that he wanted to consult me about sending a telegram to each member of the National Democratic Committee. He showed me one which he had written. It ran as follows:

MACK, TAGGART, SULLIVAN, COLE, and GOLTRA and
    OTHERS.
  Baltimore, Md.
  Clark cannot now carry Missouri, nor the country at large. Wilson can. Why not exercise political sanity in taking advantage of a rare opportunity by nominating a scholarly statesman and a conservative progressive, namely Woodrow Wilson, who can be elected?

I told him by all means to send it. He did so. It was a courageous thing for him to do, as the entire Missouri

[8]

delegation was backing Missouri's favourite son. Mr. Wells remarked that he was burning his bridges behind him. I reminded him that he had been doing that all his life, and added that he had got himself into trouble, but not into the kind he apprehended—that he would before long be called upon to render a national service in some important position.

I was not surprised when, a few days later, Mr. Wells came to see me bringing a telegram asking him to take the treasurership of the Campaign Committee. He said that he did not want the position. He gave good reasons for wishing to decline the offer, but after some insistence from Mr. Wilson, he accepted it from a sense of duty.

After Mr. Roosevelt's nomination, there was much discussion in our summer colony of the outcome of the election. Several influential Republicans asked me for my opinion and, much to their astonishment, I said emphatically that Wilson would be elected, that Mr. Taft might carry Vermont, but that I would not concede it to him.

Neither at this time, as I have said, nor for a number of weeks after the election was I dreaming that I would be called upon to take any part in the conduct of affairs. But in December, 1912, when I was in New York, Colonel House, whom I had known for many years, asked me if I would consider going into the Cabinet. I did not take the inquiry very seriously. He suggested the Treasury. I told him that, while my interests had been in economics, banking, finance, and financial history, I thought that the President-elect should get someone for the Treasury who was better known to the business world and who already had its confidence. He then asked if I would consider

[9]

the Interior or the Commerce Department. I replied that if I were called upon to take anything, I would prefer the Department of Agriculture, the one great developmental department of the government. He seemed surprised, but when I emphasized its fundamental importance to the nation, he indicated that he understood and appreciated my attitude. When I left him, I dismissed the matter from my mind as far as I could.

But, in January, the matter was brought up again. I received a letter from Mr. House, dated January 13, 1913, asking me definitely if I would consider a Cabinet position. He wrote:

> 145 East 35th Street,
> New York City.

I was at Princeton last Wednesday night and had a most interesting time.

Do you remember our talk last year about a Cabinet place? Are you still of the same mind, and would you accept one if it were tendered?

The Governor has settled none of these places even in his own mind yet, but I would like to know your feeling in regard to the matter *as soon* as it is convenient for you to let me know.

When Andrew D. White was President of Cornell he was appointed Ambassador to Germany and his Trustees gave him a four years' leave of absence. Could not this be done in your instance?

With warm regards and best wishes, I am,

> Your very sincere friend,
> E. M. HOUSE.

January 13th, 1913.

[10]

Again, on January 18th, Colonel House wrote me that Governor Wilson had spent Friday night, the seventeenth, with him, that they had talked much about me, and that he had no doubt that the matter about which he had written on the thirteenth would be arranged. He said that it was important that he see me on the twenty-second or twenty-third, or in no event later than Friday the twenty-fourth. He expected to leave Sunday for Florida to see Mr. Bryan.

I replied that the possibility of Governor Wilson's asking me to take a place in his Cabinet seemed to me to be so remote that I could scarcely allow myself to entertain it; that it would be very difficult for me to leave St. Louis; that I hoped I would not be called upon to determine the question; and that I thought the Governor could discover somebody else who could afford to serve.

When I was in New York early in February, I saw Mr. House several times. He brought up the Cabinet matter again. I asked him if the situation was at all serious so far as I was concerned, and he replied that it was very serious—that my name was one that the Governor no longer debated; that it was settled in his mind; but that, of course, he ought to have the right to change up to the last moment and would reserve the right to do so. I told him that I hoped he would change, but that evidently the matter was very threatening and that I ought to be free to discuss it with Mrs. Houston and the President of the Washington University Corporation in confidence. To this he assented.

On my return to St. Louis, I mentioned the matter to Mr. Brookings. He was not surprised, but seemed to be worried. He was good enough to say that he did not see

[11]

how he could get along without me, but that he thought I might render great service as head of a department and also as an adviser in financial, economic, and governmental matters.

On February 12th, I received the following telegram:

Savannah, Ga.,
Feb. 11, 1913.

I am writing you to-day at the suggestion of our friend. You may now confer with your board in the strictest confidence I am sure they will be patriotic and make the sacrifice   There is too much of public importance involved to admit of but one decision.

E. M. HOUSE.

The following is the letter referred to:

St. Augustine, Florida.

Confidential.

MY DEAR FRIEND:

I am just in receipt of a letter from the Governor asking me to return for a final conference on Thursday. He then adds: "Meantime, would you be kind enough to sound H. of St. Louis on the Secy. of Agriculture for me? On that case I am clear and my choice made; but I think it best for you to open the matter with him, if you will be so kind." You *must accept*. Your duty was never clearer. You do not know, as I do, how much of value to the country is involved. It is more than the one department that is at stake, and if you should fail us now, I should feel as if I had worked in vain. You may now have a more general conference with your friends, but please be firm and let them know that a higher duty now

[12]

calls. I would appreciate an early answer, and if you could veil a telegram so that its meaning would be clear to me alone that would be better. I am leaving in a few moments for New York.

Yours faithfully,
E. M. House.

After reflection, in view of the fact that I had only a few years before assumed my position in St. Louis and some important projects were at a critical stage, and of the further fact that I had limited means, I wrote that I did not see my way clear to leave and asked that another man be found. A prompt reply came to the effect that the President-elect wanted me in his Cabinet, that his plans would be thrown out of gear if I declined, and that I must accept. I answered by telegram that I would accept, if it was understood that I might retire at the end of two years without embarrassment if I decided that I ought to return to St. Louis. I added that the Administration would probably be made or marred in two years, and that I could in all likelihood get into shape within that time such ideas as I had. The reply came immediately that my suggestion was entirely acceptable. It was as follows:

New York City,
February 15.

Our friend was with me when your telegram came, and I am glad to tell you that it is entirely satisfactory. It has made me very happy. Please see that absolute secrecy is maintained.

E. M. House.

And so it was fixed.

[13]

CHAPTER II

APPOINTED SECRETARY OF AGRICULTURE

Previous Acquaintance with Wilson and House—Joining the Cabinet Without Direct Word from the President—Surprise of Governor Francis and Logan Waller Page

I FELT greatly honoured to be asked to join the President's Cabinet and to serve as Secretary of Agriculture, but for financial reasons it was a serious business for me to go to Washington in such a capacity. I knew that I could scarcely live in ordinary decency on the salary and on what little private income I had, and I did not like the idea of using my savings or of going into debt. But I felt that we were justified in going at least for a short time.

The financial problem is one which every man of limited means has to face who is called upon to serve the people in an important position either at home or abroad. We have made it possible only for men of comfortable income without undue sacrifice to serve the government in the more exacting positions and to do their appropriate and decent part in the social life of the places where they are stationed; and yet, we call ourselves a Democracy. The trouble seems to be that we fool ourselves in this as in some other matters, and that our standards are set by those who do not concern themselves about the requirements of a position, or who seem to think that to live up to the standards of simple decency is to be undemocratic.

If Democracy is the best form of government, it certainly has a right to clothe itself in seemly fashion. Our present practice is as unfair and scandalous as it is menacing. However, as George Washington emphasized the importance of a different attitude and practice in 1796 and little has been done to modify them to date, I am not optimistic about an early change. His words are worth noting and spreading. In his last Annual Message, he said:

"The compensations to the officers of the United States in various instances, and in none more than in respect to the most important stations, appear to call for legislative revision. The consequences of a defective provision are of serious import to the government. If private wealth is to supply the defect of public retribution, it will greatly contract the sphere within which the selection of character for office is to be made, and will proportionally diminish the probability of a choice of men able as well as upright. Besides that, it would be repugnant to the vital principles of our government virtually to exclude from public trusts talents and virtue unless accompanied by wealth."

I was not apprehensive about the work of the office or my general duties. I had been more or less in touch with the Department of Agriculture for a number of years, and had been dealing with the problems which it had to consider. I knew that its main function was to promote more efficient production, to improve the processes of marketing, to create better credit facilities for the farmer, to make rural life more profitable and attractive, and to make more of the benefits of modern science accrue to the rural population. In that way only could we be sure of retaining in the rural districts a sufficient number of contented, efficient, and reasonably prosperous people. I

[15]

was aware, too, that the farmers' more acute problems were in the field of economics, and in this field I was particularly interested. It was one which the economists, as a rule, had neglected. In a word, I knew that the task was one of the conservation of men and women and boys and girls in our rural districts, and that it required higher intelligence and better practices. Walter Page was fully aware of the nature of the problem, and, therefore, I wanted to see him appointed to the position, and said so. Later, I discovered that he was urging me for the place. I wish I had been able to prevail. I had said that the Department was the one great developmental agency of the government, and that it would interest me, and I believed it would interest Page more than any other man. It was the call which came to head this department under a chief like Mr. Wilson that made me willing to interrupt my work in St. Louis, which afforded a great opportunity to do something constructive in a section of the country in which it was well worth doing.

As yet I had heard nothing directly from the President-elect, himself. I had not seen him for a number of months. I had not known him very long personally, but I had known him intimately through his writings, addresses, and acts. I knew that he was trained in government, politics, and university administration; that he could think straight and clearly and could express his thoughts in excellent English; that he had high ideals and an unwavering faith in the American people; that he believed that most great reforms came from below and not from above; that with him government was an instrument for public service and ends and not for individual or class profits; that he would stand for the best things in domestic and international

[16]

life; and that we would think in similar terms on most questions. I believed that he would want the right thing, that he had great capacity for discovering what was right, and that he had the courage to follow his conclusions no matter where they might lead. I knew another thing: I knew that he was of Scotch and English ancestry and that he had been brought up in a Scotch Presbyterian atmosphere of the purest sort.

I had known members of his family intimately. His uncle, Dr. James Woodrow, was a professor in the old South Carolina College when I was a student there from 1885 to 1888. He was one of the ablest, most versatile, and most accomplished men I have ever known. I have known only a few other men who approached him in the ability to use graceful and precise English. He spoke French, German, and some Italian, and read Hebrew, Greek, and Latin easily. He had studied and taught physics and chemistry; and when I was in college, he lectured to us on geology, zoölogy, and physiology. Also, he taught theology in the Seminary in Columbia, edited the *Southern Presbyterian*, and was a director in several financial and industrial concerns. He later became president of the college. The first time I saw Woodrow Wilson was in his uncle's house in Columbia. I saw him only for a few seconds, but I never forgot him.

It was years before I met Mr. Wilson again. My next meeting was in St. Louis, when he was there to make an address before a St. Louis Club. I had the honour of introducing him. I was greatly impressed with the substance of his address, and more so with the manner of it. My third meeting with him was also in St. Louis, after he became Governor of New Jersey. This time he came to

[17]

speak before some learned society. I did not hear his address, but I met him at a luncheon at the St. Louis Club, where he made a brief talk to a group of university men. I remember only one thing, and that is that he made a rather sharp assault on experts on economics and politics, and expounded his theory that progressive impulses came from the people, and that he would look to them for support for reforms. I thought at the time that his remarks about experts were severe and unnecessary, and that he was getting, or had got, more out of his brief dip into politics than there was in it.

The only doubt I had about Mr. Wilson at the time was as to the extent of his executive ability, particularly his capacity to see a great many things in a short time, to dispose of them promptly, and to do team work. I said to Mrs. Houston, in Michigan, just after he was nominated, that I had some apprehensions about his executive ability, as it had seemed to me that, while he had been mainly right at Princeton, he had created unnecesasry friction and had finally failed to carry his point except with resulting disorganization. I raised the question whether or not the same trait, whatever it was which hampered him in Princeton, might not plague him in Washington.

My fourth and most interesting contact with him was at a dinner at Colonel House's in December, 1911. This was at the time when he was being placed before the people for the Presidency, especially by George Harvey. Colonel House had written to me asking me when I was going to be in the East again, saying that Governor Wilson wanted to have a talk with me. He added that he would give a small dinner at his house where the Governor and

I could talk without interruption. The dinner was arranged for early in December. I went to see Colonel House early and found out what was in the air. It was desired that Governor Wilson and I have a talk especially on the tariff, taxation, and currency.

Governor Wilson came in early also, and the three of us were by ourselves for a little while. Colonel House asked Wilson if he had seen George Harvey and how matters came out. The Governor, as I remember, said that he had had a talk with Harvey who asked him whether or not he thought it was true, as some had said, that his constant advocacy of him in *Harper's Weekly* was calculated to do him more harm than good; that reference was made to the suggestion that *Harper's* was supposed to be under Wall Street influence; and that he told Harvey frankly that he thought perhaps the constant urging of his name by one journal was doing some harm. Harvey, he added, said then that he would let up and seemed to look at the matter in the right spirit. The impression left on my mind was that the matter had been frankly and amicably discussed between two friends who were interested in the same thing and concerned only as to the best course to pursue.

After dinner, the Governor and I went aside in a corner of the room and were left alone for an hour or more. He asked me first what I thought ought to be done about the tariff and the currency.

I told him that I was in favour of a tariff for revenue and that, of course, the Democrats ought to come out strongly for a drastic downward revision. I added that, while I realized that the tariff must have the right of way, I considered the currency question the more important

[19]

and urgent of the two; that tariff discussion nearly always produced some industrial and financial disturbance; that in the existing partial depression, it might cause no little trouble; and that I should like to see a currency system provided before the tariff was taken up so that any storm could be more easily weathered. I said again that I recognized that this was tactically impossible, but that there was no reason why the two should not be projected at the same time and pushed to completion very nearly together. He said: "I am not an expert in economic or financial matters. In these things I shall have to get much advice. What would you do?" I answered: "To make a long story short, I would take the Monetary Commission bill, which had many good points, and decentralize the system it sought to provide; I would modify it to make its machinery simpler and more acceptable in the matter of control; it is too complex and not sufficiently popularly or governmentally controlled."

After we had discussed both topics, the Governor asked me if I would not send him a brief on each subject. I promised that I would do so, and when I went back to St. Louis I prepared the briefs and sent them to him. When I told the Governor that I would prepare the briefs, he said: "Please do not expect me to use the matter in my statements at great length or in the form in which you give it. I cannot deal with questions in that way. I want all the facts and interpretations of them I can get. I shall try to digest them—to get my thought permeated with them; and then I shall try to paint a word picture. I do not like to speak for over twenty or thirty minutes." I said to myself: "That is the artist in him."

After the last communication came from Colonel House,

[20]

telling me that my proposal to go to Washington for two years was satisfactory to Governor Wilson, I had nothing more to indicate that I was to be in the government up to the time I started for Washington, except some cards to certain functions and a note from Governor and Mrs. Wilson, from Trenton, N. J., inviting Mrs. Houston and me to lunch at the White House at 1:30 o'clock, Tuesday, March 4th.

Colonel House, through whom my negotiations with Governor Wilson had taken place, I have known for many years. I first met him when I went to Austin, Texas, from Harvard, in 1894, to lecture on economics and government at the University of Texas. I quickly contracted a great respect and admiration for him. He was then living in Austin, within a few blocks of where I found lodgings.

I soon discovered that Colonel House was very much interested in political affairs and that he was one of the most influential figures, especially for good, in the state. He had directed the campaigns of several governors, including Hogg, Culberson, and Sayers, and was easily their most trusted and useful adviser. His assistance was sought by them particularly when they got into tight places, and it was always cheerfully and unselfishly given. His interest in the whole business was unselfish. He had no ax to grind. He was human and liked the game, and, no doubt, the sense of power, and he knew how to play the game, but his first aim was to secure the best attainable thing for the people. All the public men knew that he wanted nothing and would take nothing; and they had no fear or jealousy of him.

He did his part adroitly and unobtrusively. He never

attended a political convention and disliked crowds. He was never known to make a political speech. As a rule, he saw only the leaders, and few of them at a time, and usually at his own office or residence and on his own terms. He impressed me as a most useful and valiant citizen. He could have had any position at the disposal of his state, but he would consent to have his name mentioned for none.

My contact with Colonel House did not end when I left Texas. He had already contracted a migratory habit influenced by the seasons. When it began to get hot in Austin late in the winter or early in the spring, he would migrate to New York; when the heat overtook him in New York, he would retreat to Magnolia or Manchester, Massachusetts. From there he would make a longer flight to Europe; and then, at the opportune moment, he would begin the return movement. I not infrequently encountered him at one or more of his resting places.

In the course of his travel back and forth, Colonel House spent considerable time in New York. There he began to form contacts with leaders in civic affairs; and during the months preceding the campaign of 1912 he became intimate with such men as E. S. Martin of *Life*, and Walter Page. He also became acquainted with Governor Wilson, in whom he quickly became greatly interested; and Governor Wilson as quickly discovered the value of Colonel House as an adviser. The two became intimate friends, and Colonel House was established as one of the Governor's small circle of trusted counsellors and political aids. As usual, he did his part quietly and effectively.

Mrs. Houston and I left St. Louis for Washington on the

Governor's Special, Sunday, March 2d, at 12:28. I had intended to take the regular twenty-four-hour Pennsylvania train at 12:20, and had made reservations on it for Mrs. Houston and myself. I had neglected to ask the agent not to put my name on the Pullman card. Mr. Francis, son of Governor D. R. Francis, saw it and rang me up over the telephone to ask me if I could not go on the Special at 12:28. I thought it would be simpler to accept, and I did so. Governor Major, Ex-Governor Francis, Ex-Governor Folk, National Committeeman Goltra, and lots of colonels were on board. All the leaders whom I met were very polite to me, especially Governor Francis, whom I knew well, and Governor Major; but none of them regarded me as a person of any political consequence. I wondered if they would show more interest the next day when rumours began to spread, as I knew they would.

I had been asked to say nothing about the fact that I was going to be in the Cabinet, except in strict confidence to the few people to whom, for official reasons, I was compelled to speak; and I strictly observed the request. Nobody was looking in my direction for material in their Cabinet making, and no mention had been made of me as a possibility.

I was particularly sorry, after I got on the train, that I did not feel at liberty to speak to Governor Francis, for reasons which will appear. He was, as I have intimated, an old friend of mine. He was also a member of the Board of Directors of Washington University.

I soon discovered that the Governor had something on his mind. He sat down by me the first afternoon and asked if I knew Mr. Wilson. I told him I did. He asked

[23]

if I knew him well. I replied that I did. He inquired if I had seen him lately. I said: "Not for several months." Then, sensing trouble, I asked him to excuse me, as I wanted to see if Mrs. Houston was ready to go in to dinner. After dinner, the Governor came to me again and asked more questions about my relations with Mr. Wilson. Had I been in college with him? How long had I known him? Had I had any communication with him during the campaign? I answered each question fully and then excused myself to join Mrs. Houston.

The next morning, after breakfast, I joined Mrs. Houston in our compartment. She greeted me with a smile and an injunction not to talk very loud. I asked her what was troubling her. She said that she had just had an amusing experience; that she was resting, almost napping, after a somewhat sleepless night, when she began to hear two men talking in the adjoining compartment. One of them she thought from his voice was Governor Francis. She heard him say that apparently the President-elect had not yet selected his Secretary of Agriculture; that he was anxious to see President Waters, of the Kansas State College, appointed; and that he thought he could land him at the last moment with the aid of Senator Stone and Speaker Clark. She said she could not avoid hearing that statement, but that, when the conversation continued in rather loud tones, she left the compartment.

A little while later, Governor Francis again joined me. Again he turned the talk to Mr. Wilson. Did I say that I had seen him recently? Did I expect to see him soon after I reached Washington? Did I know the men who were particularly close to him? I answered each question in the affirmative, and then beat a hasty retreat. Perhaps

[24]

I ought then to have told him that I was going to be in the Cabinet, but, at the moment, it seemed to me that I ought to observe the request made of me to say nothing.

When we got to Washington, Mrs. Houston and I went immediately to our hotel. The Governor hurried away in another direction. As I learned next day, or that afternoon, he went immediately to the Capitol to see Speaker Clark and Senator Stone to take up the task of landing Waters. A reporter of the St. Louis *Republic*, the paper in which the Governor was interested financially, met him and asked him if he knew that Missouri was to have a member in the Cabinet. The Governor said: "Not yet. Who is it?" The reporter answered: "Houston." I do not know what the Governor's comment was, but I can imagine it. My guess is that he used words to this effect: "I do not believe it. Houston was on the train with me all the way from St. Louis. He would have said something to me about it."

When he got to the Capitol, he asked Stone if he knew Missouri was to have a representative in the Cabinet. Stone said: "No; who is it?" Francis replied: "Houston." Stone flashed out with: "Who the hell is Houston?" Francis enlightened him.

Before I had finished dressing, Francis rang me up and said: "You are the meanest man in America." I laughingly asked what had changed his opinion. He said: "You need not try to keep the matter a secret any longer. The report is all over town. I am coming up to see you." When he came to the hotel, I told him all about the matter and how distressed I had been that I had not felt free to tell him long before. He accepted the situation gracefully. He said that if he had known that I would take

[25]

the place or that I was being considered for it, he would have been glad to do everything he could do to assist. He gave his paper and the reporters a very complimentary statement about me. Later he gave me a dinner at the Metropolitan Club.

Another incident grew out of my reticence in the matter. No person in the Department of Agriculture, itself, had had any intimation that I was to be the head of it until the third of March. I had met many of the chief officers of the Department, including the secretary and the chief of the office of Public Roads, the man who had created and developed it, Logan Waller Page, who was an old Harvard friend of mine. I had written to him telling him that Mrs. Houston and I would be in Washington during the inauguration and asking him if he would be kind enough to reserve quarters for us at a good hotel. He wired that there were no rooms at the Shoreham or the Raleigh, that no hotel would let quarters for less than a week; that all the prices were outrageous; but that he had reserved a room at the Powhatan which he thought might be comfortable. He had also taken the precaution to get us some tickets for seats on Pennsylvania Avenue, where we might sit to view the parade.

Late on the morning of the third, Secretary Wilson called his staff together to say farewell to them after many years of association. During the meeting, he asked if anybody had authoritative news as to his successor. Nobody said anything for a few seconds; and then Doctor Galloway said that he had heard a somewhat direct statement that a man of the name of Houston, of St. Louis, had been selected. The Secretary asked what Houston it was. Galloway replied: "The Houston who was at one time President of the State College of Agriculture of Texas. You met him when you visited Texas, and you saw him several years ago in Washington when he attended the meeting of the Association of Land Grant Colleges." Page quickly recalled my correspondence with him. He put two and two together, and Sam Blythe reports that he exclaimed: "Give me air and plenty of it and put me on the 'phone instantly. I know now that Houston is going to be Secretary of Agriculture. And think of it! I have reserved a couple of cots at the Powhatan for him and Mrs. Houston and bought them seats along the Avenue so that they may have a chance to see the parade! Get me that Powhatan clerk and help me to get the best rooms in the hotel." A few minutes before one, at any rate, Page appeared at the hotel serene and satisfied, having succeeded in getting us comfortable quarters; and expressed his joy that I was to be associated with the Department and his work.

At the hotel, we were kept very busy greeting old friends and acquaintances, including Albert Burleson and J. W. Gregory, whom we had known so well in Austin. Both had only a little while before heard that I was to be in the Cabinet, and they had called to express their satisfaction. Mrs. Burleson, Mrs. Gregory, and Mrs. Houston had known one another for many years, all having been born in Austin.

Tuesday morning, March 4th, the day of the Inauguration, the newspapers carried a list of the names of the members of the new Cabinet; but there still seemed to be some doubt about one or two names. This was resolved later in the morning when the Senate assembled for the exercises of the day. It is customary for those who

[27]

are to constitute the new Cabinet to be placed together in one corner of the Senate Chamber—many eyes are kept on that corner. Before the Senate convened, ten of us were in our corner, and it was officially demonstrated that the published list was correct; but as yet we had no official status. We were where we were by courtesy. Mr. Bryan was the busiest person in the group, and apparently one of the happiest; but McAdoo, Daniels, Burleson, and Lane, were running him a good race. I was kept busy receiving the congratulations of my old friends from the states where I had lived—Missouri, Texas, and North and South Carolina. Each state was polite enough to say that it claimed me. Politically, Missouri, in Washington especially, was a trifle backward, but letters and telegrams began to pour in from my friends in St. Louis.

CHAPTER III

The First Cabinet Meeting—Contrast Between Wilson and Bryan—Wilson on Patronage—The Six-power Loan to China

TUESDAY, March 4th, marked the beginning of the first Democratic Administration since March 4, 1897, when Cleveland finished his second term. It was significan t that the first Democrat to follow Grover Cleveland was a man who, I believed, would illustrate Cleveland's best qualities and add a few admirable ones of his own.

The day was fine, just a trifle cloudy. It was balmy. Washington never looked prettier. Flowers were beginning to make their appearance. As usual, there were great crowds in the city, and a holiday spirit pervaded it.

We first witnessed the exercises in the Senate. The oath of office was administered to new Senators and to the Vice President-elect. Marshall made a brief address, in the course of which he caused the dignity of the Senate to crack a little by comparing it to a bridle with blinders.

At the appointed time, we filed out with the Senate procession to the stand where th e President-elect was to take the oath. Mr. Wilson and the President, Mr. Taft, were soon in evidence. The la tter looked well but appeared to be much more solemn than usual. Mr. Wilson was self-controlled, but he seemed to me to show signs of

[29]

strain. The sight from the stand was inspiring. Almost as far as one could see in every direction, there were people—men, women, and children. The West Point Cadets and the Annapolis Middies were drawn up near the stand protecting a large vacant space. At a command, they opened avenues, and this great space was quickly flooded with the plain people, who thus really had the position of honour, as was proper. Of them Mr. Wilson was thinking; to them his message was addressed; their voice was the one for which, in the years to come, he would listen; and theirs was the only dictation he would tolerate. He would administer the government with an eye single to their interest, the interest of the whole people. There would be no "intermediary" between the people and their government.

As the President delivered his Inaugural Message, I became definitely impressed with the thought that, in writing it, he had had two men specifically in mind— Jackson and Lincoln. He evidenced their attitude toward the people and the same faith in them. Two of his sentences were reminiscent of Lincoln: "This is the high enterprise of the new day: To lift everything that concerns our life as a nation to the light that shines from the hearth fire of every man's conscience and vision of right"; and, "The feelings with which we face this new age of right and opportunity sweep across our heartstrings like some air out of God's own presence, where justice and mercy are reconciled and the judge and brother are one." Lincoln closed his first Inaugural Message with these words: "The mystic chords of memory, stretching from every battlefield and patriot grave to every living heart and hearthstone all over this broad land, will yet swell the chorus of the Union, when again touched, as they surely will be, by the better angels of our nature."

To me the significant statements in the address were these:

"There has been a change of government. What does the change mean? It means much more than the success of a party. The success of a party means little except when the nation is using that party for a large and definite purpose. No one can mistake the purpose for which the nation now seeks to use the Democratic party. It seeks to use it to interpret a change in its own plans and point of view. The great government we love has too often been used for private and selfish purposes, and those who used it had forgotten the people. Our duty is to cleanse, to reconsider, to restore, to correct the evil without impairing the good, to purify and humanize every process of our common life without weakening or sentimentalizing it. We have made up our minds to square every process of our national life again with the standard we so proudly set up in the beginning and have always coined in our hearts. . . .

"The firm basis of government is justice, not pity. There can be no equality of opportunity, the first essential of justice in the body politic, if men and women and children be not shielded in their lives, their very vitality, from the consequences of great industrial and social processes which they cannot alter, control, or singly cope with. Society must see to it that it does not itself crush or weaken or damage its constituent parts. The first duty of law is to keep sound the society it serves. . . .

"This is not a day of triumph: it is a day of dedication. Here muster, not the forces of party, but the forces of humanity. Men's hearts wait upon us; men's lives hang

[31]

in the balance; men's hopes call upon us to say what we will do. God helping me, I will not fail them, if they will but counsel and sustain me."

And thus a great nation changed its government! And how orderly it all was, and by well-established law and custom, after all the turmoil, extravagant utterance, and heated passions. And this, too, in the face of the fact that the new government was a minority government, Mr. Wilson having received 2,350,000 less votes than had all his opponents combined. I could not help thinking that the lesson ought to be a very impressive one to the representatives of those nations where changes of government are frequently not only accompanied by violence but are the products of violence. Most so-called Republics and Democracies are shams and farces, and the peoples of few nations are capable of conducting a Democracy. We need to take great pains to see that our people are kept up to the standard; and to this end that they are not too greatly diluted with elements which lack, and probably are temperamentally incapable of acquiring, the requisite aptitude, states of mind, and habits of thought and action. We do not need to fill up the nation immediately, anyhow. We have already been too long in the hands of real-estate agents and people who want what they call cheap labour. They little consider how expensive a thing it may be in the long run. They, in fact, do not think at all. They simply feel something about their present comfort or profits.

After the Inaugural Ceremonies, we drove immediately to the White House, where we lunched. There was a large company present, including all the members of the new Cabinet and their wives. I spoke to the President but there was no chance to do more than to offer my congratulations and good wishes. He made no reference to the fact that he had invited me to be in his Cabinet, or that he expected me to be associated with him, and so I still had no word—personal, direct word—from him about the matter. From the luncheon, we went to the President's stand to view the parade, which was an interesting spectacle. The most striking figure in the parade was the Governor of Virginia, Governor Mann, I think it was, a large, white-haired, dignified gentleman, who rode a beautiful gray horse. The horse seemed to sense the importance of the occasion and to be determined to do credit to his state. The Governor was a graceful rider. He and the horse seemed to be parts of a harmonious whole; and as they passed the President's stand, the Governor saluted with a charming wave of his large hat and a low bow in which the horse seemed to join.

The most amusing and ridiculous figure was Governor Sulzer, of New York, who, riding a prancing horse, was bowing with great energy to the left and to the right to the lines of people who really ignored him.

About ten o'clock, Wednesday morning, March 5th, I was called on the telephone by Tumulty at the Executive Offices, who said that the President wanted to have an informal meeting of those who were to be in his Cabinet in the Cabinet room at eleven o'clock. We had not yet taken the oath of office, and the meeting necessarily had to be informal. The actual heads of departments and, therefore, those who could have attended a formal Cabinet meeting were the hold-over Republicans.

This was to me a very interesting call. Naturally, I was not a little affected by it. There was to me an ele-

[33]

ment of unreality about the situation. It seemed that I was taking part in a play. It is a novel thing to be about to become a part of a great government. Very many Americans have this novel experience, since we have no governing class which stays in public life. Men participate for a while in the administration of the nation's business, and then, as a rule, disappear permanently. This is one of our sources of weakness.

I went to the Executive Offices a little before eleven o'clock. There were still many visitors in the city; and they were thick on the sidewalks near the White House and about the White House grounds. They eagerly gazed at everybody who went into the White House just as I would have done; and, in fact, as I seemed to feel myself doing. I seemed to be two persons, one of them going in to take his place at the conference table of the President of the United States, the other watching him from the side lines.

When I appeared at the main door of the Executive Offices, the attendants, by some magic, recognized me, and one of them conducted me to the door of the Cabinet room. This room is on the right of the President's office at the end toward the White House. It is rectangular and is sufficiently large to hold comfortably the long broad table at the end of which the President sits with five members of the Cabinet on each side arranged in order of precedence, that is, according to the date of the creation of the departments, as follows: the Secretary of State on the right, the Secretary of the Treasury on the left, next to the President, then the Secretary of War and the Attorney General, the Postmaster General and the Secretary of the Navy, the Secretary of the Interior and the Secretary of

Agriculture, and the Secretary of Commerce and the Secretary of Labour.

When I reached the Cabinet room I found there most of my associates. Josephus Daniels appeared to be hugely enjoying the experience. He was having sensations at the rate of a dozen a minute. He came toward me, exclaiming: "Isn't it great? Isn't it wonderful?" Secretary Redfield also was having numerous palpitations, with Burleson and Garrison as close seconds. McReynolds, Lane, and William B. Wilson were taking the experience calmly. McAdoo, I imagined, was saying to himself: "How in the mischief did I get here and what am I doing?" And Bryan!!

The President slipped in quietly, looking very trim, alert, and well, greeted us charmingly, and took his seat at the head of the table. He acted as naturally as if he had been doing the same thing all his life. He was not in the least nervous. He seemed to have a firm grip on himself and on the situation. I felt that he knew where he was going and how he proposed to get there. I recalled that he had been studying government all his life, and that he had had several years of experience as Governor of New Jersey. There was no mark of the recruit about him.

After a brief pause, he said: "Gentlemen, I thought we had better come together and talk about getting started on our way."

After a few good stories and some witty remarks from the President, Bryan, and others, we discussed when we should take the oath of office. It was agreed that as many as possible should be sworn in that afternoon, if the Senate had acted and confirmed our nominations. Each

[35]

of the others said that, in conformity with custom, the head of his department had called and had asked his pleasure about assuming his duties. As yet I had had no word of any kind from Secretary Wilson of the Department of Agriculture. Some matters of patronage were mentioned, but nothing of consequence was considered. The President decided that the first regular Cabinet would be held the next day, Thursday, at eleven o'clock.

As I sat at my place at the table, I found myself looking constantly at the man at the big end of it and at the man at his right, his Secretary of State. I had long known and watched both of them. I knew that they were about as different as it was possible for men to be. I had watched Bryan for more than twenty years. My attention was first called to him when he made a speech on the tariff in Congress about 1892. Some time afterward, I was visiting in Darlington, S. C. I called to see an old friend, Congressman George W. Dargan. This gentleman belonged to one of the old Carolina families and to the old school, and was one of its finest types. He was a charming man, a fine lawyer, and a student of affairs. He had great self-respect and, therefore, great courage. He was one of the best representatives South Carolina or any other state ever had. He was a Cleveland Democrat. Nearly every precinct in his district, after the free-silver movement got well under way, instructed Mr. Dargan to vote for the free coinage of silver at sixteen to one; but he not only did not do so; he made one of the three best speeches against the proposal that were heard in Congress during that struggle. Of course, he was left at home in the next election, much to the loss of the state and the nation.

© *Harris & Ewing*

The first meeting of President Wilson's Cabinet in 1913

When I saw Mr. Dargan, I spoke of the Mr. Bryan who had made a speech on the tariff and asked him what he thought of him. He answered: "He has a fine voice and a good presence, but he really doesn't know anything at all." I was to be reminded of this opinion many a time —the first time in Fort Worth, Texas, early in 1895, when I heard Bryan for more than two hours on the silver question. I discovered that one could drive a prairie schooner through any part of his argument and never scrape against a fact or a sound statement.

Well, this man was now sitting on Woodrow Wilson's right as his Secretary of State—on the right of the man who had leaped into the place which Bryan had tried for twenty years to reach. He had never been successful, or tried out, in anything except in speaking or writing; while Wilson excelled him certainly as a writer and had demonstrated his ability also to act and to act wisely. Wilson, I reflected, is a student: Bryan is not. Wilson searches for facts, masters them, and interprets them. He knows history and has its teachings at his command. Bryan has never been a student. He has natural ability, but is untrained. He does not examine a question with a view to get all the pertinent facts, to analyse them, to interpret them, and to draw the fair and sound conclusion from them. Rather, he has impulses, mainly in the field of morals, and is constantly on the alert to get something which has been represented to him as a fact to support or to sustain his impulses. Wilson has a keen sense of direction; Bryan an uncanny sense for the wrong direction. Both, I believe, are men of high character and good intentions. Bryan, I believe, is honest. I think he is merely ignorant and unpractical. They are

[37]

among the best public speakers in America, each in his own field: Bryan shining before a popular audience, Wilson before a discriminating one. Both are religious—Christians of a type now somewhat rare.

Which of these men will be the master? Which will dominate? There is no real doubt in my own mind. If there had been, it would have been dispelled within the first few minutes of our meeting. It is apparent that Mr. Bryan is setting out to follow the President's lead. He is obviously gentle natured, unsophisticated, and deferential to the office—unless he is playing a game. He seems to be happy in his position, the second he has held in the Federal government.

Not having heard from Secretary Wilson, I sent word to him that, if it would be convenient to him, I would take the oath of office Thursday morning at ten o'clock. He replied that he would make the necessary arrangements. When I appeared at the office of the Secretary at the appointed time, I found him, the Chiefs of the Bureaux, a delegation of Missourians, headed by Governors Francis, Major, and Folk, and Edward Goltra, National Committeeman, and a few of my old friends.

The oath was administered by a notary public attached to one of the divisions—the affair was distinctly informal, and, in a sense, casual. I appeared at the office without anybody to vouch for me. I had no credentials in my hands. My commission had been signed, but I did not have it in my possession. In fact, up to that moment I had no direct word from the President, oral or written, that I was to be the Secretary of Agriculture. In such fashion I became head of this important department of the government.

[38]

At the close of the function, after the visitors disappeared, Secretary Wilson spoke to me about a number of the employees of his immediate office and said that, if I wished to retain them, I would find them efficient and loyal. I told him that I did not expect to make any changes. Fortunately, nearly all the positions in the Department are in the classified service; and there is little chance for the office seeker. As the Secretary was leaving, I offered him the use of the Department carriage and team as long as he remained in the city; but he declined it, saying that he would not need it. He looked at me an instant and whispered: "You can save half your salary, if you make up your mind to do so." That was the Scotsman in him. I knew that I could not do so, because I knew that I could not live as he lived. The Secretary, who was a widower, had restricted quarters in an inconspicuous apartment hotel and did little or nothing in the way of entertaining.

I discovered that there were two perquisites attaching to the office: several carriages and pairs of horses, and flowers from the greenhouses of the Bureau of Plant Industry. It is customary for the Bureau to send some of its flowers about twice a week to the houses of the members of the Cabinet, of the Vice President, and the Speaker.

At eleven o'clock, Thursday, March 6th, I attended our first regular Cabinet meeting. First of all, we had to submit to being photographed by about fifteen photographers. They were a persistent lot and kept up a steady fire till the President became impatient and told them that we had had enough.

After they left, he said that he was reminded of a very irascible man of erratic habits and dangerous practices

[39]

who became converted at a revival. The necessity of his being patient and restraining his temper had been emphasized by his spiritual adviser. He made a mighty resolution to control himself. Several days later, in a meeting of his old associates over which he was presiding, the discussion grew very heated; vehement protests were made against some of his rulings. Finally, members began to throw things. For a time, the convert maintained his poise, but when a few particularly decayed eggs reached him, he drew out his revolver and shouted: "This damn Job business is going to last just two seconds longer."

In looking over the Cabinet group as the pictures were being taken, several things occurred to me. It was not a bad-looking group of men. The President, Bryan, McAdoo, McReynolds, Garrison, and Burleson, would be noticeable in any crowd. It had very few well-known figures; in fact, only three, the President, Bryan, and McAdoo. I decided without much difficulty that it was not a particularly able group of men—Cabinets seldom are. Those immediately preceding, on the whole, were noticeably weak.

As we settled down, the President quietly remarked: "Gentlemen, I shall have to give my attention to the graver problems of the nation, and I shall not have time to see the swarms of people who want office. I shall have to ask you to sift the applicants for me and to make your recommendations. I think I owe this to the people." He said this as simply as if he were telling us that he would have to drink several glasses of water before breakfast; but its significance was obvious. The President will have time to do his work. The heads of departments will be strengthened before Congress and the public. It was clearly the right course to pursue. I knew that I would not be bothered much with office seekers because there are only four or five officers in the Department of Agriculture who are not in the classified service, that is, who are not appointed for merit: the Secretary, the Assistant Secretary, the Chief of the Weather Bureau, the Solicitor, and a private secretary or two. I determined not to bother with people seeking places in other departments. I have made it a rule not to take the initiative in any matter falling under the jurisdiction of another department and to try to be of assistance only when my aid was sought.

The Postmaster General brought up some of his troubles in connection with appointments. He said: "Mr. President, I shall not present the name of anybody who fought you." The President did not wait to get exactly what Burleson had in mind. He quickly answered: "It makes no difference whether a man stood for me or not. All I want is a man who is fit for the place, a man who stands for clean government and progressive policies." This was a blow straight from the shoulder. It was electrifying. It was only what I expected from Woodrow Wilson. That night, Bryan asked me if I was not shocked by that statement by the President. I said: "I was not shocked. I was thrilled and pleased." Burleson evidently had in mind men who had fought the President on personal grounds and who might be personally antagonistic to him. Bryan thought he included Republicans.

(The Postmaster General was, from the beginning to the end, an advocate of the merit system. President Taft had covered the fourth-class postmasterships as well as

[41]

their occupants in the classified service. The fourth-class postmasterships were retained in the classified service, but an executive order was issued by President Wilson, requiring the positions to be filled as the result of competitive examinations conducted by the Civil Service Commission. The Postmaster General, in his report for 1913, emphasized the fact that the Post Office Department is essentially a business institution, and that the merit system should be adhered to, to secure the very highest standards of efficiency in the conduct of its affairs. In 1914, he recommended a change in the law so that third-class postmasters might be appointed by the Postmaster General under the merit system. In 1915, he extended his recommendation to cover second-class postmasters. On his recommendation, the President, in 1917, by executive order required that vacancies in the first-, second-, and third-class postmasterships should be filled as the result of open competitive examination. In 1919, the Postmaster General pointed out that the Department had gone as far as it could in placing appointments on the merit basis, and that it remained for Congress to enact legislation extending the system to include postmasters in offices of the Presidential classes. He again recommended the necessary legislation. In his Annual Report for 1920, he returned to the subject and renewed his recommendation.)

Bryan is an old-fashioned partisan. If he were President he would flood the departments with his henchmen; and all his friends look alike to him. Each one is equal to every other one. He has no sense of discrimination. His appointments would wreck the government, if it could be wrecked. He smilingly remarked that we need not be surprised if he asked us to find places in our departments for his supporters. He said that he was in a different position from any of us—that 6,000,000 people had voted for him for President three times and many of them would like to serve the nation.

That afternoon, he carried out his thought in my direction by writing me a note asking me if I could not find a place for "Coin" Harvey. He could not have tried it on a less susceptible person. I had been opposed to the free coinage of silver proposal from its inception, and had regarded "Coin" Harvey and his Financial School as huge jokes. Of course, I had no place for the candidate.

Speaker Clark also made an effort to have me appoint a nonentity to the important position of Solicitor of the Department of Agriculture. He brought the man with him into my office to see me. I explained to him that the Department had the second largest law force in the government; that there were many important laws to administer; that the position was a sensitive one; that it was very close to me personally; and that I could not select any one who was not a good lawyer and who I did not know from personal experience was clean and courageous. I said that I already had a man in mind whom I intended to appoint if he would accept, but that he might decline. I said: "Will this man stand his ground under fire?" He replied: "He will stand it if you will back him up." I immediately responded: "He will not suit me. I want a man who will stand if I run."

At the Cabinet meetings Friday and Tuesday, March the 7th and 11th, the disturbed conditions in certain South American countries came up for discussion. The

President on Tuesday read a statement which he had prepared, on the Latin-American matter. This interested me at this time particularly because it clearly indicated that the President was going to be his own Secretary of State. I do not know to what extent the President had consulted Bryan, but Bryan had not presented the matter; and the President did the reading. Bryan listened with a smile on his face and nodded approval as the President read. Several members were inclined to think that no statement was called for and that we might be looked upon as amateurs. The President said that something had to be said, that the agitators in certain countries wanted revolutions and were inclined to try it on with the new Administration. He intimated that he was not going to let them have one if he could prevent it.

The President and Bryan were thinking of handing the statement to the diplomats of all the Latin-American countries. I asked why they wanted to offend Chile and Argentina, and suggested that they might as well call in the Ministers from Rumania and Bulgaria. I pointed out changes I thought ought to be made in the phraseology and urged that the statement be given to the press. This was assented to.

At the following meeting, Friday the 14th, an interesting matter was brought up by Mr. Bryan. He said that he had had a visit from a group of representative New York bankers who wished to know what the attitude of the Administration would be toward the Six-power Loan to China by banks of the countries mentioned. He had no very clear notion of the proposal. It was suggested that he present the matter at the meeting on Tuesday the 18th. He did so, saying that the proposal was that our

[44]

banks should join banks of the other nations in lending money to China, largely to pay the army, that certain antiquated taxes were to be pledged to meet the payments of interest, that the matter was to be supervised by foreign agents, and that it was to be understood that, in case of difficulty in collecting, our army and navy might be used to make a demonstration. There was only one opinion, and that was that the Administration would not give its approval, thus reversing the position taken by the Taft Administration just before it went out.

The Pres dent had prepared a statement to be used. In it he mentioned certain nations by name and by implication, and rather severely criticized them. Several of us suggested modifications, and finally it was in shape satisfactory to the President and to the members of the Cabinet. After we had suggested the changes toning the statement down, the President remarked that we were clearly an anti-acid society.

The President gave his Chinese Loan statement to the press, instead of sending it through the State Department to foreign governments. At the meeting on Tuesday, March the 25th, he referred to the matter and said that it was a mistake to have given it to the press before its receipt by foreign governments, but the oversight was not serious. The Japanese Ambassador had called upon him and asked to know his "full mind" on the matter.

This Loan policy was one phase of Knox's diplomacy. It is a question whether it would have resulted in any good for China.

The President remarked that social matters seemed to constitute the chief serious business for the greater part of Washington and indicated that he would have to limit his indulgence in them. He said: "While I am not ill, my health is not exceptionally good, and I have signed a protocol of peace with my doctor. I must be good." He added that his health was really better than it had been.

CHAPTER IV

THE TARIFF

Wilson's Message Delivered in Person—The Sugar Lobby—Farmers' Demands for Treasury Aid

THE tariff formed the chief topic of discussion at the meeting Friday, March the 28th. The President read his message and smilingly asked: "Are there any object ons?"

The tariff bill, the Underwood bill, had already been definitely formulated and approved by the President. Two of its principal features were the wool and woollens schedules and the income tax. The President said that the party was united on the tariff and divided on the currency. He said that the party pledge on the tariff must be kept, and that it would be necessary to get the party behind a wise currency measure. He added that it was possible that the Administration would work its ruin trying to serve the real interests of the people. He thought it was possible that a hostile state of mind might develop; that the next election might be lost; but that there would be a reaction. One member was opposed to his making any reference to the currency. The President and the rest of us, except Bryan, emphatically differed. The President said that he would deal with the currency problem. It was interesting to me to watch Bryan while we were discussing currency. He said nothing. I asked myself what he was thinking and what he would do. Many were predicting that if the Administra-

[47]

tion took a firm stand for a sound currency system, Bryan would break with the President and resign. As I watched him, I formed the impression that he would subordinate his views on specific economic issues.

The President referred to his message as a very innocent document. He said that he was considering delivering it in person. This greatly interested me. It would be a return to the practice inaugurated by Washington and abandoned by Jefferson, who was a poor speaker. No man would revive it with a better chance of success than Mr. Wilson. It is singular that Roosevelt did not think of it and do it.

One of the members of the Cabinet suggested that, in view of the industrial situation, the Administration ought to go slowly in the matter of reducing the tariff. The President said that a number of people had urged caution. He added: "This reminds me of a cartoon in a Western paper. It pictures a great beast of a man standing over me saying: 'What do you mean by meaning what you said?' I must say now what I said before election." This is a somewhat new note in American political life. It is refreshing. I fear that a man who thinks straight, means what he says, says what he means, and continues to say it, may possibly puzzle the politicians. It is too honest and simple for many of them to accept it.

The President referred to the rule he had made that he would see no office seekers; and remarked that he intended to adhere to it. He told us that, the day before, a man had got in to see him on pretext of public business. "After a few minutes he informed me that he desired to be appointed Governor of the Canal Zone. I simply said: 'Good-morning, sir,' and went to my office."

[48]

At the Cabinet meeting, Tuesday, April 1st, it was reported that representatives of a group of banks had been asked if they would agree to an extension of time of their loan to China. They said that they would be glad to coöperate with the government "so far as was consistent with sound business." This caused much amusement. It was a slap at the Chinese Loan attitude of the Administration—an intimation that it was amateurish and sentimental in business matters.

The matter of the recognition of China was raised. Apparently, Russia had suggested that we follow her lead in China just as she followed our lead in Mexico. The suggestion was dismissed without discussion. It was pointed out that the Chinese Assembly would meet Tuesday, April 8th, and that the convening of this body would furnish a suitable occasion for action. The President was anxious to act as soon as possib'e, because he wished to see China establish a stable government and he was afraid that certain great powers were trying to prevent her from doing so. I suggested that we had no means of knowing what course the Assembly would take, and that it would be better to wait for more light.

Somebody raised the question as to whether we had any assurance that China would really establish a republic and could operate one. The President remarked that, after years of study, he had only one final conviction on government, and that was that the same sort of government was not suitable for all nations.

This matter was again under consideration at the meeting, Friday, April 4th. It was agreed that we should await further developments in China.

The President said that he had had a death grapple with

the sugar people. Evidently the sugar people got killed. The question of the tariff on sugar had been put up to him. He thought that free sugar was not fair immediately. A duty of 1 per cent. on raw sugar after the differential had been subtracted had been proposed, and this for a period of three years. The Democrats would still be in power at the end of that time and could take what further action they saw fit. He was willing to stand for this; and if it was not accepted, then he would insist on free sugar. If this was not accepted, there would be no single bill, but a number of schedules and the wreck of the party would follow.

At this time, a representative of the sugar interest called to see me at my office. He was stupid enough to ask me if I would not go before the Committee on Ways and Means and ask it to retain the duty on sugar. I said: "Your request is most surprising. Of course I shall not go before the Committee. It has not requested me to do so. It is not likely to request me to do so. If it should, I would urge it to reduce the duties." He was insistent. He began to argue the matter. I told him that it was utterly out of the question for me to comply with his request. He began to urge the matter again when I interrupted him and told him that he did not seem to understand plain English. I finally told him he would have to excuse me as I had important business to attend to.

Two days later I received a letter from the person saying: "I greatly enjoyed my visit to your office a few days ago socially, but I was greatly disappointed from a business point of view. Heretofore, I had always found in the Secretary of Agriculture a sympathetic friend of the farmer." I replied: "If to follow without question the

suggestion of a representative of one of the most highly
protected industries of the nation is to be a friend of the
farmer, you may write me down as one of his greatest
enemies. I resent your note and your attitude." A few
days later I received an apology.

The Japanese question, the President said at the meeting Tuesday, April 8th, was again becoming very trouble-
some. The Japanese were taking offence at the purpose,
and especially the wording, of the proposed California law.
The objectionable part was the declaration about aliens
who did not declare their intention of becoming citizens.
Such persons could hold no title to land. The Japanese
could not become citizens. Apparently, California is
bent, not only on preventing more Japanese from settling
in her borders, but on getting rid of those she has. She
asserts that she will not have a large number of people of
a race radically different from the mass of Americans. I
sympathize with California in that purpose if she seriously
holds it; but on this point I have my doubts. I have
talked to numbers of Californians, and have found that
many of them object to the Japanese, not only because they
are radically different, but also because they are efficient,
thrifty, ambitious, saving, and unwilling to remain "mud-
sillers." It is their economic ability, in part, which they
dread. Many of these same people tell me that they
would not object to Chinese, because they are thrifty,
will work for little, and are content to remain in humble
stations. They object to Negroes, not because they are
of a different race, but because they, as a rule, are of
low mental capacity and lazy. Those who take such a
position are not thinking primarily of the welfare of the
state in the long run, but of their profits and comfort. I

think it highly unfortunate that there should be anywhere in this nation large groups of other peoples such as Negroes, Chinese, or Japanese. It is not a question mainly of superiority or of inferiority, but one of hopeless difference. They cannot live side by side to the advantage of both races; and intermarriage, I believe, tends to produce unhappiness and, if one race is inferior, to reduce the population to its level.

The Californians do assert that the Japanese are objectionable on other than economic grounds: that they are unmoral and should not be in contact with white girls and boys in schools. They do not say that this is true of the better class of Japanese, but of those who try to settle in California.

The difficulty in handling the situation is great. The Japanese assert that their honour as a nation is involved; but the state of California has power to make land laws affecting natives and aliens. Such laws are found in Texas, Arizona, New York, and perhaps in other states. The trouble with the proposed California law is that it discriminates against the Japanese. Another trouble, according to Lane and other Californians, is that there are in California demagogues who, even if it should cause serious embarrassment, would not hesitate to make political capital out of this situation.

The discussion was interrupted because the President had to leave at twelve o'clock to go to the Capitol to read his Tariff Message. I had a distinct sensation when this departure was brought thus sharply to my mind. I recognized both its political and historical significance. Some members of the Cabinet seemed to be a trifle shaky about the venture. The President showed no sign that he was aware, as of course he was, that anything unusual was about to happen.

The President regards himself as the head of his party and its political leader. He believes that he can lead better, can get nearer to Congress, and convey his message more impressively to the people by delivering his message in person. He is right; and his example will probably be followed till we get a President who is timid and a poor or indifferent speaker.

Most of the members of the Cabinet went to the Capitol to hear the President read his message. I reached the House just before the Senate filed in. Its members were given seats on either side in the front rows. The Vice President, as usual in joint sessions, sat with the Speaker. Each officer, on behalf of his body, appointed a committee to wait upon the President and to conduct him to the floor. Members of the Cabinet occupied seats to the left of the Speaker's desk, looking toward the body of the House. Diplomats and the public crowded the galleries. Speaker Clark, Wilson's defeated rival for the Democratic nomination, was in his place.

There seemed to me to be a distinctly tense atmosphere, as if strange things were about to happen. Members of Congress appeared to be a trifle nervous, and something of a chill pervaded the air. Some members of Congress, I thought, had a sullen look. Suddenly the President of the United States was announced and the Speaker rapped loudly with his gavel. The whole body stood up. The President, looking, I thought, a trifle pale and tense, quickly entered with the Committee, stepped upon the Speaker's stand in the space between the Vice President and Speaker at the rear and the secretary or reading clerk in front, and turned to greet the Vice President and the Speaker. Then he faced the body and began speaking; and thus it was happening again for the first time since November 22, 1800, when Adams delivered his fourth annual address.

The beauty of the President's English was instantly felt; and his first sentences relieved the strain and made for easier feeling. They were:

"I am very glad indeed to have this opportunity to address the two Houses directly and to verify for myself the impression that the President of the United States is a person, not a mere department of the government, hailing Congress from some isolated island of jealous power, sending messages, not speaking naturally and with his own voice—that he is a human being trying to coöperate with other human beings in a common service. After this pleasant experience I shall feel quite normal in all our dealings with one another."

The message was short. It pointed out that the tariff burden should be lightened; that, while the whole face of our commercial life had altered, tariff schedules had remained the same or had moved in the direction they had been given when no large circumstance of our industrial development was what it appeared to-day, and that our task was to square them with the facts. Tariff legislation had wandered very far afield. We had passed beyond the notion of protecting industry. We had come to hold that it was entitled to the direct patronage of the government. We were giving to each group of manufacturers what they thought they needed to maintain a closed market. We had built a set of privileges and fostered monopoly, "until at last nothing is normal, nothing is obliged to stand the test of efficiency and economy, in our world of big business, but everything thrives by concerted agreement.

"We must abolish everything that bears even the semblance of privilege or of any kind of artificial advantage, and put our business men and our producers under the stimulation of a constant necessity to be efficient, economical, and enterprising, masters of competitive supremacy, better merchants and better traders than any in the world." The object of duties henceforth must be to promote effective competition. We must accomplish our purpose without reckless haste. We must build up our foreign trade. We more than ever need an outlet for our energies.

"We can render the nation a service in more directions than one. We are to deal with the facts of our own day. We begin with the tariff. Nothing should obscure this undertaking. Later, currency reforms will press for action."

The next time I saw the President was at Cabinet meeting on Friday, April 11th. When he came in, I congratulated him on his address and on the success of his personally appearing before Congress. He thanked me and smilingly remarked: "Congress looked embarrassed. I did not feel so."

It would be interesting if this step of the President should lead to another—the appearance in both Houses of members of the Cabinet to participate in discussions and to answer questions. I hope that it will not. I much prefer the present practice of having them appear before committees to express their views and to aid in shaping legislation, unless we are willing to go the whole distance

[55]

and adopt a responsible government system, the parliamentary system. Nothing will be gained by trying to mix the two. We cannot get the advantages of the parliamentary system without taking everything that goes with it; and this would mean changes of a very radical nature for which our people are not ready. Such a system is more democratic in that it imposes scarcely any check to the expression of the will of the people. It would be more in harmony with our claims that we are a democratic people capable of governing ourselves, but it is not likely to be seriously considered now.

The presence of members of the Cabinet on the floor of either House, so long as they are not selected from the majority and responsible to Congress, would not greatly expedite business or improve the situation. They could not be accepted as leaders and might be subjected to an annoying hazing. Furthermore, many Cabinet officers would make a rather sorry spectacle of themselves in exposition and debate. Certainly, the majority of those in all the Cabinets I have knowledge of would. If the practice were adopted, the President would have to take parliamentary leadership and capacity to speak and to handle a difficult crowd more largely into account in selecting his aids, and in doing so might have to subordinate other essential qualities, such as administrative capacity. Good speakers are seldom men of great executive ability.

It is a question in my mind whether the President can long continue to be the formal head of the government, the chief of his party, and the leader of Congress. It may be a task too great for any human being to stand up under; and Congress will resent his attempt to lead it. He must at least have the Presidency better organized. He should have as his first aid one of the ablest men in the country, and under him three or four men of exceptional ability, one to see that problems affecting a number of departments are dealt with promptly and in the right fashion, one to establish the necessary contacts with Congress and the public, including the press, and the other to supervise the executive offices. The President should ask Congress to authorize him to do this and to give him money enough to pay a respectable salary to each of them, that is, a salary of from $25,000 to $40,000.

If the President's own party is in power in both Houses and he is willing to be a gentle leader of Congress, if he is willing to play the game of the professional politician, he may at times bend Congress to his purpose, especially if he is inclined to use patronage as a bribe; but otherwise he is likely to have trouble. And if the opposing party is in power in one or both Houses, an absurd situation, which is the rule rather than the exception, the President is certain not to be able to lead. At critical junctures, when the President has been a strong character and has seriously tried to lead, the Congress has refused to follow and chaos has resulted At such times there have developed difficult situations, menacing, humiliating deadlocks or defeats; and not infrequently there have appeared, in the President's own party, groups which were more hostile to him than were many of the opposing party. We need only recall the administrations of Jackson, Johnson, and Cleveland. After the "Light in the West" appeared, many Democrats came to dislike Cleveland more than they disliked Republicans, and more than Republicans disliked him. And it may well be doubted whether, if Lincoln had lived, he would not have suffered a worse martyrdom at the hands of his party, led by Thaddeus Stevens and Charles Sumner, than he did at the hands of Booth. Congress, and particularly the Senate, does not like a "boss."

I brought up the matter of the drift of legislative proposals in Congress in the field of agriculture, the tendency to appropriate great sums of money to the farmers out of the Treasury or to grant bounties directly to the states. I mentioned especially the proposals to lend the farmers $2,000,000 out of the Treasury at 4 per cent., to appropriate to the states large sums for extension work, and also for public roads. I said that we must meet these crude measures with those which were carefully considered and on sound lines. To this the President assented and told me to proceed to frame them.

CHAPTER V

Bryan's Trip to California on Japanese Question—Possibility of War—The Mexican Problem Looms up

FOREIGN problems continued to occupy much time and thought. China was again pressing for attention. After much discussion, it developed, as the President remarked, that it was the sense of the meeting that China should be recognized if the Assembly convened in regular and orderly session on April 15th. This was to be done through the Secretary of the Legation in Peking.

At the ensuing meeting, on April 15th, the President said that he had been giving much thought to the matter of Panama Canal tolls and that he was inclined to be against the existing exemption of American ships on both economic and moral grounds. I quickly expressed my concurrence. Bryan was inclined to oppose the repeal of the exemption. He feared that the railroads wanted tolls charged for their own ends! He thought they could, in that event, either secure more traffic or increase their rates!

The situation was especially difficult. The Democratic party had declared for exemption, possibly on Bryan's initiative, and this made it embarrassing to act. The President was in favour of rescinding the action outright, frankly and immediately. He did not wish to suggest arbitration. The Senate, he thought, was probably against either course. Mr. Bryce had suggested that the President make a statement favouring arbitration, if the law could not be repealed, but this was regarded as unreasonable.

Foreign questions were uppermost at the meeting, Friday, April 18th. China had not been recognized. The Assembly had not organized. Most of us urged that we wait further developments and information, but Bryan was in favour of immediate action. The President decided that the matter should be deferred.

On Tuesday, the 22d, when the Japanese question was raised, Bryan asked if it would not be possible to have the matter submitted to a referendum in California. This was opposed because of the known attitude of the California people and the danger of intemperate discussion. Asked what his opinion would be on a proposal to insert in the law the phrase, "ineligible to citizenship," Mr. Bryan said: "I would oppose the insertion of that phrase, unless the President has a different opinion. In that case, I might have another opinion. I am here solely to help and to carry my part of the burden."

The President spoke of having asked Mr. Bryan to go to California. Mr. Bryan said that he was far from being anxious to go, but that he would do so if the President requested him to go. It was then decided that he should make the trip, if the Governor was favourable to it, and that the Governor should be sounded. We were not hopeful that the California situation could be improved; but it was thought that Japan would be convinced that the Federal government was friendly and disposed to do all it could.

Bryan went to California, and at the Cabinet meeting, April 29th, a dispatch from him was read in which he placed before the President a hypothetical statement and asked for his views. The President declined to give answers to hypothetical questions and reaffirmed his position. Mr. John Bassett Moore was in Bryan's chair. He expressed the opinion that the United States courts could set aside a state law against alien holding of land.

At the meeting after Bryan's return from California, he gave a detailed account of what happened and stated his impressions. Politically, he asserted, there was everything to aggravate the situation. The Democrats in their platform had demanded the enactment of an exclusion law. They had made a hot fight and had forced the Republicans to declare themselves. They had put them on the rack.

The protest of the Japanese Government was read. Its terms were strong. They asked the Federal Government to declare the California law invalid. They demanded prompt and decisive action, terming the law obnoxious, discriminatory, unfair, unfriendly, and in violation of the treaty. The offensive character of the protest was something of a shock, especially in view of what the government had done and was doing and of Japan's own laws against aliens.

There was much doubt as to Japan's real purpose and meaning. Some thought that the protest was for home consumption; others that Japan wanted trouble before the Panama Canal was opened. It was asserted that Japan was in too great financial straits to enter into a fight with the United States. I expressed the view that poverty constituted no reason against her fighting if she wanted to fight—that history furnished many instances of nations waging war when they seemed to be down and out financially, and waging it successfully. I added that I credited Japan with some sense and therefore did not believe that she seriously intended to go to the limit. As to the fear expressed that Japan could take the Philippines and land an army in California, I said jokingly that I would almost be willing to whip her to make her take the Philippines, and that I would eat every Jap who landed in California as part of an invading force.

Bryan again suggested a California referendum. This was passed over. The President called the Japanese statement unfair—all treaty rights were specifically safeguarded in the law itself. It was agreed that it would be unwise to publish the statement, as it would inflame the public. Bryan was authorized to tell the Japanese Ambassador informally that the language used was objectionable, especially the words referring to California.

The President suggested that Bryan take particular pains to attempt to form an opinion from the Japanese Ambassador's manner and expressions how much there was in the protest. If Japan meant what she said, it was impossible to exaggerate the seriousness of the situation.

A few days after his confirmation by the Senate, as I was walking on Pennsylvania Avenue in front of the White House, I met our new Ambassador to the Court of St. James's, in the person of my old friend, Walter Hines Page. He was just coming through the gate from the White House grounds. As he came toward me, he was smiling. He gave one of his characteristic chuckles and said: "Doesn't it beat the devil?" I asked him what the joke was. He replied: "I am. Did you see that fellow come out of the White House grounds a few seconds ago? Did you notice the people staring at him? Did you see me among them looking at him with my mouth open? They tell me I am that man—that I am the Ambassador from the United States to the Court of St. James's. It isn't true. It's a dream. It's worse; it's a joke. I can't get used to this sort of show." I told him that I had been functioning for nearly two months and that I could not get rid of the feeling that there was more appearance than reality in the experience.

At this meeting, I was reminded of a somewhat similar experience. Before Page's appointment was announced, about March 28th, I went to New York on business. For a few days before my trip, there were rumours in the press that Page might be selected by the President to go to London. I knew that he expected to do so and would, unless some unexpected change occurred. After I got through with my mission, I called Page up to tell him I would drop in to see him, and incidentally I said: "Have you packed your trunk?" He asked: "What do you mean?" I replied: "You know what I mean." He said: "Are you serious? Is there really anything in these rumours?" I told him there was so much that he would soon be on the high seas. He asked me to stay where I was and said that he would join me in a few minutes. When he came into my room, he said: "But it can't be true. I have heard nothing direct from the President." I told him I had been in the Cabinet for a number of weeks, and had seen the President a number of times, and that I had not yet had any word from him about my taking the position. He said: "Do you mean to tell me that he did not write you asking you if you would take the

[63]

position and that he has not said a word directly to you about it?" I told him that he had guessed right and that he might be on his way to London without any word from the President, himself. But he said: "I can't go. I can't get away. I have some new important matters in hand." I replied that I could not go to Washington; that I had had some very important undertakings which stood in the way, and had said so, but that I had been in Washington for some time. "But," he insisted, "I can't afford to go. The thing will cost a lot of money. The salary will not pay house rent. The mission would bankrupt me." I told him that I had said that I could not afford to go to Washington; that I had no money to speak of; that I knew it would be impossible for me to live in Washington as a member of the Cabinet ought to live on the salary; but that I had been wrestling with the enterprise for some time. I added: "I know nothing has been said to you. Nothing may be said to you by the President himself. I know that you cannot leave your business. I am sure that you cannot afford it, but all the same, you will soon be in London, and you had better be packing. You cannot afford not to go. You are the very man for the place. You will understand and like the British, and they will understand and fall in love with you."

"That is another story," he said. "Come on. Let's go out to Long Island and talk to Mrs. Page about the matter. She will be very much interested in what you say." We went. We got nowhere. I left for Washington the next day. About two or three days later Page received a message from the President telling him that he wanted his services, and, of course, Page accepted.

[64]

On May 13th, the Japanese protest was further considered. It had been revised. The words which were offensive to California had been omitted, as had the demand that the Federal Government declare the law invalid. It was reported that Great Britain had called upon the Japanese Ambassador to see that something was done to allay feeling in his country.

The President asked advice on his answer to Japan, if he decided to make one, adding that he thought that Japan's case was a very weak one.

The possibility of war was discussed. The President thought that there would be no war, and that it would be mischievous to hint that there might be, but that, of course, we should keep our eyes open. Daniels gave his naval staff's analysis of the situation. The Japanese could take the Philippines, Hawaii, and Alaska, as we were not prepared. The President said that they might do so, but that they could not keep them—that eventually we would have our way. This, I said, might depend on the plans and ambitions of European nations and whether they would interfere for reasons of their own on Japan's side. The President reiterated his view that there would be no war.

At the following meeting, May 16th, the President presented his draft of an answer. I pointed out an apparent contradiction in one place. The statement regretted that Japan should regard the California law as creating "unfair discrimination." The next sentence practically admitted that we thought so too by indicating that we had tried to get California to forego or radically to alter the law. The necessary alterations were made.

The President pointed out that the law itself, by very

[65]

precise statement, was based on the theory of necessarily conforming to the Treaty, and purported to conform to it; and that, in any event, if it did not conform to it, it was invalid. This was a matter for the courts, and the Japanese had the same rights before them that Americans have. They could ask no more.

Again the possible course of Japan was considered. The President stated that he had not seriously entertained the thought of such a criminal possibility as war till Thursday, the 15th, when he noticed the extreme perturbation of the Japanese Ambassador. It was possible that this was due to his fear of what might happen to his home government. Garrison stated that he had canvassed the matter of defending the Philippines, and that the War Council, while thinking war a remote possibility, thought we ought to be prepared, and that Manila could be defended for a year, if some ships then in Chinese waters were sent to Manila. These could prevent the Japanese from crossing the neck of land.

Garrison intimated that our views on military matters were not particularly valuable—that his Board of Army and Navy Officers were the people who were competent to pass on such things. At this, Bryan flared up for the first time. He got red in the face and was very emphatic. He thundered out that army and navy officers could not be trusted to say what we should or should not do, till we actually got into war; that we were discussing not how to wage war, but how not to get into war, and that, if ships were moved about in the East, it would incite to war. Several members said that they could not see why we could not move our own ships from where they were to our own ports. My view was that we could, but that the real question was whether the ships could get to Manila and could be of any real use if they did.

The President said that he would direct the ships to stay where they were and would do so, knowing full well that there would be bitter criticism if war should come and he had not done everything possible to prepare for it.

At a garden party at the White House a day or so later, Bryan thanked me for not getting excited at the Cabinet meeting. He added: "There will be no war. I have seen the Japanese Ambassador, and I am letting the old man down easy."

At lunch after Cabinet meeting, May 20th, we discussed the tariff and particularly the duty on sugar. All seemed to think it a mistake for Congress to place a three-year limit on the one-cent sugar rate. It was believed that it would injure domestic producers without benefitting the consumer. Lane thought that it would result in the Democrats losing the Senate and possibly the House.

It was noted that lobbyists, and particularly sugar lobbyists, were everywhere. It was impossible to move around without bumping into them—at hotels, clubs, and even private houses. They are pests, but they seem worried. They are not making their usual headway.

Somebody pointed out that all our discussions, or nearly all, had been over foreign matters; that domestic problems of importance such as the tariff and currency were never raised by the President. Lane, in particular, was critical. I pointed out that the President had evidently and of necessity given his thoughts primarily to pressing foreign questions, that he regarded this as his particular field, one in respect to which he had unusual powers and responsibilities, that he was evidently depending upon the heads of

[67]

departments initially to handle domestic economic questions each in his particular field, and that he complimented us by presenting many matters for discussion and advice while some heads of departments did not. The President always welcomed such topics, but he did not have them immediately in hand. The truth is that the two important domestic measures at the time, the tariff and currency, are under the Treasury and that McAdoo is a solitaire player. He possesses many of the qualities of leadership. He is self-reliant and has dash, boldness, and courage, but he does not cultivate Cabinet team work and does not invite discussion or suggestion from the Cabinet as a whole.

In reference to the sugar situation, I had come to certain definite conclusions after thoroughly canvassing it with experts of the Department of Agriculture. Briefly stated, they were that Louisiana farmers ought not to be encouraged to grow sugar exclusively; that they should grow it only as an incident and not as a main or the sole reliance, and that beet sugar should not be produced unless as an incident in diversified farming except in California, Montana in places, Colorado, Idaho, and Wyoming. The Louisiana climate is not favourable for sugar production. It is too damp. There is not enough sunshine. The sugar content of the cane is low. The season for milling is too short, being about six weeks as against five months in the tropics. Labour is not efficient and is not well supervised; and the business methods are not good. Louisiana would be vastly better off in the long run if she would resort to diversified farming, specializing in live stock for which excellent foundations exist or can be laid.

In like manner, except in the states mentioned, beet

[68]

sugar cannot be produced to advantage. There are permanent disadvantages. There is no need of protecting people against nature or simply to permit them to make a profit out of an undertaking to which they happen to take a fancy. Only in the mountain states are the conditions favourable to a high sugar content in the beets. There with good farming, with decent treatment of growers by the manufacturers, who have good machinery and good business methods, sugar can be produced and distributed through a large area at a reasonable profit in competition with foreign sugar, without artificial aid.

Mexico loomed up at the Cabinet meeting, May 23d, as an ugly problem. Several members expressed themselves as being in favour of the recognition of Huerta. The President and Bryan were opposed to recognition. I emphatically opposed it as immoral. I asserted that the Huerta government was bad both in origin and in purpose, that neither Huerta nor his crowd had any interest in the Mexican people; and that recognition would probably make us indirectly responsible for a large loan to Huerta which would fasten him upon the Mexicans. It was replied that he would get the money anyway and hold the people down, and that, if he did so and suppressed the revolutionists we would have to recognize him. I said that this would not necessarily follow and that, if it did, we would not be responsible for him. It was agreed that Bryan should sound the English and French ambassadors, to see if their governments were back of the loan and to warn them that they could not enforce a loan guaranteed by a pledge of customs duties.

The provision of the Sundry Civil bill containing a proviso exempting labour and farm organizations from

[69]

prosecution with the aid of the $300,000 carried by it for the Department of Justice was referred to. Apparently the President had said to two Senators that he would not veto the bill because of the provision. I made an emphatic protest against the item as vicious in principle. In a way, the provision was harmless because it exempted the two sorts of organizations from prosecution, if they did not do unlawful things, with the use of the amount carried in the item. The Department, of course, had other funds. My objection was primarily that the motive was bad, that there was an appearance of deception, and that, if it meant anything, it was against justice and equality.

On Saturday, three of us met at lunch and agreed that the President ought to send for the two Senators and tell them that he had acted hastily in saying that he would approve the bill with the item in it and that he would not sign it.

At the next meeting, on May 27th, this matter was immediately brought up. Several of us urged that the bill be not signed; or that, if the President thought that in the circumstances he had to let it become a law, he file with it and publish a statement pointing out his objection to such legislation, that in reality it did not permit the organizations to do anything other organizations could not do, and that the law would be enforced against all alike.

Subsequently, I prepared and sent to the President a memorandum, adding the thought that the practice of amending a general statute of long standing in this way was vicious; and that Congress should by separate legislation deal with labour and farm organizations, defining their relation to the public and limiting their field of operations to legitimate undertakings. The President replied that he preferred not to argue the question in his note.

I read with delight the statement given out by the President on the lobby. It was short and to the point. He said:

"I think that the public ought to know the extraordinary exertions being made by the lobby in Washington to gain recognition for certain alterations of the tariff bill. Washington has seldom seen so numerous, so industrious, or so insidious a lobby. The newspapers are being filled with paid advertisements calculated to mislead the judgment of public men not only, but also the public opinion of the country itself. There is every evidence that money without limit is being spent to sustain this lobby and to create an appearance of pressure of opinion antagonistic to some of the chief items of the tariff bill.

"It is of serious interest to the country that the people at large should have no lobby and be voiceless in these matters, while great bodies of astute men seek to create an artificial opinion and to overcome the interests of the public for their private profit. It is thoroughly worth the while of the people of this country to take knowledge of this matter. Only public opinion can check and destroy it.

"The government in all its branches ought to be relieved from this intolerable burden and this constant interruption to the calm progress of debate. I know that in this I am speaking for the members of the two Houses, who would rejoice as much as I would to be released from this unbearable situation."

The effect of this statement was immediately noticeable.

[71]

The crowd scattered like rats, and business could be transacted without interference from the pests.

On June 6th, the second Japanese note was brought before us by the President and the Secretary. It contended that the courts would not be satisfactory; that the law violated the Treaty and was adverse to good relations; that California could not confiscate property; that the objection did not rest wholly on economic grounds; that Japanese were not naturalizable; and that the situation was mortifying to Japanese. The President said that the Counsellor would examine the whole matter; that, if necessary, the question could be taken to the courts; and that if the Japanese had suffered damage, the United States might make good the amount.

It was agreed that there would be no further regular meetings till fall, and that we were subject to call.

Mexico continued to be a disturbing factor; and there were many people in this country who for purposes of their own were trying to get us to go into Mexico. Certain papers even carried the story that five great powers had notified us that if we did not intervene, they would. The President did have in mind the possibility of attempting mediation.

Mediation was tried. Lind, of Minnesota, a singular choice, one of Bryan's friends, was sent to Mexico. Huerta seemed to be about at the end of his rope. He had got a loan of $30,000,000 from bankers, but he could not get any more. It was doubtful if he could hold his own even with recognition by the United States, and with the aid of a further loan.

Congress plodded on with the tariff as its steady regular business; and the Committee on Banking and Currency of the House was busy shaping a currency measure.

On June 23d, the President appeared before a joint session of Congress and delivered his address on the currency. He pleaded for a banking system which would be elastic with the control vested in the government, "so that the banks may be the instruments, not the masters, of business and of individual enterprise and initiative."

On August 27th, he appeared again before Congress, this time to keep it in touch with the Mexican situation and his policy. He pointed out that there was little prospect of peace in Mexico under the existing provisional authorities. Their control over territory was growing weaker and was contracting. We had volunteered our good offices through Mr. Lind, but our proposals were rejected. They were rejected, he thought, because the Mexican authorities did not realize the spirit of friendship of the American people and their sober determination and because they did not believe that the present Administration represented the people of the United States. This left them isolated and without friends who could aid them. We must give the situation a little more time to work itself out.

In the meantime, everything we do must be rooted in patience. "Impatience on our part would be childish, and would be fraught with every risk of wrong and folly. We can afford to exercise the self-restraint of a really great nation which realizes its own strength and scorns to use it. It was our duty to offer our active assistance." The door was not closed against further coöperative action if opportunity should offer.

He stated that, while he would omit nothing to safeguard the lives and interests of Americans in Mexico, he would urge them to leave the country, because there would be hazard to them while the country was upset. He would act under the law of March 14, 1912, to see that neither party received aid from the United States. He would forbid the exportation of arms or munitions to any part of Mexico.

Several of the great governments of the world had given the United States their support in urging upon the provisional authorities the acceptance of our good offices. "All the world expects us in such circumstances to act as Mexico's nearest friend and intimate adviser. . . . If further motive were necessary than our own good-will toward a sister republic, and our own deep concern to see peace and order prevail in Central America, this consent of mankind to what we are attempting to do, this attitude of the great nations of the world toward what we may attempt in dealing with this distressed people at our doors, should make us feel the more solemnly bound to go to the utmost length of patience and forbearance in this painful and anxious business. The steady pressure of moral forces will before many days break the barriers of pride and prejudice down, and we shall triumph as Mexico's friends sooner than we could triumph as her enemies— and how much more handsomely, with how much higher and finer satisfactions of conscience and honour!"[2]

This message was intended no less for the jingoes in this country, the oil interests, the American public, South America, and Europe than for the Mexicans themselves. It was a policy of "watchful waiting."

On October 3, 1913, President Wilson approved the Tariff Act, known as the Underwood-Simmons Act. Thus the Democratic party kept its first and most specific pledge to the people of the nation. Thus the discontent of the people over the practice of legislating for, and under pressure from, special interests, which had been growing for years and was intensified by the failure of the Republicans in 1909 to keep their promise to revise the tariff downward, found expression. It was the fruit of effective coöperation of the Democrats under the skilful and determined leadership of a man who knows where he wishes to go and how he proposes to get there. It is the first instance, so far as I recall, at least for many years, in which the rates insisted upon by the Senate were lower than those agreed to by the House; and the first in which the legislation was not substantially dictated by the Conference Committee. It is also the first in fifty-six years, or since 1857, to carry generally decidedly lower rates, although it had been the expectation after the Civil War that the rates imposed during that struggle would be materially reduced. The average rate on dutiable goods was lowered from a little more than 40 per cent. to a little less than $33\frac{1}{2}$ per cent.

The notable features were these: Schedule K, embracing wool and woollens, was revised. Wool was put on the free list; and the rates on woollens were reduced from one half to two thirds; those on cottons, from one third to one half; and large reductions were made in the schedule on food imports, with a view to lower the cost of food. The Act particularly discriminated against luxuries in favour of necessities. Many increases were made in the free list, and many substitutions of *ad valorem* duties which could be more easily understood were made for specific and mixed rates.

If no great disturbance occurs, such as a great war, this measure will be followed in time by further enactments

[75]

carrying still lower rates. If a great explosion should occur, rates will again be increased, and the whole miserable fight will have to be made once more.

Even more important than the reduction of customs duties was another feature of the law: the direct tax on incomes. The struggle to get such a tax as a permanent part of our Federal system of taxes was a very long one. Such a tax was imposed in 1862. It was apportioned and proved to be undesirable. It was repealed in 1872, and we were left with a system of indirect taxes, mainly on consumption. Another income tax was imposed in the Tariff Act of 1894, but it was declared unconstitutional by the Supreme Court. Finally, the Seventeenth Amendment to the Constitution was ratified, and the way was open for the adoption of a direct income tax. Very properly, the tax was made progressive; and thus the foundation of a sound Federal tax system was laid. It remains to be seen whether those who prefer to have indirect taxes which the people cannot so easily estimate, who fear that use will be made of direct taxes to take from the better-to-do classes a fair percentage of their income, and who wish to insist particularly upon higher customs duties for protection, will seek to repeal the income tax when they come into power, as they repealed direct taxes after the Civil War to make place for high protective duties. There will, on the other hand, be those who will desire and try to use the income tax as a levelling measure rather than as a revenue measure without regard to equity. They will have to be controlled by those who believe in equal justice.

On October 27, 1913, the President, in an address before the Southern Commercial Congress at Mobile, Alabama, took occasion to state the Administration's friendly in-

[76]

terest in, and attitude toward, the Latin-American nations. He pointed out the dangers to these states from their policy of granting concessions to foreign capitalists. The danger, he said, was that foreigners securing concessions were apt to dominate their domestic affairs. These states, he believed, were about to witness an emancipation from such subordination. "They have had harder bargains driven with them in the matter of loans than any other peoples in the world." We must prove ourselves their friends upon terms of equality and honour. "You cannot be friends upon any other terms than upon the terms of equality. You cannot be friends at all except upon the terms of honour." There is something behind all this which is dearer than anything else to the thoughtful men of America. "I mean the development of constitutional liberty in the world. Human rights, national integrity, and opportunity, as against national interests— that, ladies and gentlemen, is the issue which we now have to face. I want to take this occasion to say that the United States will never again seek one additional foot of territory by conquest." He added that he knew what the response of America to his programme would be, because America was created to realize such a programme. "This is not America because it is rich. This is America because it has set up for a great population great opportunities of material prosperity. I would rather belong to a poor nation that was free than to a rich nation that had ceased to be in love with liberty. But we shall not be poor if we love liberty, because the nation that loves liberty truly sets every man free to do his best and to be his best, and that means the release of all the splendid energies of a great people who think for themselves."

[77]

There were no meetings of the Cabinet from the sixth till the latter part of September. At the meetings during the fall, nothing of a novel nature was discussed. No change was made in the policy toward Mexico. In his First Annual Message to Congress, the President touched upon the situation and stated that he would not alter his "policy of watchful waiting."

"There is but one cloud upon the horizon. That has shown itself to the south of us and hangs over Mexico. There can be no certain prospect of peace in America until General Huerta has surrendered his usurped authority in Mexico; until it is understood on all hands, indeed, that such pretended governments will not be countenanced or dealt with by the Government of the United States. . . . Mexico has no government. The attempt to maintain one at the City of Mexico has broken down, and a mere military despotism has been set up which has hardly more than the semblance of national authority. . . . Even if the usurper had succeeded in his purposes, in despite of the Constitution of the Republic, and the rights of its people, he would have set up nothing but a precarious and hateful power, which could have lasted but a little while, and whose eventual downfall would have left the country in a more deplorable condition than ever. But he has not succeeded. He has forfeited the respect and the moral support even of those who were at one time willing to see him succeed. Little by little he has been completely isolated. By a little every day his power and prestige are crumbling, and the collapse is not far away. We shall not, I believe, be obliged to alter our policy of watchful waiting."

There was much uproar among certain elements in the

[78]

United States over this policy of watchful waiting. There were many who were anxious to see Huerta recognized. They thought that if he were supported he might sustain himself, restore order, and become a second Diaz. That is unlikely; and those who think that Diaz was a great asset to anybody except the Concessionaires and a small ruling class in Mexico have always seemed to me to be mistaken. The biggest indictment against rulers like Diaz and his associates everywhere in the world, and there are many such in eastern Europe, Asia, and Central America, is that they scarcely have the intelligent interest in the masses of the people that a good farmer has in a good hog. They do nothing, plan nothing constructive, to train the people little by little to better ways of living and action. Why, after so many centuries, are 80 per cent. of the people in countries like Russia, and a large per cent. in countries like Mexico, illiterate, able neither to read nor to write? What real concern have the ruling classes in Rumania or Prussia, the great landlords, for the welfare and development of the rank and file? I understand the difficulty of doing much in a short time for such people as the Mexicans. It would take generations to bring them very far along the road to self-government and higher living; but they will never get anywhere unless they have leaders who have the right attitude and are willing to try to lay the foundation. A good police force in Mexico, a system which would give the masses an interest in the land and in their products, an elementary vocational educational system, and an agricultural agency such as our Federal Department, would work great changes in Mexico within a reasonable time.

CHAPTER VI

THE FEDERAL RESERVE ACT

Bryan's Ability to Understand Finance—Indiscretions of Cabinet Members—The President's Patience

THE President, in his message, stressed the need of early action on the currency measure, asking the Senate to concentrate its whole energy upon it till it was successfully disposed of.

He then pointed out the need of better credit facilities for farmers.

"The pending currency bill does the farmers a great service. It puts them upon an equal footing with other business men and masters of enterprise, as it should; and upon its passage they will find themselves quit of many of the difficulties which now hamper them in the field of credit. The farmers, of course, ask and should be given no special privilege, such as extending to them the credit of the government itself. What they need and should obtain is legislation which will make their own abundant and substantial credit resources available as a foundation for joint, concerted local action in their own behalf in getting the capital they must use.

"It has, singularly enough, come to pass that we have allowed the industry of our farms to lag behind the other activities of the country in its development. I need not stop to tell you how fundamental to the life of the nation is the production of its food. Our thoughts may ordinarily be concentrated upon the cities and upon the hives of industry, upon the cries of the crowded market-place and the clangour of the factory, but it is from the quiet inter-spaces of the open valleys and the free hillsides that we draw the sources of life and prosperity, from the farm and from the ranch, from the forest and the mine. Without these, every street would be silent, every office deserted, every factory fallen into disrepair. And yet, the farmer does not stand on the same footing with the forester and the miner in the market of credit. He is the servant of the seasons. Nature determines how long he must wait for his crops and will not be hurried in her processes. He may give his note, but the season of its maturity depends upon the season when his crop matures, lies at the gates of the market when his products are sold. And the security he gives is a character not known in the broker's office as familiarly as it might be on the counter of the banker."

Poetic and true!

In connection with the discussion of rural credits, I will give two incidents which enabled me finally to determine to my satisfaction Bryan's mental make-up. I had been studying him, as I have indicated, since 1896. I had been puzzled about him, but had been slowly arriving at an estimate. These incidents fixed him for me once and for all.

There had been appointed as a member of the Rural Credits Commission to visit Europe a very energetic person, one of those people who, like the beetle, mistake energy for efficiency. He was a sort of professional organizer. He was constantly constituting bodies or committees, which he used with a noise out of all proportion to their influence, to impress Congress and the public.

He could make more noise than a coyote. There are many similar characters in Washington, and they usually flourish under the guise of farmers' friends.

The Commission had been given an appropriation by Congress to meet expenses. The person who was most active thought the allotment was too small. He wanted more. He was quite a plunger and a grandiose person. He knew that there was an appropriation in the State Department's budget for the International Institute of Agriculture at Rome. It was customary for us to send a delegation to Rome each year, the Secretary of State handling the appropriation and calling upon the Secretary of Agriculture to select the delegates. Mr. Bryan was ignorant of this. The busybody on the Commission came to me and asked if I would designate to the State Department his Commission as the delegation to Rome. I told him I would not, as I thought it was too large and not properly constituted for such a purpose, that I would suggest a few experts from the Federal Department and the Land Grant institutions. He left much disgruntled. A little later, my secretary came in and said he understood that the Secretary of State had agreed to designate the Commission as the delegation to Rome. I told him I would see about the matter at Cabinet meeting. When I saw Bryan talking to the President at the meeting that day, I spoke of the matter, saying that it would not do to have that body selected for the reasons I have indicated, and for the further reason that Congress had given it all the money it wanted it to use and would resent, and properly so, its using two funds. The President said it should not be done. Bryan looked puzzled and said that he would take the matter up.

A few days later, my secretary came in again and said that he understood that the commissions had been made out in the State Department for the members of the Commission as delegates. I asked him to get for me on the telephone the officer who had them in hand. He did so, and I told the officer not to issue the commissions, or, rather, not to send them to the President, till I could again see the Secretary and the President, and that I would assume all the responsibility. When I saw the President and Mr. Bryan, I stated the facts and insisted that the commissions be not issued. The President said they would not be. Bryan said: "Why, I thought the matter was all right. Senator ——," giving the name of a Senator whose name was nearly the same as the busybody's, "came to me and assured me that the thing was all right and that the delegation should be designated." I told him that he was being fooled, that it was the busybody himself and not Senator ——, and I reminded him that the President had agreed a few days before that the delegation should not be appointed. I had to intervene again before the matter was finally settled; and then Bryan asked me if I would not let him name a man from the Land Grant Institution in his home town as one of the delegates. As a matter of fact, he had power to name all the delegates. I told him that his man was a suitable man, and that he might be selected.

The busybody was persistent. From the middle of the Atlantic, he sent a wireless to the Department, requesting that the Commission be allowed the thousand dollars of the appropriation from the State Department's item.

This incident throws light on Bryan's administrative capacity.

[83]

The other incident, or series of incidents, was this: It was my custom to keep the President informed of the principal undertakings of the Department of Agriculture and of the course of legislation in the field of rural life. A bill had been introduced in Congress to lend the farmers two billion dollars out of the Treasury at 4 per cent. I mentioned the matter and said that, although it was an unwise measure and class legislation, I was afraid it was making headway. "Why shouldn't Congress lend the farmers money out of the Treasury at 4 per cent.?" Bryan asked belligerently. "You have created the National Banking System" (he referred to the National Bank Act) "in the interest of bankers and lend the bankers money at 2 per cent. Why not lend the farmers money at 4 per cent.?" This would have got a yell from a country audience. I said: "I seem to have been labouring under a misapprehension. I understood that the National Bank Laws were passed to assure good and safe banking in the interest of the public, and that, not wishing to keep public funds tied up in the Treasury, we permit the banks to take the trouble and go to the expense of keeping them for us subject to withdrawal on demand, and make them pay us 2 per cent. for the trouble." I then outlined the kind of legislation I thought we should have in the field of rural credits, giving the essentials of a good farm loan act. Bryan sat back in his chair with a satisfied smile. Ten days later, I mentioned the vicious measure again, indicating the terms. Bryan said: "Why not lend the farmers——" I gave my explanation again and he subsided, apparently pleased. A third time, the same thing occurred. When I finished, Bryan asked me if I would write out my statement for him. I did so that afternoon very carefully, taking four typewritten pages, and sent it over to him by a messenger. In the course of two hours, he called me up and said: "This is fine. May I use it?" I replied: "Yes, it is yours. Use it when and where you please." In due course, I received a marked copy of his paper, the *Commoner*, and I found my statement printed as his leading editorial, which was all right. I felt that I had done a good job, an educational one. I had the thing nailed down.

I was too optimistic. At the next meeting of the Cabinet, when the matter came up again, and I stated that it had made progress, Bryan chirped up with: "Why not——?" I said: "Good Lord!" and gave it up.

When the currency bill came up in the Senate, certain Democratic Senators were not sympathetic. They aligned themselves more or less with the Republicans. They were disgruntled over appointments. In view of certain political happenings in New York, Massachusetts, New Jersey, Maryland, and elsewhere, these Senators began to swing around. The Democrats, becoming weary of partisan tactics of the Republicans who were professing to be very non-partisan, held a caucus and decided to put the currency bill through promptly. It was clear that it would go through as the President wanted it.

For several meetings of the Cabinet after it became clear that the currency measure was safe, there was much discussion as to what measures to take up next. It was suggested that it would be desirable to let the country get its breath, to let it adjust itself to the new tariff and currency legislation. There had been and was an industrial chill due to world-wide causes. It had spread over the world. I was of the opinion that we should take no step till some

[85]

readjustments had occurred and the currency system could be organized. I thought it better to make haste slowly. We might lose what we had secured if we tried to run too fast; and I said as much to a number of members of the Cabinet and at Cabinet meeting. If we went a little slowly for a while, we might be able to make a certain goal even more quickly in the end.

At the Cabinet meeting Tuesday, December 16th, statements were made by several of us along the lines just indicated. When we finished, Bryan said very cleverly: "I agree with everything you say, but with nothing you mean. There are only two times when the problem you raise, what to do about trusts, should not be touched: one is when business is good, the other when business is bad and ought not to be made worse." He insisted that the party keep its promise on trusts as it was keeping those on currency and the tariff.

The matter of railway rates was considered at some length. It was agreed that the situation ought to be met squarely and promptly. One of the members (Lane) said that some of the rates on certain goods were too low. They had been made in the interest of owners of industries along the line: Those he said should certainly be raised, but those on all competing roads would have to be raised also. Bryan, with a surprised look, asked why. He apparently could not see that if they were not, the competing roads would get all the business and the others would die.

It was agreed that the matter was one for the Interstate Commerce Commission and that it should either raise or reclassify rates or insist on greater efficiency in management. It was agreed that no pressure of any sort could be brought to bear on the Commission. The impropriety of approaching it or its members was recognized.

For some time some members of the Cabinet had been doing no little speaking on many topics, one in particular talking for the edification of social groups in Washington. Also, notwithstanding the fact that Cabinet members are supposed to say nothing about Cabinet discussions unless the President desires someone to make a statement, and that the publishing of anything be otherwise left entirely to the President, one or two members had persisted in letting things out. Newspaper men always waylaid us and tried to get hints. Most of us kept our mouths shut, but a few could not do so. They were in constant touch with the newspaper men, either after Cabinet meetings or at other times. Apparently, they could not resist the temptation to be obliging.

As I went to Cabinet meeting Friday, December 19th, the President sent word to me that he would like to see me for a moment. When I stepped into his office, he said that he wanted me to do him a little favour. He was, he remarked, embarrassed by the fact that one or two members of the Cabinet who I knew were talking too freely about matters of a non-departmental nature in respect to which naturally he had to assume the immediate responsibility. He thought they ought to be more guarded and ought to advise with him as to whether it was opportune to discuss such matters and as to his policy and purposes. Again, he said: "I am embarrassed by the fact that one or two members seem to be unable to refrain from telling everybody what happens in Cabinet meetings. I wish to advise with the Cabinet freely. Some things cannot be given publicity; at any rate, at once. It is important to consider what shall be said, and how and when. I ought to have the privilege of determinining this. The discussions should be free and full. If they cannot be kept within the family, leaving it to my discretion when and what to give out, it will make it difficult for me to canvass confidential matters as I should like." I told him that I understood the situation and exactly where the trouble lay. I said that I would raise the two questions in the meeting and give him an opportunity to express his views as emphatically as he wished.

At the proper time, I brought up the two matters and asked the President if he would not state his wishes for our guidance. He did so pointedly. The members generally quickly agreed that it was not desirable to talk on general policies unless they were requested by the President to discuss them. It was also understood that what was to be given out be left to the President.

It was clear from what the President said to me that he knew the members who were chiefly responsible for talking on the outside about Cabinet matters. One of these it seemed made it a point to cultivate the press. He was particularly strong before its representatives on matters as to which he had no responsibility. And so he gets much advertising. As a matter of fact, he is of very little help in a discussion. He listens to gossip, attaches importance to it, and labours under the impression that he must cultivate Senators and Congressmen to get measures through; and, if they fail, he usually ascribes it to the fact that some member is offended. He has no great administrative ability and gives too much of his attention to general matters over which he has no control.

The President is amazingly considerate. He is even

more amazingly patient and tolerant. I admire his ability to restrain himself at times. I wonder that he does
not explode sometimes when he has to listen to a lot
of ill-considered, confused, and irrelevant advice. How
refreshing his clear, concise, and well-expressed views!
Generally, he takes the initiative only in his special field,
that of foreign affairs, but he is ready to discuss any matter
presented from any quarter and have any questions
raised about foreign matters or anything else. He depends on heads of departments to take the initiative in
matters under their jurisdiction and leaves them the utmost freedom in bringing matters before the Cabinet or
in acting on their own judgment. He evidently desires
that they shall assume full responsibility and bother him
only when in their judgment it is essential. If a head of a
department is competent, if he has first-rate executive
ability, he can spare the President much time and worry.
The trouble is that the average head of a department is
not highly competent and has not first-rate executive
ability. Not one man in a hundred occupying a high position anywhere has first-rate administrative talent. If
Presidents of the United States had more efficient aids
and were better served, they might live longer. But some
Cabinet officers who have executive ability do not spare
the President as they should. They like to keep themselves in the President's thoughts and before the public,
and to appear to the public to be high in the President's
counsels. A surgical operation is the only remedy in such
cases.

In thinking of a head of a department as an executive,
one must bear in mind not only the routine handling and
determination of a vast variety of internal departmental

[89]

matters, including the selection of higher officials, which is a matter of first importance, but also contacts with Congress, the initiation or discussion of legislative proposals, and constant conferences with members of the House and Senate, running errands and acting as messengers for constituents. One must remember also the many demands made by visiting individuals and delegations from all parts of the nation with matters of little or of great importance—great at least to them—and also the insistent pressure from all sorts of organizations to go somewhere and speak, or look at something, or open something. If a head of a department knows especially how to handle his problems before Congress; if, for instance, he is able to look ahead and frame a better bill than anybody in Congress can get up, and defend it, and if he can and will dispose of visiting delegations effectively, he can render the President aid and relief.

Also, if he is able and well informed and has good judgment, he can be of great value to the President in Cabinet discussions. In proportion as he lacks such qualities, he merely contributes to the Presidential wear and tear and is a liability instead of an asset. I think, on the average, about one third at least must be liabilities.

The impossible has happened. To-day, Tuesday, December 23d, the currency measure became a law. The President approved it a few minutes after six o'clock in the afternoon. It was passed by a Congress dominated by the Democrats, two thirds of whom had been unsound on currency questions and a majority of whom can scarcely be said to have understood what the measure meant and would accomplish. The majority of the Republicans had also had an unenviable record on the currency. Bryan and several other members of the Cabinet had supported free silver, as had the Vice President, Marshall, the Speaker, Champ Clark, and many Democratic Senators. The measure itself was the result of the labours of many men, extending over a long period, but its passage at this time in its present form was due to Woodrow Wilson, ably supported by McAdoo, Glass, and a few others.

This was the second great Administration victory. It was the culmination of efforts for a sound national banking system extending over one hundred and twenty-four years. The First National Bank of the United States served the country well from December, 1791, till its charter expired in 1811 and Congress declined to extend it. Politics, ignorance killed it. It closed its doors at a critical juncture. The war with Great Britain began in 1812, and there being no banking system, and the fiscal arrangements being defective, specie payments were suspended in 1814. Chaos reigned till after the Second Bank of the United States began operation in 1816. Politics played havoc with this Bank during Jackson's Administration, and it died when its charter expired in 1836. It continued to operate for a time under a charter from the State of Pennsylvania; but chaos in banking again reigned. The Crisis of 1837 developed, and the Bank itself suspended specie payments in that year. It suspended again in 1838, and a third time in 1841. Its process of liquidation covered fifteen years. The government had ceased to be a shareholder, its stock having been paid off at a premium. The private shareholders lost all their holdings, as did its president. There was no real banking system for many years.

The Civil War came on. Specie payments were promptly suspended and were not resumed till 1879. The national banks provided for by the Act of 1863 in time furnished partial relief, but they did not and could not prevent panics and public hardships. There were panics in 1873, 1893, and 1907. The advocates of unsound currency continued to be active and came very near to committing the nation to the vicious policy of free coinage of silver at sixteen to one and prevented any real reform till the passage of the Federal Reserve Act in 1913.

It is interesting that, when this act was passed, Bryan, who was the head and front of the forces of unsound currency and money, was in the Cabinet. He had a large following still in the country and in the Congress, and there was much question as to what his course would be and whether a measure could be adopted if he was in opposition. He was certainly less of a danger in the Cabinet than he would have been on the outside. The story of how his support was secured is one for others to tell. It is said that, because the act provided for the issuance of notes through the Federal Reserve Board, he acquired the notion that the act really incorporated his theories and that he, therefore, was willing to stand for it. What could be more strange than that Bryan should have been a conspicuous member of the administration which gave the nation its first sound currency system?

Whether the system will survive is, of course, a question. Whether it can be kept out of politics or politics can be kept out of it remains to be seen. The ignorant and the demagogues we still have with us. The test will come in some period of great stress. If prices should fall and many people, for causes over which banks have no control, should come to grief, there will be those who will ascribe their ills to evil designs of whose who direct the system. It will be pictured as the monster "who plays upon the hopes and fears of the masses of the plain people." We shall then see what we shall see. We shall see whether we have developed enough popular intelligence and courageous leadership to save us from our folly. We shall see whether we have learned anything from experience.

CHAPTER VII

CHOOSING THE FEDERAL RESERVE CITIES

Touring the Country with McAdoo—Strength of Boston, Richmond, and Texas—Weakness of New Orleans, Baltimore, and Washington—President Urges Clayton Act

THE Federal Reserve Act contained a section creating an organization committee, in part as follows:

"As soon as practicable, the Secretary of the Treasury, the Secretary of Agriculture, and the Comptroller of the Currency, acting as 'The Reserve Bank Organization Committee,' shall designate not less than eight nor more than twelve cities to be known as Federal Reserve Cities, and shall divide the continental United States, excluding Alaska, into districts, each district to contain only one of such Federal Reserve Cities. The determination of said Organization Committee shall not be subject to review except by the Federal Reserve Board, when organized: Provided, That the districts shall be apportioned with due regard to the convenience and customary course of business and shall not necessarily be coterminous with any state or states. The districts thus created may be readjusted, and new districts may from time to time be created by the Federal Reserve Board, not to exceed twelve in all. . . . A majority of the Organization Committee shall constitute a quorum with authority to act."

The Committee was directed to prescribe regulations

under which every National Banking Association in the United States was required, and every eligible bank in the United States and Trust Company within the District of Columbia was authorized, to signify in writing, within sixty days after the passage of the Act, its acceptance of its terms and provisions. After the Committee had designated the Reserve Bank Cities and fixed the limits of the districts, it was its duty to notify the banks; and within thirty days thereafter, each bank was required to subscribe to the Capital Stock of the Reserve Bank within its district a sum equal to 6 per cent. of its paid-up capital and surplus. If the subscriptions to the stock of the Reserve Banks or any one or more of them was insufficient in the judgment of the Committee to provide the required capital, the Committee was authorized to offer to public subscription such amount of stock in any one or more districts as it might determine. If this failed, then the Committee might allot to the United States such an amount as it might determine.

When the Committee had established the districts, it was required to file with the Comptroller of the Currency a certificate showing the limits of each district and the Federal Reserve City designated in each. Then, after the minimum amount of capital stock had been subscribed and allotted, the Committee was required to designate any five banks whose applications had been received, to execute a certificate of organization, and thereupon such banks were to make an organization certificate specifying certain things, such as the name of the Reserve Bank. Upon the filing of such certificate with the Comptroller of the Currency, the Reserve Bank was to become a body corporate with the powers conferred by the Act. The

Committee was further authorized in organizing the banks to call meetings of bank directors in the districts and to exercise the functions of chairman of the Board of Directors of each bank pending complete organization. It was empowered, pending the organization of the Federal Reserve Board, to make regulations for the admission of state banks and to admit those which satisfied the requirements.

Because of my long study of currency and banking and of my great interest in the new legislation, I was glad to be made by the law, as Secretary of Agriculture, a member of the Organization Committee and therefore to have a part in the preliminary work of organizing the new system and getting it started. It had originally been suggested that the Secretary of Agriculture be made by law a member of the Reserve Board. It was finally decided that it would be unwise to do so. The Secretary of Agriculture might be a man who would have no qualifications for membership on the Board; and, as it had been decided to make the Secretary of the Treasury and the Comptroller of the Currency members, it was thought, and wisely, that a third member who was a political appointee would overload the Board with politics.

McAdoo and I decided that the best and quickest way for us to proceed was to make a trip through the country to give all sections an opportunity to be heard and fully to present their claims and such supporting data as they might desire.

We arranged for hearings in New York and Boston covering the week of January 4th to the 11th. The leading bankers in both cities appeared, and a number of them gave us their views. Some of them seemed not to have given the law very careful study and were clearly not sympathetic with its plan.

I was particularly interested in the testimony of a member of one of New York's leading banking institutions. I was presiding when he appeared. I asked him if he had read the law. He said that he had and would be glad to be of assistance to the Committee. This, in substance, was the course of the conversation:

"Have you decided how many banks should be created?" I asked.

"I have," he replied. "I would create the minimum number, eight. I would create a smaller number, if the law permitted." "Why the minimum number?" "Because there is not enough banking capital and surplus in the nation to justify more," he replied. I said: "Are you thinking of to-day or to-morrow?" He asked what I meant. I said: "Do you know how many people this nation has gained in fourteen years?" He replied that he had not looked it up. I told him that the increase had been more than twenty-two millions. I asked: "Do you know how much the nation's banking resources had in the same period?" He answered in the negative. I said: "From about nine and a half to more than eighteen billions." I said that we must look to the future; and that it seemed likely that the conditions would justify the creation of at least eight banks. He said that he doubted if as many as eight banks would pay. I then asked: "Have you thought where you would locate the banks?" He said he had found it easy to locate a few—one in New York, one in Chicago, one in San Francisco, and perhaps one in New Orleans. "What territory would you attach to the New York bank?" He replied: "Maine, New

Hampshire—the New England States, New York, New Jersey—the Atlantic seaboard."

I called his attention to the fact that this would take up more than 50 per cent. of the national banking capital and surplus and would leave the other districts rather lean. He said that that was true and the area would have to be restricted. I inquired why he wanted such a big bank in New York. He replied that it ought to be as big as the biggest private bank in the city so as to be able to hold its own with it, to control discount rates, and to inspire respect abroad. When I called his attention to the fact that the Reserve Bank would not be a competing bank, that the law contemplated a national reserve of banking power of at least $600,000,000 at the outset, distributed in from eight to twelve centres, under the direction, in part, of a central agency, that it would not be the function of any one particular bank to control discounts by itself, and that the foreign bankers would be very careful to analyse the facts, and then inquired if he still thought there should be a bank in New York of such overwhelming strength he said that it was not essential and that a branch might answer every purpose.

It was fairly clear that his thoughts were still running on a great central agency and not on a decentralized system such as the law contemplated. The New York bankers as a whole did not expect a district larger than New York State and parts of Connecticut and New Jersey.

There was a question in my mind whether the New England bankers would want a bank in Boston or would prefer to be attached to New York. It had been asserted that the big New England banks really desired the latter; but when we got to Boston, it became clear that nobody would openly advocate this. A claim was put in for a bank in Boston embracing in its district all New England; but the bankers of western Connecticut requested that they be attached to New York.

Our next hearing was held in Washington, with delegations from Philadelphia, Pittsburgh, Baltimore, Washington, West Virginia, Richmond, and North and South Carolina. Each state appeared with its claim for a Reserve Bank City, and one had two applications, Pennsylvania. It became clear that the section from Virginia to New Jersey was going to be difficult to arrange to the satisfaction of many people.

On January 18, 1914, we left for a long trip through the Middle West, West, and South. We took a private car as a matter of convenience and necessity as we had to travel about ten thousand miles and make many stops. We held hearings in Chicago, St. Louis, Kansas City, Lincoln, Denver, Seattle, Portland, San Francisco, Los Angeles, El Paso, Austin, New Orleans, Atlanta, Cincinnati, and Cleveland. Usually, we held hearings throughout the day and spoke at luncheons at noon and dinners in the evenings. Everywhere the people were interested and courteous. It soon appeared that city, state, and sectional pride was involved; and that we were in for a great deal of roasting no matter what we decided. It also became obvious that if we created fewer banks than the maximum fixed by law, the Reserve Board would have no peace till that number was reached.

One of our objects in making the trip was to do some educational work. There was no little misunderstanding of the meaning and purposes of the law. McAdoo and I therefore accepted all the invitations to luncheons and dinners our schedule permitted. We explained in our speeches and in our hearings the purpose of the act and its probable operation. We pointed out the weakness of the banking situation as it had existed, the fact that there were no reserves when a pinch came, the drawing of resources from the country to New York where funds were used to the limit, the failure of the attempt to secure a satisfactory currency by basing note issues on a contracting national debt, the too exclusive attention which had been given to banknotes, and the need of considering checks and the whole credit structure.

I explained why we could not model our banking system and practices on those of Europe, touching upon the size of the country, its rapid growth, the constant movement and change, and the difference in institutions and in "the character and habits of our people." I have found few people who have imagination enough to keep up with the United States or the ability to understand the needs of all sections of the nation, to know what is happening, and to act intelligently on problems which arise from all quarters. These considerations pointed to the desirability, not of a single great central bank, but of a system of regional banks under the direction of competent local business men, functioning under the supervision of a central agency.

The difference between our banking habits and those of Europe is marked and has a larger significance than is commonly realized. Too much of the discussion of banking in the United States has been in European terms and by people who know Europe better than they know this country. The habit of depositing and checking is rudimentary on the Continent of Europe. It is less so in Great Britain, but there it is by no means so highly developed as here. In 1913, for instance, the Bank of France had $285,000,000 deposits with a note circulation of $1,000,000,000, while we had deposits of $17,000,000,000 and a note circulation of only $725,000,000.

Checks serve in the main the same purpose as bank-notes. In the United States, the great mass of our transactions is effected through the use of checks. They are of greater importance as credit instruments than bank-notes and yet we have in the past contented ourselves with legislation to secure the safety only of our note issues; and in the Federal Reserve Act no attempt is made to deal with that part of our credit instruments created by state institutions which remain outside the system. If great numbers of state banks stay out of the system, obviously our credit structure will be only partially safeguarded. In time of financial distress this defect may well prove to be an element of great weakness and danger. The condition of the state institutions may jeopardize our whole financial structure and cause widespread suffering and distress.

We are too much given to deceiving ourselves, to sacrificing the essentials for appearances of freedom, and to thinking that we can safeguard liberty by diffusing power and obscuring responsibility. The Federal Government ought to exercise supervision over all agencies that create credit instruments which serve as media of exchange. Checks, like banknotes, are money, or are representatives of money, and affect its value. Congress cannot discharge its constitutional duty of coining money and regulating its value as long as it permits state banks with their enormous resources to carry on the business of deposit and checking free from its regulation. As long as it permits this, it will fail to live up to its constitutional

[101]

rights and duty. Our national financial system will be unsound and unsafe till Congress does its duty. Its power in this field is exclusive, as it is over interstate commerce and therefore over interstate railway rates. As every railway rate, with negligible exceptions, affects interstate rates, Congress has exclusive power over all railway rates. National agencies should be nationally regulated. We gain nothing but trouble by reliance in whole or in part on local bodies in such matters, just as we endanger our interests and institutions by imposing upon the Federal Government things which should be assumed by the states.

Before we started on our trip, I had in a general way run my mind over the country to see if I could locate from eight to twelve banks, but without attempting to form any fixed opinions. Of course, Boston, New York, Chicago, and San Francisco, were obvious. In a somewhat definite fashion, St. Louis, New Orleans, and Washington were in my thoughts, with Baltimore and Philadelphia as competitors with Washington. Richmond scarcely occurred to me as a possibility. New Orleans was doubtful, because I knew that Texas had relatively little to do with New Orleans financially, and that the banks to the east of New Orleans would not want to be attached to her. I assumed that Texas would want to be attached to St. Louis or Chicago. Atlanta and Nashville I thought of as possibilities. I recognized that, if twelve banks were created, we should have to give the South at least two. I did not see how we could give her three without making the districts unduly weak, or locating one of them in St. Louis, and another in Louisville, Washington, or Baltimore.

I had great difficulty in even tentatively indicating more than seven reserve centres. Denver, Seattle, Minneapolis, Cincinnati, Cleveland, Pittsburgh, Louisville, and Omaha all claimed attention, but I could not at all satisfactorily define their districts. There was nothing west of Denver to speak of till California was reached, and I knew that the banks to the east of Denver would look eastward. Seattle seemed to be out of the question because there was nothing at all west of it, and there was nothing north of it. I suspected that Minnesota and Iowa and Nebraska would really want to be attached to Chicago.

I knew that we would have difficulty in arranging more than eight or nine strong districts; and yet I felt that, since the law permitted twelve, it might be better, as I have said, to fix that number and be done with it. Kansas City, I considered, since I knew that she served a distinctive territory and constituency, but I felt that she would probably not be selected, partly because she was too near St. Louis, which was a larger and a more impressive banking centre.

I got a good many surprises. There was little enthusiasm for St. Louis anywhere. The Southwest and West—that is, most of Texas, Oklahoma, Kansas, and part of Arkansas—preferred Kansas City. I was not surprised that nobody to speak of wanted Omaha. Portland put in her claim, but I got the impression that her leading bankers really preferred San Francisco. Denver, as I expected, could not make a case. Nobody in particular wanted New Orleans, and Louisiana had strikingly little national banking capital and surplus.

Texas wanted neither New Orleans, St. Louis, nor

Kansas City. She wanted a bank of her own. Her leading witness was very effective and alert. I said: "Would it not be best to attach Texas to some city to the north or northeast, so that the district may be diversified, that is, have both manufacturing and agricultural interest, with the pressure more uniform throughout the year?" He answered: "There is something in that suggestion, but where would you find the industrial part of the district, west of Ohio and Pennsylvania? We might not kick if you attached us to New York." I asked: "Why not attach you to St. Louis with Missouri?" He quickly countered with this: "Why not attach Missouri to Texas? Why suggest that the tail wag the dog? Texas has more national banking capital and surplus than Missouri by $21,000,000 and much more state banking capital and surplus, even though Missouri has both Kansas City and St. Louis. Texas can take care of herself better than she would be taken care of if she were tied to St. Louis, or certainly better than St. Louis, or Chicago, or New York, or all of them have taken care of her in the past. Texas was all right herself in 1907, but she could not get her balances from those cities. One bank in Chicago in 1907 had $100,000,000 of balances, but could lend only $7,000,000; one in New York had $110,000,000, and could lend only $10,000,000; and five reserve cities had $145,000,000 from thirteen Southern states and could make available only $39,000,000." He made a strong presentation. He urged that a bank be located in Texas: he did not care where especially, but preferred Dallas. El Paso asserted that her fortunes were tied up with Arizona and New Mexico and that she did not care so much where she was attached as that she should go with those two states.

The case of New Orleans was almost pathetic. She was a big and important city; and she felt that her position and her past and future entitled her to a bank. It was clear that her pride would be very much hurt if she were not selected. As I have stated, I had thought of her as a possibility, but the difficulties were even greater than I had anticipated. Scarcely any banks wanted to be attached to her. Of 1,200 or more banks in the district suggested as her possible territory, only 51 did not protest against being connected with her. Texas had three times the banking power of Louisiana. She had 500 national banks alone, while Louisiana had only 26.

Washington and Baltimore, to my surprise, made a very bad showing. Banks to the north of them wanted to go to Philadelphia or even more to New York, while those to the south and west, as a rule, wanted Richmond. It was difficult to discover that either Baltimore or Washington did any substantial financing in the territory to the south and southwest of them, while Richmond had marked and growing financial and industrial ties. Baltimore's loans in the South were reported to be only $6,700,000, while Richmond's were $35,000,000, and the latter was not a reserve city. Furthermore, Virginia had more national banking capital and surplus than Maryland. North Carolina, South Carolina, and West Virginia, preferred Richmond; and there was only one line of railways connecting two of these states with Baltimore.

It was clear to me that within limits it did not make a vast deal of difference, except in a few cases such as New York, Boston, Chicago, and San Francisco, which cities were selected. The considerations were those of convenience, of railway, telephone, and telegraph facilities, the drift of banking and customary practices. With these limits in mind, I associated also the thought that the districts were so many reservoir agencies, under the general supervision of the general staff, the Federal Reserve Board, which could bring one or more districts to the aid of any other.

There was a vast amount of state and city pride revealed to us in the hearings; and to hear some of the speeches one would have thought that not to select the city of the advocate would mean its ruin and that of its territory. We had floods of oratory, and particularly from Senators and Congressmen who appeared, in many cases, for their states and without much technical knowledge. They could prove to their satisfaction in every case and to that of their constituents that all roads led to their city and that it was the supreme factor in its environment.

After a while, we determined that we had to do something to save our time and our nerves; and we adopted a simple but effective course. We were getting tired of hearing over and over again things which we knew better than any of our witnesses. So we did this: We would state at the beginning of each hearing: "We request that you limit yourself to concrete matters peculiar to your particular section. We do not wish anybody to repeat what someone else has said. We shall read your full and carefully prepared brief and examine your maps. We are collecting a great deal of information in Washington. We are familiar with the general situation. We will concede that your city is the centre of the surrounding country and the most important one in it from your point of view. We admire your fine local spirit and your loyalty. We will concede all your oratory. Now, with this preface, will you proceed in your own way?"

It was amusing to note the effect of this. It took much wind out of some very big sails, which thereafter sagged and flapped greatly. One further request put the finishing touch on oratory. It was that each speaker make his statement sitting down, so that the audience could have a better view.

One thing was quickly demonstrated, as we suspected it would be, that is, that no one can be an orator sitting down. We had an amusing illustration of this in New Orleans. There we heard the claims of Louisville, and that stalwart Blue Grass orator, Senator Ollie James, appeared for his city, Louisville. When he came forward McAdoo said quietly with a smile: "Senator, will you be good enough to take a seat and speak sitting down, so that the audience may be able to see the Committee?" The Senator complied and began talking. As he warmed up, he unconsciously rose from his seat and put on more steam. He began to work with his customary effectiveness which had been decidedly lacking before. We saw that we were in for a long and eloquent address. McAdoo interrupted and asked him if he would object to sitting down again. He did so and vainly tried to go forward. Finally he stopped and said: "Mr. Secretary, I cannot make a speech sitting down. I shall have to ask you to let me stand, and I promise you that I shall be brief." We let him have his way, and he made a good address and kept within limits.

When we got back to Washington on February 18th, we decided to work out maps showing districts that we thought ought to be created, with the Reserve City indicated for each, to do this separately, and then to meet and compare maps and exchange views. We had had about fifty maps presented to us by different individuals or groups, but we quickly discarded all of them. We found them impossible, revealing ignorance of conditions in most parts of the Union, of lines of communications, currents of trade, and banking habits. Most of these maps, of course, were prepared to make a case for some city, and, therefore, were not based on broad and disinterested considerations. We have polled the banks directly from the Comptroller's Office, and the tabulation of the votes or expressions aided us immensely, helping to confirm opinions which we had developed during our trip.

I drew about thirteen different maps. I was not satisfied with any of them, but I was willing to submit two for consideration. I had finally settled on eleven districts, leaving room for one later to be created for the Northwest, which was developing very rapidly. When we met, I found that McAdoo had a map providing for twelve districts which John Skelton Williams was willing to assent to. Williams had very little to say, as he had not been with us on our trip except for a few of the last hearings. After a full discussion, I accepted the view that there should be twelve districts.

When we came to matters of detail, we had to do some adjusting. McAdoo and Williams were inclined to select Cincinnati for the Ohio District. I insisted on Cleveland. I pointed out that we could not send Pittsburgh to Cincinnati while we could send her to Cleveland, and that if Cincinnati was to be the Reserve City, Pittsburgh should go to Philadelphia, which would leave the proposed Cincinnati district too small. McAdoo agreed with me and Williams assented. Arrangements which I preferred but which were not accepted were these: Most of Wisconsin and part of northern Michigan to go with Chicago, only northwest Wisconsin and northwest Michigan going to Minneapolis; northern New Jersey to New York, which was opposed because the New York district without northern New Jersey had about one fifth of the national banking resources; and western Connecticut to go with New York.

After reaching an agreement, we had our report prepared and published and then proceeded with the work of organization.

During our absence in the West, the tariff and the currency being out of the way, the President, who had been giving much thought to the matter, on January 20, 1914, laid before Congress his views on the trust question. Bills covering the subject had already been prepared under the direction of the Judiciary Committee of the House, headed by Henry D. Clayton, of Alabama. The President began by pointing out that public opinion had long been directed to the matter of monopolies, and that the time had come to give effect to that opinion. He emphasized the important principle that successful legislation is the embodiment of mature opinion and convincing experience. "Constructive legislation, when successful, is always the embodiment of convincing experience and of mature public opinion which finally springs out of that experience. Legislation is a business of interpretation, not of origination; and it is now plain what the opinion is to which we must give effect in this matter. It is not recent or hasty opinion. It springs out of the experience of a whole generation. It has clarified itself by long content, and those who for a long time battled with it and sought to change it are now frankly and honourably yielding to it and seeking to conform their actions to it.

[109]

"What we are purposing to do, therefore, is, happily, not to hamper or interfere with business as enlightened business men prefer to do it, or in any sense to put it under a ban. The antagonism between business and government is over. We are now about to give expression to the best business judgment of America, to what we know to be the business conscience and honour of the land."

Specifically, he pleaded for laws which would prohibit interlocking of the personnel of directorates of great corporations. Railroads, particularly, should be released from their subordination to great financial interests and should hereafter be run solely as transportation agencies in the interest of the public. "The country is ready, therefore, to accept, and accept with relief as well as approval, a law which will confer upon the Interstate Commerce Commission the power to superintend and regulate the financial operations by which the railroads are henceforth to be supplied with the money they need for their proper development to meet the rapidly growing requirements of the country for increased and improved facilities of transportation."

The country, he insisted, awaited a more explicit definition of anti-trust law. It was afflicted with uncertainty and "nothing hampers business like uncertainty." Business men demand "something more than the menace of legal process. They desire the advice, the definite guidance, and information which can be supplied by an administrative body, an Interstate Trade Commission." He might have pointed out that business men had frequently said that they found it exceedingly trying to conduct their affairs with the frequent interruptions of our court proceedings and were demanding that the government inform them as to the "rules of the game."

Furthermore, he urged, punishments should fall, not upon business itself but upon individuals who use business instrumentalities to do things condemned by public policy and sound business practice. "Every act of business is done at the command or upon the initiative of some ascertainable person or group of persons. These should be held individually responsible and the punishment should fall upon them, not upon the business organization of which they make illegal use. It should be one of the main objects of our legislation to divest such persons of their corporate cloak and deal with them as those who do not represent their corporations, but merely by deliberate intention break the law."

In this last suggestion, particularly, the President was seeking to project into the national legislation a distinctive feature of laws which, as Governor, he had succeeded in forcing through the New Jersey legislature.

CHAPTER VIII

OUTBREAK OF THE WAR

Repeal of Panama Tolls—Mexico—The Coming of the War: Its Effect on the United States—President Urges War Taxation —Questions of Water Power, Shipping, and National Defence —Disagreement with President on Immigration Restriction Veto

ON March 5, 1914, the President appeared before Congress and read his brief message on the repeal of the law exempting American coastwise ships from paying tolls at the Panama Canal. He begged Congress not to measure his message by the number of sentences it contained. He had addressed to Congress no communication, he said, which carried with it graver implications. The matter was one with regard to which he was charged by the Constitution with personal responsibility. The exemption, in his judgment, constituted a mistaken economic policy and a plain violation of a treaty with Great Britain concerning the Canal, concluded on November 18, 1901. Whatever might be the view held in the United States, the meaning of the Treaty was not debated outside the United States. We ought to be too self-respecting to interpret with a too strained reading the words of our promises just because we have power enough to give us leave to read them as we please. "We ought to reverse our action without raising the question whether we were right or wrong, and so once more deserve our reputation for generosity and for the redemption of every obligation without quibble or hesitation."

"I ask this of you in support of the foreign policy of the Administration. I shall not know how to deal with other matters of even greater delicacy and nearer consequence if you do not grant it to me in ungrudging measure."

The President read this message to Congress without having laid it before the Cabinet. We had discussed the matter, as I have indicated, in the spring of 1913. He had not mentioned the matter since that time. All of us were somewhat puzzled by his reference to matters of even greater delicacy and by the seriousness of his manner and language. My guess is that he is meeting with resistance in his handling of Mexican and other matters from Great Britain, especially because she doubts our sincerity and good faith; partly because of our action on the tolls matter. I know that Page is constantly representing that he is very little use in England because we do not take the course which will show that we mean to be decent. Lane thought that bringing up the repeal was bad politics, that it would create resistance and block other more important things. Bryan, who referred to the fact that the Democratic platform had a plank opposing the repeal, had discovered a way out to his satisfaction. The tolls exemption was in effect a subsidy to American ships. The Democratic platform declared against subsidies. There was a conflict. The subsidy business was a long-standing principle; the tolls exemption was an occasional or passing matter, and had been little considered, and could not be said to embody a mature demand of the rank and file of the party. The declaration in favour of tolls, therefore, ought to yield to the plank against subsidies.

[113]

Mexico had for some time occupied very little attention at Cabinet meetings, when an incident occurred which brought it to the centre of the stage. This was the arrest of a paymaster of the U. S. S. *Dolphin* and its boats' crew at the Iturbide bridge landing at Tampico, April 8, 1914. The arrest was made by a subordinate officer. As he was proceeding up one of the streets of the town, he was met by a superior, who ordered him to return to the landing and to await instructions. In an hour and a half, orders came from the commander of the forces of Huerta in Tampico to release the men. The commander apologized and Huerta expressed regret. He explained that martial law prevailed at the time and that orders had been given that no one was to land at the bridge. Our officers had not been notified of this; and, in any event, arrest of our men was not the remedy. Admiral Mayo regarded the action as a grave insult and demanded that our flag be saluted with special ceremony. The demand was referred to Huerta, who ordered a refusal to comply. President Wilson, on April 14th, dispatched the American fleet to Mexican waters. Notes were exchanged, and Huerta agreed to salute our flag if we would return the courtesy. The President declined and demanded an unconditional salute by six o'clock in the afternoon of April 19th. Huerta refused, and it was reported that a German steamer with munitions of war was approaching Vera Cruz.

Meantime, there had been other incidents, such as the arrest of an orderly of the U. S. battleship *Minnesota* and the interception of a message from our government to its embassy in Mexico City, which indicated a studied purpose of Huerta and his people to single out the United

States for insult. On April 20th, the President appeared before Congress to ask its advice and coöperation. He specifically asked its approval of the use of "the armed forces of the United States in such ways and to such extent as may be necessary to obtain from General Huerta and his adherents the fullest recognition of the rights and dignity of the United States." The President expressed the hope that this country could not be forced into a war with the Mexican people. They were not to blame. They had no government. The conflict would be only with Huerta and his adherents, if it came; and our object would be only to have respect shown to our flag and to restore to the people of Mexico the opportunity to set up again their own laws.

The President was in Hot Springs, Virginia, when the incident occurred. Admiral Mayo could quickly have reached the Navy Department and have asked for instructions before demanding a salute. I think he ought to have been authorized to demand a salute, but I doubt if it ought to have been possible for him to do so without specific advice. In this case, it may lead to war which would amount to very little. In other cases, such a course might involve the nation and the world in a great and prolonged war. Ought a military or naval commander to have the right to take action which would lead two nations into war? I think not. The President thought that even he ought to have the previous advice and approval of the people's representatives before he took the logical and necessary step to make good his support of Mayo's demand.

The affair, in the absence of a demand by Mayo of a salute, might well have closed after the apology of the

[115]

Tampico commander and the expression of regret from Huerta, if the additional incidents had not occurred. The situation was delicate. We had stated that Mexico had no government. The arrest was made by an insignificant officer who was promptly called down by his superior. It was scarcely compatible with our dignity to make war on a person, a usurper. There was nothing for the President to do, however, after Mayo made his demand, except to support him. Our position before the Mexican people would have been an impossible one.

On April 21st, on orders from the President under protection from the fleet, a force of Marines from the United States warships landed at Vera Cruz, seized the Customs House, and later occupied the whole city. Diplomatic relations were promptly severed.

In connection with this affair, there happened at one of the Cabinet meetings an interesting episode. It was obvious that the situation was critical. The time had come to take military action or to back down. It was clear that Mexico could give us little effective military resistance, but it was not known what the attitude of certain great powers would be. In any event, a decision to go into Mexico would mean loss of life. The President was profoundly disturbed. He said with much feeling that it was a terrible responsibility to decide on a course which might take the nation into a war and cause the loss of the lives of many men, and then he added suddenly: "If there are any of you who still believe in prayer, I wish you would think seriously over this matter between now and our next meeting." This came with something of a shock and sent us from the Cabinet room with decidedly solemn faces.

[116]

The capture of Vera Cruz was followed by the severance of diplomatic relations. The American chargé d'affaires was handed his passports. The special envoy, Mr. Lind, had already abandoned his mission and was on his way home. At this juncture, an offer of mediation was made by Argentina, Brazil, and Chile, the A. B. C. powers, and it was accepted by the United States and Huerta. It is difficult to see what they can accomplish beyond making it clear to Pan-America that we have no selfish purposes and that, if we go into Mexico, it will be because we cannot avoid doing so, that we shall simply undertake to establish order and set Mexico on her feet.

The whole Mexican situation is a mess. Huerta must go; but when he does go, nobody can forecast what will happen. Zapata, a bandit, is operating in the south and is headed for Mexico City. If he gets in, things will happen which will enrage the American people and the world. Villa is making headway in the north, and seems to be holding his men pretty well in hand in deference largely to the wishes of his friend, General Hugh L. Scott. Villa has an economic programme which has some merit in it, but it cannot be carried out without grave trouble. He intends to give the masses of the Mexican people some interest in the land and in the fruits of their labour; but they are densely ignorant and probably would make little use of their opportunities. It will take generations to lay the foundations of order and to develop and direct constructive programmes which will bring the masses of the Mexicans to the point where they can use land or run a government; and the requisite number of intelligent and forceful men in Mexico to furnish leadership is not in sight. If Villa should get in there might be an unpleasant mo-

[117]

ment with Great Britain, because she notified us a month ago that she would demand satisfaction of Villa for the murder of one of her subjects.

It is possible that we may have to go into Mexico. We are not dealing with people who think in our terms or in those of most nations with which we have many dealings.

Early in the summer of 1914, we again abandoned the holding of Cabinet meetings at the stated times with the understanding that we would be subject to the President's call. I was much occupied with the affairs of the Department of Agriculture, to some extent with my duties as a member of the Reserve Bank Organization Committee, and other domestic problems.

On the second of August, 1914, I left Washington to join Mrs. Houston the following day in Boston, as we had accepted an invitation to spend a week or ten days with friends at York Corner, Maine. The days immediately following were full of rumours and excitement. Word came that the German steamship, the *Kronprinzessen Cecilie*, with a large stock of gold on board, had put into Bar Harbor. The reason given was that war had formally been declared by Germany, France, Belgium, and England.

I had watched the development of the trouble between Austria and Serbia. I had noted with passing interest the news of the assassination of the Austrian Archduke, Francis Ferdinand, and his wife at Sarajevo, Bosnia, on June 30th, Austria's ultimatum to Serbia on July 23d, her declaration of war against Serbia on July 28th, Russia's mobilization on the twenty-ninth, and Germany's declaration of war against Russia the day before I left Washington. But as I had had no rest for many months, and as

[118]

there was no clear indication that the developments would be brought very near home to us or that there was anything I could do if I remained in Washington, I decided to take a short vacation.

There had been so much fighting and turmoil in the Balkans that I had become accustomed to them. For the moment, it looked like more of the same thing on a larger and more serious scale. I had known that the Slavs in the Southeast had been especially restless since the annexation of Bosnia-Herzegovina in 1909. I felt that Serbia had become more aggressive since the Balkan wars, that she aspired to larger territory and was desirous of securing the adhesion of parts of the Slavic peoples in the Austrian dominions. It was clear that Austria would hold on to what she had in order to have access to the sea. The great trouble is that these nations have as their leading motive, not so much the welfare of their people as expansion of their territories and the enhancement of their prestige and power, under the leadership of their princely houses and their aristocratic militaristic adherents. The curse of central and southern Europe is the desire of the reigning dynasties to expand their power. To this end, they keep alive racial and national jealousies and hatreds. The foolish mediæval notion is rampant that the prosperity of one state is a menace to every other, and that military force is the only guarantee of safety and greatness. There was no appearance anywhere of the idea that the welfare of the people of Europe lies in the nations' living together in neighbourly and Christian fashion and that it is to the interest of all for each to keep a clean national house and to help every other to make its fullest economic and political contribution to civilization. The ruling classes are obsessed with a sense of their own importance and regard the masses as so many cattle. They boast of their superior civilization and have no awareness that it means the maximum of ease and luxury for themselves and the minimum for the multitude. Politically, economically, and socially, Continental Europe, with the exception of a few small countries, is still mediæval; and yet there are Americans who accept the boast of this Europe that it is civilized while their country is crude and common.

When I reached York, I saw from the papers that Germany had practically without a declaration of war taken the offensive against France through Luxembourg and had made a base proposal to Belgium, which the latter had bravely spurned. Belgium's heroic answer thrilled me, but still the horror was not brought directly home to me in all its tragic meaning. There came England's ultimatum and declaration of war; and I had a feeling that the end of things had come. Figuratively speaking, I stopped in my tracks, dazed and horror-stricken.

After a few days' rest, I motored to Woods Hole, and when I reached there I found a telegram awaiting me telling me of the death of the President's wife. I had had no warning that her condition was serious, although I had seen Doctor Grayson at rather frequent intervals before I left Washington. The President himself had given no hint that he was alarmed, although, as I afterward learned, he and Doctor Grayson had felt since May that the end was not far off. What a terrible strain for the President during all the intervening days, and with what courage and fortitude he faced the inevitable.

The effect of the war on industry and finance in this

country in 1914 was terrific. There was a temporary paralysis. The United States, by reason of her dependence on foreign ships, was either isolated or dependent on the plans and necessities of foreign nations. It was obvious that temporarily the farming sections, and particularly the South, would be hard hit. Germany would be cut off and would no longer take from three to three and three quarter million bales of cotton. As chance would have it, our crops were almost, if not quite, the largest in our history. Their movement had already begun. In a short time, our warehouse and terminal facilities were overrun. It was reported that more than fourteen hundred cars were on the tracks on the way to Galveston. If the control of the sea had long remained in doubt, a tremendously serious situation would have developed. By reason of the fact that England and France not only controlled the sea with their navies, but also had immense shipping facilities, the movement of foodstuffs and munitions soon set up in volume, and relief was afforded in certain directions.

The interruption of trade had an immediate effect on the government's revenues. Custom duties began to drop greatly. In August alone there had been a falling off in customs of more than ten million five hundred thousand dollars as compared with the corresponding month of 1913.

The President, therefore, on September 4th, appeared before Congress to urge additional legislation. He pointed out the danger of delay and warned against reliance on loans, the usual resort, especially of non-democratic countries, in time of emergency, and too frequently of democracies.

I was particularly pleased by what the President had to say on the wisdom of taxing. It is, in part, as follows: "And we ought not to borrow. We ought to resort to taxation, however we may regret the necessity of putting additional temporary burdens on our people. . . . The country is able to pay any just and reasonable taxes without distress. . . . The people of this country are both intelligent and profoundly patriotic. They are ready to meet the present conditions in the right way and to support the government with generous self-denial. They know and understand, and will be intolerant only of those who dodge responsibility or are not frank with them." He closed by urging Congress to provide an additional revenue of $100,000,000 through internal taxes.

The elections occupied much of the time of the professional politicians through the latter part of September and October of 1914. The results, on the whole, were favourable, but not what I expected. I thought that the Democrats would maintain a larger lead in the House. However, they gained in the Senate and will have control of it, at any rate till 1919. If conditions improve, they should carry the elections in 1916.

The President, in his Second Annual Message to Congress, December, 1914, gave much time to a discussion of steps which he thought should be taken to improve production and transportation, especially by sea, which had been so greatly deranged by war. He urged haste in water-power legislation and pleaded for the prompt passage of the shipping bill. The topic, however, which attracted most attention was national defence. There were many who were urging large measures of preparedness. They were insistent on the creation of a regular army of considerable strength and the Secretary of War apparently was committed to a marked enlargement of the regular establishment. The President's principal points were these: We are not prepared for war in the sense that we can put a trained nation in the field. We shall never be ready in time of peace to do this as long as we retain our present political institutions. We are at peace with the world. Our independence and our territory are not in danger. We are champions of peace. "This is the time above all others when we should wish and resolve to keep our strength by self-possession, our influence by preserving our ancient principles of action." We have never had a large standing army. "We will not ask our young men to spend the best years of their lives making soldiers of themselves." We will depend upon a citizenry trained and accustomed to arms. We should "provide a system by which every citizen who will volunteer for training may be made familiar with the use of modern arms, the rudiments of drill and manœuvre, and the maintenance and sanitation of camps." We should develop and strengthen the National Guard. More than this would be a reversal of our policy. "More than this proposed at this time, permit me to say, would mean merely that we had lost our self-possession, that we had been thrown off our balance by a war with which we have nothing to do, whose causes cannot touch us, whose very existence affords us opportunities of friendship and disinterested service which should make us ashamed of any thought of hostility or fearful preparations for trouble." We shall take leave to be strong upon the seas in the future as in the past. "Our ships are our national bulwarks. But who shall tell us what sort of navy to build? Who can tell

[123]

us what the changes we see going on will demand? But I turn away from the subject. It is not new. There is no need to discuss it. We shall not alter our attitude toward it because some amongst us are nervous and excited."

The President's closing words were eloquent. He pictured the tasks on which a nation's energies might worthily be expended. He unfolded the ideals of a great free nation. How different the situation of the world might be if Europe had had for generations leadership in such directions! He said: "To develop our life and our resources; to supply our own people and the people of the world as their need arises from the abundant plenty of our fields and our marts of trade; to enrich the commerce of our own states and of the world with the products of our mines, our farms, and our factories, with the creations of our thought and the fruits of our character—this is what will hold our attention and our enthusiasm steadily, now and in the years to come, as we strive to show in our life as a nation what liberty and the inspirations of an emancipated spirit may do for men and for societies, for individuals, for states, and for mankind."

The President had not read this message to us. When I heard it, I had very mingled feelings. The rural credits problem and the shipping act we had discussed. As to the latter, I was more than doubtful. I doubted whether we had reached the point in our economic development when it would pay us to put capital and labour in shipping. We have vast opportunities in other directions as evidenced by our high productivity and high wages. I felt confident that it would be foolish to attempt to develop a merchant marine for international trade and retain some of our trade restrictions. I was inclined to believe that a merchant marine would be a very expensive luxury, or necessity, and that we could justify the undertaking only on grounds of national defence and preparedness. For this reason, I urged that the use of the ships as possible naval auxiliaries or as transports be emphasized. What a pity we cannot have, without danger, the benefits of a world division of labour and, in this instance, use the ships of England, France, Germany, Italy, and other nations for our overseas trade.

One of the two measures to which the President referred as finely conceived I was by no means satisfied with: the one dealing with water power. This had been taken up by the Interior Department without consultation either with me or with the Secretary of War, although the Interior Department controlled only about 8 per cent. of the nation's water power, while Agriculture through the Forest Service controlled about 42 per cent., and the War Department, all our navigable streams. Lane had called me up at the last moment to say that a committee was going to hold a final meeting on water power in his office and that he would like to have me present. I replied that it was too late, that I was opposed to what the Committee had in mind, that I could only express my opposition, and that, in the circumstances, I had better stay away. Incidentally, the bill proposed to take the jurisdiction of all water power from the other two departments and place it under the Interior. This, I believed, would set up endless confusion and conflicts.

The national forests, in which there is 42 per cent. of the water power, are in the Department of Agriculture, where they belong. In these there are many important activities, such as the regulation of grazing of millions of animals, timber sales, reforestation, fire protection, recreation, and other uses; and these it would be difficult to administer, if another department had jurisdiction over waterways and water development. Of course, the Interior Department's answer was obvious: Transfer the national forests to that department in which the parks and public domain are administered. This would be a crime. The Interior Department had the forests once. They were steadily running down and were supporting only about one million five hundred thousand animals. Since the Department of Agriculture has had them, the grazing has steadily improved and they are supporting six or seven times as many animals. All the other features of forest administration are agricultural—roads, reforestation, insect control, and irrigation. And furthermore, the personnel of the Agricultural Department is trained for this work and is non-political, while that of the Interior, except of a few bureaus like the Geological Survey and Mines, is political and relatively inefficient. And, furthermore, the Interior Department's attitude and record on conservation have not been and are not now satisfactory.

As a matter of fact, instead of moving over the national forests to the Department of the Interior, Congress ought to transfer the national parks to the Department of Agriculture and ought to empower that Department to regulate grazing on the public domain. The solution of the problem of administering water power will be found in the creation of a Commission consisting of the three Heads of Departments concerned: War, Interior, and Agriculture.

I did not feel easy over the President's remarks on national defence. I agreed that "in time of peace" the American people would be indisposed to prepare for war or to have a great standing army. I agreed that we are now (1914) at peace with all the world, that our independence is not now threatened, that we intend to live our own lives, and that we want nobody's territory; but I could not forget that half the world was afire, and I could not assent to the view that the war was one "whose causes cannot touch us." I was particularly disturbed by the declaration that we must depend in time of peril, not upon a standing army, nor yet upon a reserve army, but "upon a citizenry trained and accustomed to arms." I assented to the view that we should have a trained "citizenry," and I was far from being partial to a large standing army, but in the circumstances I thought that we should have something more than our small regular army, scarcely more than a respectable police force in number, and that we should not depend on volunteers. I thought that we ought to enlarge our army, provide for the training of more officers, develop a large reserve force, improve the National Guard, and lay the foundations for an adequate supply of equipment, munitions, and big and little guns.

At the Cabinet meeting on Tuesday, January 26th, the Immigration Bill again claimed attention. It had been mentioned at the preceding meeting, and Secretary Wilson had intimated that he was looking into the situation. At this meeting, he had his comment prepared but did not read it, as the President announced that he would veto the bill. I do not know what the Secretary's view is. There was little discussion of the matter, as the President had evidently already finally chosen his position.

I was against a veto and said so. The measure is not

an ideal one, but it would serve as a foundation and could be amended. Immigration ought to be checked, and particularly from the southeastern and eastern parts of Europe. We are getting entirely too many people who have no aptitude or qualifications for participating in our political activities and may never acquire any. I think we have overworked the asylum business. We may owe some duty to people in less fortunate countries, but we owe it to ourselves to see that our institutions are sound and strong, and they will be menaced if the numbers of those of radically different experiences and habits continue to mount up, and particularly if they are permitted to congregate in race groups in our great cities or even in the rural districts. If we allow them to come, we should see that they are dispersed.

These people furnish not only many of our worst agitators, but also very fruitful soil for the seed of revolution. In their countries, they have been accustomed to resort to violence to secure what they want; and what they sought at home we began with and have greatly extended. At home they were governed by a minority, the ruling class; and they do not know that things are reversed here. They are easily deceived by names and appearances. They do not know that the majority here can peacefully secure anything it wants; that any cause can get a hearing; that all any advocates have to do is to convert the majority to their way of thinking; and that, if they cannot do so, they must hold their peace. They cannot understand that not to do this is treason to the majority, to democracy, and they do not know that the American people are not going to permit any misguided minority to have its way by violence.

An educational test is not a wholly satisfactory test, but it is one test. A people whose government has failed to make provision for their development along educational lines are written down by that fact as an unsatisfactory people; and lack of education in such people seeking admission here is at least symptomatic. The education test is not merely a test of opportunity. It is also a test of purpose and character. A people of the requisite character and purpose see to it that educational opportunity is not lacking. This is true of individuals in large measure. With us, sections where educational opportunity has not been provided may justly be charged with measurable lack of character, purpose, and will. Eighty per cent. of the Russian people are illiterate. Millions of people who, after centuries, will stand for such indifference and failure on the part of their government and have not the initiative to do anything for themselves in an educational direction, will stand for anything, and we do not need many additions to our population from them.

A restrictive measure has passed Congress three times. This evidences sufficient deliberation, and this last action ought to have been acquiesced in. I do not assent to the view indicated in the veto message that a measure should not be accepted unless the people have previously given their mandate on it.

CHAPTER IX

BRYAN'S RESIGNATION

*Garrison Dissatisfied—The Sinking of the "Lusitania"—
Apathy in the West—Bryan Refuses to Face Issue—His Last
Attendance at Cabinet Meeting*

SECRETARY GARRISON, for some time before
April, 1915, had been showing signs of restiveness,
but I was surprised when he came to see me and
told me that he was going to resign. He had his
resignation written and was set on sending it in. He told
me that he had found that he was not in sympathy with
the Administration. The atmosphere, he thought, was not
good. It was too Bryanistic. There was a strong note
of hostility to business. He was not in accord on Mexico.
He resented the attitude on preparedness.

Garrison, as usual, stated his views clearly and strongly,
but I thought that he took an extreme position. I
could not agree that the Administration was Bryanistic.
The President was doing the leading and Bryan the following. There had been little or nothing new in respect
to policies since the fall, when Garrison made his speech
at Trenton which was a strong defence of the Administration. He was not justified, I thought, in saying that his
defence views were not being given full consideration.
He was presenting them vigorously before the Congressional Committee, and it seemed not unlikely that they
would be accepted in the main.

Members of the Cabinet discussed Garrison's case at length among themselves. The opinion was that Garrison's attitude had no sufficient justification, that it was too rigid, and that he was too impatient. I felt that it was best that he should carry out his purpose and quit. I did not see how he could remain in the Cabinet feeling as he did, and, knowing him to be a gentleman of high character and fine feeling, I was sure he would not stay unless he could give his full and loyal support to the President. I knew that, if he resigned, the partisan press would make a great to-do about it, but I believed that the tempest would be of short duration and would do little damage. Most of the members thought it would be best if Garrison resigned later. Burleson was strongly of this view and presented his reasons at length. It was suggested to Tumulty that he tell the President that Garrison might quit at any moment, and that it would be well for him to have a strong man in mind to appoint immediately upon his resignation, preferably an outstanding man from New England, Ex-Secretary Olney, if he would serve.

In April, 1915, I left Washington for the West to make a business trip through the national forests. I was in southern California when the news came that the *Lusitania* had been sunk on May 7th. I instantly realized the seriousness of this tragedy from the point of view of our international relations. The press reports indicated that a considerable number of Americans had lost their lives, and raised the question as to whether the ship could be regarded as a war vessel if the rumour that she carried arms and munitions were true. I had a wire from a friend asking for my views. I replied that I did not have sufficient information to justify me in forming an opinion.

I added that certain things were clear to me. Nothing could justify the sinking of a vessel carrying passengers, except after visit and search, and, even if it were discovered that it was carrying contraband, except after seeing that passengers and crew were placed in a position of safety. I added that it was questionable wisdom for Americans to sail on belligerent ships and run the risk of involving their country in a serious situation, but that they had a perfect right to do so. I advised reliance on the wisdom and courage of the President.

I found that the sentiment in the West was strongly with the President in his course The war seemed out there to be far very away. Nobody was thinking about intervention either in Mexico or in Europe. The people were not seriously contemplating the possibility of our becoming involved in the war in Europe; but, at the same time, they wanted our rights safeguarded.

The morning I received the news of the sinking of the *Lusitania,* a delegation from Los Angeles with which I had an appointment for breakfast and a trip into the mountains, made its appearance. The members of the delegation talked for a few minutes about the tragedy without excitement, and then turned the discussion to irrigation, citrous fruit, roads, water power, and forest-fire protection, and did not again while I was with them refer to the *Lusitania.* Nor did any reporter of any local paper seek to interview me on the matter, and no citizen brought it up during the remainder of my stay in the West, which lasted several weeks.

I returned to Washington in time for the Cabinet meeting Tuesday, June 1st. Bryan was a few minutes late. He seemed to be labouring under a great strain and sat back in his chair most of the time with his eyes closed.

The President read a draft of a proposed warning to the Mexican factions. Lane thought the President ought to make it clear that the government would get behind another Mexican leader, Iturbide, and that steps ought to be taken to get him in touch with financiers who would back him. Bryan thought the way ought to be left open to recognize one of the men, Carranza, who had been fighting so long for liberty, and not take up a man who would probably play in with the reactionaries. Another member suggested that we ought to have clearly in mind the steps we would take in case nothing happened, and not commit ourselves in the note to any individual. The President seemed much surprised at the many and divergent suggestions, and said so with some emphasis, adding that the note embodied what seemed to him to be the consensus of opinion of the last Cabinet meeting. He asked for an explanation of the "singular change of mind." Nobody ventured to enlighten him.

I reminded him that I had been absent from the last few meetings and expressed the hope that what I might say would not be based on a misapprehension.

"The note purports to be a solemn warning. From its phraseology, the people would, of course, regard it as such, and also as a change of policy. But I find no indication of a change of policy and no hint that anything else will happen. In effect it says: 'We have tried Carranza, and hoped for something from Villa and others. They have failed us. Now, we will look around and see if we can find another promising bandit. Perhaps Iturbide would do.' This does not mean a change of policy. It is a continuance of the present policy. We simply propose to play our cards on a new man. I know the new man. He is the best of the outfit I have seen, but I have no real faith in him. Like most of his kind, he is vain and vainglorious. I do not believe he can do anything. He has not the right fibre, and if he prevailed he would do nothing for the Mexican people. He wants to get in, not for their sake, but for his own. To that extent I agree with Mr. Bryan.

"I have no faith in Carranza. He is dull and pigheaded. If he has any intelligence, he takes great pains to conceal it. Villa is a roughneck and a murderer. He is clearly impossible.

"If you propose to back a new man, do not announce a change of policy or issue a solemn warning. Simply quickly go ahead, back him, and let the proper parties know that you will approve their support of him. I notice you conclude by saying that if the leaders do not get together, you will turn elsewhere for suggestions. What does this mean? Who will give them? This will scarcely appear to be an adequate conclusion of a note conveying a solemn warning and announcing a change of policy. The people will have a right to believe that you have definitely in mind a real solution of the problem and are prepared to see it through. They will expect to see you take drastic action if necessary. The people may or may not now wish intervention, but they would have a right to conclude from this statement that you have it in mind in case your warning is not heeded."

At this Bryan vigorously shook his head.

The President asked what I would suggest. I said: "Either do not issue the statement, or conclude it with a

[134]

definite intimation that if the Mexican situation does not
clear, you will be compelled to recommend to Congress
the steps which this government should take to bring an
intolerable condition of things to an end."² The message
was sent on June 2nd.

The President presented his draft of his reply to the
German note on the sinking of the *Lusitania*. The first
note had been sent while I was in California. In it we
had warned Germany that her measures could not "operate as in any degree an abbreviation of the rights of American shipmasters or of American citizens bound on lawful
errands as passengers on merchant ships of belligerent
nationality; and that it [our government] must hold the
Imperial German Government to a strict accountability
for any infringement of those rights, intentional or inci-
dental."² Our government assumed that the German
government "accepted" as of course the rule that the
lives of noncombatants, whether they be of neutral citizenship or citizens of one of the nations at war, cannot lawfully or rightfully be put in jeopardy by the capture or
destruction of an unarmed merchantman, and recognize
also, as all other nations do, the obligation to take the
usual precaution of visit and search to ascertain whether a
suspected merchantman is in fact of belligerent nationality
or is in fact carrying contraband of war under a neutral
flag."² The objection to the German method of attack
against enemy trade "lies in the practical impossibility
of employing submarines in the distinction of commerce
without disregarding those rules of fairness, reason, justice, and humanity, which all modern opinion regards as
imperative. . . . American citizens act within their
indisputable rights in taking their ships and in travelling

[135]

wherever their legitimate business calls them upon the high seas, and exercise those rights in what should be the well-justified confidence that their lives will not be endangered by acts done in clear violation of universally acknowledged international obligations, and certainly with the confidence that their own government will sustain them in the exercise of those rights."

The note closed with an expression of confident expectation that the German Government would disavow the acts of which this government complained, make all possible reparation, and take steps to prevent a recurrence of them, and with a warning that this government would omit no act necessary to its performance of a sacred duty to maintain the rights of American citizens.

This note was signed "Bryan."

The German reply was unsatisfactory. It was insincere and cynical. It contained a statement to the effect that a great liner had no right to sink so quickly merely from the effect of a torpedo, that it must have resulted from the explosion of ammunition, and that the *Lusitania* had been armed. A final statement was reserved pending the receipt of further information from this government.

Secretary Garrison urged that the rejoinder contain no discussion of details or facts. Germany should be made to say, first, whether or not she accepted the principle we stood for. If she did not, there was nothing to discuss; if she did, we could then canvass details with her.

One member wanted to know what we were going to do about England's interference with our trade. He wanted a strong note sent to her protesting against her illegal action in holding up our exports, particularly our cotton. There was an instant objection to such a course from several members of the Cabinet. They strongly resisted the proposal that our material interests be considered at the same moment when we were discussing a grave matter involving human lives.

Bryan got excited. He said that he had all along insisted on a note to England; that she was illegally preventing our exports from going where we had a right to send them; and that the Cabinet seemed to be pro-Ally. All the rest of the Cabinet strongly protested against a note to England, and no note was sent. The President sharply rebuked Bryan, saying that his remarks were unfair and unjust. He had no right to say that any one was pro-Ally or pro-German. Each one was merely trying to be a good American. We had lodged a protest with England and might do so again at the proper time, but this would be a singularly inappropriate time to take up such a matter with her. Furthermore, he had had indications that the control of shipping would be taken out of the hands of the Admiralty, out of Lord Fisher's hands, that there would be Cabinet changes, and that our reasonable demands would be met. Certainly, in any event, when we had before us a grave issue with the Germans, it would be folly to force an issue of such character with England. We were merely trying to look at our duty and all our problems objectively. He added that certain things were clear and that as to them his mind was made up.

Here Bryan handed the President a note, and I said to myself: "That must be an intimation that he expects to quit." Apparently, it was something else.

Redfield said that Bryan was in error in saying that England had actually stopped our exports. As a matter of fact, he insisted, they are larger than ever and are

[137]

growing. Bryan asked if that was not true only so far as the Allies were concerned. We all instantly answered emphatically in the negative, and someone suggested that such interruptions as had taken place were due in no small measure to the foolish action of some of our merchants in trying to conceal contraband and of some of our ships in attempting to evade the English regulations.

Bryan then asked, with a show of heat, if we thought we ought to ask the English authorities what we might do. We replied that the English regulations were framed to expedite the shipment of non-contraband goods and not to delay them. A certificate from the proper authorities exempted them from interference. We had to face the facts of a difficult situation. We pointed out particularly that our cotton had gone out in much larger quantities than we had expected, in quantities almost equal to those of the preceding year, that 8,000,000 bales would have been shipped by July 1st when we had expected that less than 6,000,000 would go. Sweden, Holland, Spain, and Italy had imported 1,900,000 bales more than in the preceding year; Italy 900,000 against 450,000; Sweden 732,000 instead of 44,000; and Holland 500,000 against 30,000. It seemed highly likely that much of this cotton had found its way to Germany. It was true also that immensely larger quantities than usual of lard and foodstuffs had gone to certain neutral countries, and the presumption was that much of it was for transshipment. These facts seemed to make little or no impression on Bryan.

I suggested that the President in his note assume that the German reply accepted the principle for which we were contending. I added that Germany had delayed saying so pending the receipt of information from us as to the arming of the *Lusitania* and as to its carrying munitions, and suggested that he give them the facts and reiterate the demand of his first note.

As we left the meeting, I said to two of my colleagues that Bryan would "fly the coop" if the President showed firmness toward either Mexico or Germany, or even if Bryan became convinced that the President meant what he said in his first note. Bryan evidently had not taken the first note very seriously. He imagined, apparently, either that nothing further would happen, or that Germany would comply with our wishes as a matter of course, or that we would back down. I had the feeling after the meeting that, if necessary to avoid trouble, Bryan would be willing to tell Germany that we did not mean anything by the first note and that she should not take it seriously.

On Friday, the fourth, we met the President in his study, the old Cabinet room, in the White House proper. The President spent several minutes looking up something and a confused and somewhat tiresome discussion followed. It tried the President's patience greatly and tired him perceptibly. It did not help him. I spoke to him for a few minutes along the same line as at the preceding meeting, and several of us suggested that the main thing for him to do was to stand by his first note. The meeting did not last long.

The following day, Saturday, the fifth, at 12:15, the President called me over the telephone and asked me what I thought the settled sentiment of the Cabinet was. He said that he had been able to get no clear notion of the view of the body at the last meeting. I told him that the general judgment was that his note was admirable and needed only slight modification. I suggested that it would be useless to demand flatly that Germany give up the use of the submarine, but that it was imperative that he demand that she use it in accordance with the law of nations and the dictates of humanity, and that she must not imperil or destroy our ships, or endanger the lives of our citizens travelling on ships on which they had a right to travel. I suggested that he lay the emphasis on our own ships and on the safety of our own citizens on whatever ships they were lawfully travelling, and that other neutral nations might be trusted to do their own protesting about their ships and citizens. I told him, also, that one member was in favour simply of making Germany say "yes" or "no," without referring at all to the issue of fact which had been raised. He said that that would not do at all; that it was too technical a view.

On Sunday, June 6th, at the President's request, I went to the White House with McAdoo to see him. When he came in, he said immediately that Bryan was going to resign. I told him that I was not surprised; that I had thought at the Friday meeting that Bryan's note to him was an intimation that he was going to quit, and that I had said to McAdoo and Lane as we were leaving the meeting that Bryan was going to "fly the coop."

McAdoo had seen Bryan Saturday. Bryan was in the throes of writing his resignation. McAdoo told him that it would not be fair to the nation, to the President, or to himself to resign in the circumstances. The President expressed some apprehension that, if Bryan resigned immediately, it might create the impression among our people and in Germany that the Administration wanted trouble and was bent on forcing an issue. I said that I thought that most of our people would put another interpretation on it, and that nobody could understand the psychology of the Germans. It was agreed that there was no use or wisdom in trying to change Bryan's mind.

The President was confident that Bryan would resign and was on personal grounds genuinely sorry. He said that he had a real affection and admiration for Bryan, but that he was doing wrong to quit in the circumstances.

The President asked us to think of a man for Bryan's successor, saying that he had canvassed the field and could not hit upon a satisfactory outside man. He said that Colonel House would be a good man, but that his health probably would not permit him to take the place, and that his appointment would make Texas loom too large. He remarked that Lansing would not do, that he was not a big enough man, did not have enough imagination, and would not sufficiently vigorously combat or question his views, and that he was lacking in initiative. I agreed with him and said that I thought that Lansing was useful where he was but that he would be of no real assistance to him in the position of Secretary of State.

Both McAdoo and the President had a talk with Bryan on Monday but there was no change in his attitude.

The Cabinet met on Tuesday, June 8th, at the usual hour. Bryan was absent. We began discussing the revised note to Germany. There was further discussion of the suggestion that the note ought merely to hold Germany to the principle involved without a reference to the issue of fact she had raised. This point was soon passed over, and then the question was raised as to whether the note was sufficiently firm.

At this point, the President was interrupted by a message. A few minutes later, another messenger came in, and the President said: "Gentlemen, Mr. Bryan has re-signed as Secretary of State to take effect when the German note is sent. He is on the telephone and wants to know whether it would be desirable or agreeable for him to attend the Cabinet meeting. Would it be embarrassing? What do you think?"

There was a general expression to the effect that his presence would not embarrass any of us, that it would be entirely agreeable to us for him to attend, but that he ought to feel free to follow his own inclination.

In a few minutes, Bryan came in. All the members stood up; there was no evidence of embarrassment in any direction; the President greeted Bryan very graciously and then we resumed our seats and the discussion. Bryan, looking exhausted and appearing to be under a great emotional strain, leaned back in his chair with his eyes closed.

I took up the discussion and said in substance:

"I find myself in some difficulty because your first note is not entirely clear to me. I first read it when I was in California, and I endeavoured then to discover just what it meant.

"In one place it says that this government cannot admit that the German policy and measures can operate as in any degree an abbreviation of the rights of American shipmasters or of American citizens bound on lawful errands as passengers on merchant ships of belligerent nationality and that it will hold the German Government to a strict accountability. In the next paragraph, it says that we assume that the German Government accepts the rule that the lives of non-combatants, neutral or belligerent, cannot rightfully be put in jeopardy by the capture

[142]

or destruction of an unarmed merchantman, and that it recognizes the obligation to take the precaution of visit and search to ascertain whether a suspected ship is in fact of belligerent nationality and is carrying contraband under a neutral flag. Lower down, the note says that the objection to the present method of attack is the practical impossibility of using submarines against merchant vessels without violating the rules of justice and humanity.

"How far do you propose to go? Do you demand that Germany give up the use of the submarine in her efforts to destroy British trade? You speak of the practical impossibility of her using it in accordance with the rules of justice and humanity. I agree that it is unlikely that she can do so; but that is a matter she will have to resolve. We can insist that she observe such rules, but can we demand specifically that she give up the use of this new device? I do think that we can demand that she strictly comply with the rule of visit and search. We can demand that she make no mistakes and that she safeguard the lives of passengers and crew. This war will present many new problems. England is violating the three-mile blockade. She is blockading at a distance. The long-range gun and the submarine make the three-mile rule obsolete. If I were England, I would do just as England is doing, and, if I were Germany, I would use the submarine if I could justly and humanely do so to stop English trade. I would not, if I were England, let any supplies of any sort reach Germany, if I could prevent it. It is silly for the Germans to cry that England is starving her women and children. It is impossible in modern war to separate, in the matter of food and other supplies, the civilian from the soldier. War now is the war of whole

[143]

nations. Conditions are different from what they were when a few thousand men went to war and passed back and forth. You cannot feed a mass of civilians and not feed armies also. If you cripple the civilian population, you cripple the army. The contest is one of resources. Nobody knows this better than the Germans, and they know that they are being cut off from the outside world. What they demand is, in effect, that the Allies be prevented from using their fleets. They ought to have thought of this and of their women and children before they entered upon their present enterprise. Of course, they did think of it, but either they did not believe that England would go in, or they are waiting with their tongues in their cheeks, assuming that we are fools.

"I understand that you do not specifically demand that submarines be not used against British trade but that you say that they cannot be used to impair the rights of Americans or to jeopardize their lives. You do insist, however, in general, that in using them against merchant vessels they do so in accord with accepted rules. This is a proper protest. There is no need of repeating this protest for the record.

"We have now come to a show-down. What you now say or do may mean war. You are speaking for the American nation. You must have its united backing. At present, the masses of the poeple are not dreaming of our becoming involved in the war. As a rule, they know very little about the issues and are not thinking much about it except so far as it affects their particular individual fortunes. This is particularly true in the South and West. I realized it everywhere during my recent trip. It is only in the Northeast, and there among relatively small groups, that there is a real understanding of the broad issues involved and of the seriousness of the present situation. The nation will follow leadership in the right direction on a show-down, but the people are now relatively little interested, not at all excited, and would not be a unit. They are getting educated, and they need it. Let the people understand that the issue is an American issue, that it is now very definitely a matter of American rights and American lives. There are and have been very broad issues involved since the beginning, but they are now as broad as American rights and involve American lives.

"When you make your demand, let it have specific and exclusive reference to the rights and lives of American shipmasters and American citizens. Do not discuss belligerent or neutral rights and ships, or visit and search, or the discontinuance of the use of the submarine. Simply demand that they take no action which will impair the lawful rights of American citizens in trade or travel or which may imperil their lives. And interpret the German reply as an acceptance of the principle you stand for and demand a prompt confirmation in view of the facts which you recite in response to their request."

The President indicated that he was in agreement. He asked me to restate my principal points. I did so. He made notes as I spoke, and then we adjourned.

As we were leaving the Cabinet room, Bryan asked us to lunch with him at the University Club. Lane, Daniels, Burleson, Wilson, Garrison, and I accepted. For a considerable time after we seated ourselves at the table, we engaged in general conversation. Bryan was preoccupied. He seemed to be communing with himself. As we were finishing our lunch, Bryan said: "Gentlemen, this is our last meeting together. I have valued our association and friendship. I have had to take the course I have chosen. The President has had one view. I have had a different one. I do not censure him for thinking and acting as he thinks best. I have had to act as I have thought best. I cannot go along with him in this note. I think it makes for war. I believe that I can do more on the outside to prevent war than I can on the inside. I think I can help the President more on the outside. I can work to control popular opinion so that it will not exert pressure for extreme action which the President does not want. We both want the same thing, Peace."

Each of us said some pleasant things to Bryan along conventional lines. Lane said: "You are the most real Christian I know." Burleson expressed agreement. Bryan continued: "I must act according to my conscience. I go out into the dark. The President has the Prestige and the Power on his side." Then he broke down completely and stopped. After a few seconds he added this: "I have many friends who would die for me."

I did not like these last expressions. They did not run on all fours with his earlier ones. They did not square with his statement that he and the President wanted the same thing. The President wanted peace, but an honourable peace. Bryan apparently wanted peace at any price. He was, in effect, telling Germany and the world that we had not meant what we had said, and that we would not stand up for our rights. He was quitting under fire. Of course, he could not logically refuse to sign the proposed note after signing the first one. If he was in doubt, he ought to have resigned when the first note was agreed upon. The only explanation is that he had not thought that the first note was dangerous, while this one, in his judgment, meant trouble—that is, that Germany would not accept our view and, in effect, back down. Therefore, we must back down.

Bryan is mistaken if he thinks that he can promote his programme on the outside and not be drawn into opposition to the President. This will be impossible. He is already in opposition. The only thing which can ease his situation will be a conciliatory and satisfactory answer from Germany, and this I am inclined to expect, because Germany has some sense and she must know that her game will be over if she forces us into the war. Nothing which her submarines can do to the Allies will be at all comparable to what we will do to her.

I expect to see Bryan take a stand against any increase of armament, favour keeping our citizens off the seas, and urge prohibition and woman suffrage. I shall not be surprised if he urges these in the next campaign and insists that they be incorporated in the next Democratic platform and that a candidate be selected who will be generally known to have vigorously advocated them.

At nine o'clock, extras announcing Bryan's resignation and giving his letter and the President's reply were cried through the streets. There were great interest and excitement on all sides, the greatest, perhaps, since our arrival in Washington.

The same evening, the President rang me up at my home. He said he wished to read me certain passages of the revised note to see whether his changes met the views I expressed in Cabinet meeting. He read the passages, and I told him that they fully embodied my suggestions,

[147]

of which the principal ones were: (1) that he make it clear that we assumed that Germany did not raise a question of principle, (2) that he inform Germany that she was mistaken as to the *Lusitania's* being in effect a British naval auxiliary; (3) that he point out that a number of her contentions were irrelevant; (4) that he again emphasize the point that we were contending for something higher than rights of property or of commerce, namely, the rights of humanity; (5) that he renew the representations and warnings of the first note; (6) but that, in this note, he limit his statements to the rights of American shipmasters and American citizens and demand assurances that they will be respected.

This note was dated June 9th, and on this day Bryan's statement appeared. It was disturbing in its conception and implications.

When the President's note was published, it made Bryan's statement look silly. But Bryan talked incessantly. The press, except the German part of it, was a unit against him. It supported the President and the cause of civilization and decency.

CHAPTER X

DIPLOMATIC NOTES AND NATIONAL DEFENCE

Lansing Appointed Secretary of State—Diplomacy with Germany—Garrison's Plan for Defence—The President's Change of Mind—The Hay Bill

THE President left the city Thursday, the twenty-fourth, and there was a notice in the late afternoon papers saying that Lansing had been selected. Lansing will be the President's Private Secretary for Foreign Affairs. He will not be of much more assistance than he would have been as an expert in the Department. With the growing burdens, I do not see how the President can stand the strain. He will have to do all the thinking and planning. What a pity he could not get a man like Ex-Secretary Olney.

The period from June, 1915, to the middle of December was one of great and growing activity and strain; but, in the field of foreign relations, there was no departure in policy which caused or demanded much discussion or consideration at the hands of the Cabinet, or which I felt it particularly necessary to note. The happenings of most moment were the development of the submarine controversy with Germany, the growing recognition of the need of preparedness, the change of the President's attitude as conditions became more critical, his struggle with the pacifists in and out of Congress, the development of the preparedness programme for the army and navy, including the creation of the Council of National Defence, the Garrison resignation incident over a difference as to an important item, the strengthening of the financial structure, and the election of 1916. Each of these I shall touch upon in order.

Germany replied to this government's second *Lusitania* note under date of July 8th. She professed her sympathy with our views as to the need of recognizing and enforcing the principles of humanity. Her whole history, she contended, demonstrated that she stood and had always stood for the freedom of the seas and peaceable trade. If the principles had been traversed, she was not guilty. England had blockaded neutral coasts and intercepted neutral trade with Germany, and had driven her to submarine warfare. England was bent on starving Germany's civilian population. She had been compelled to retaliate in self-defence.

The *Lusitania* incident showed "with horrible clearness to what jeopardizing of human lives the manner of conducting war employed by our adversaries leads." Britain had obliterated distinctions between merchantmen and war vessels by arming the former. If the German submarine commander had caused the crew and travellers of the *Lusitania* to put off in boats before firing the torpedo, his own vessel would have been destroyed. "After the experience in the sinking of much smaller and less seaworthy vessels it was to be expected that a mighty ship like the *Lusitania* would remain above water long enough, even after the torpedoing, to permit the passengers to enter the ship's boats"!! The explosion of munitions defeated this.

But the German Government would do all it could to

[150]

prevent the jeopardizing of the lives of American citizens. "The Imperial Government therefore repeats the assurances that American ships will not be hindered in the prosecution of legitimate shipping, and the lives of American citizens on neutral vessels shall not be placed in jeopardy."[2] German submarines would be instructed to permit safe passage to American ships if they were marked with special markings and notice was given in advance. American citizens did not have to travel to Europe on enemy merchantmen. The United States could acquire a sufficient number of neutral ships if her own were inadequate. We might place under our flag four enemy passenger vessels.

This note was unsatisfactory. It was offensive. It paid no attention to our statement that the *Lusitania* was not armed. It denied our right to travel on merchant vessels of belligerent nationality and the need of assuring the safety of passengers and crews. And it directed us to mark our own ships as Germany dictated.

This reply was, of course, not accepted, and it was necessary only to point out that it did not square with our principles already stated and our former demands.

On July 21st, our third note was sent. It reminded Germany that we could discuss Great Britain's policy with reference to trade only with her. If Germany could not retaliate without injuring not only the property but also the lives of neutrals she should discontinue her course. Events had indicated that submarine operations such as Germany had carried on in the war zone could be in substantial accord with regulated warfare. It was hoped that Germany would no longer refrain from disavowing the wanton act of its naval commander in sinking the

[151]

Lusitania and from offering reparation for the loss of American lives. This government could not accept the suggestion that our vessels be designated as this would be an acknowledgment of a curtailment and an abandonment of our principles. Friendship prompted us to say that repetition by German submarines of acts in contravention of our rights would "be regarded by the Government of the United States, when they affect American citizens, as deliberately unfriendly."

This note was followed by assurance from Germany that she would so modify her submarine operations as to remove our grounds of objection; but on August 19th, the *Arabic*, a White Star liner, was sunk with the loss of American lives. Before details were received, Bernstorff, on August 24th, informed the Secretary of State that he had been instructed to ask that this government take no stand till after reports were heard from both sides, to say that, in case any "Americans should actually have lost their lives, this would be contrary to the intention of the German Government, who would deeply regret this fact, and to extend its sincerest sympathies to the government of the United States."

On September 1, 1915, Bernstorff, referring to a conversation with the Secretary of State, informed him in writing that his instructions concerning his government's answer to the last *Lusitania* note contained this passage: "Liners will not be sunk by our submarines without warning and without safety of the lives of non-combatants, provided that the liners do not try to escape or offer resistance." He added that this policy was decided upon before the *Arabic* was sunk.

About a month later, on October 5th, the German Ambassador reported to the State Department that such stringent orders had been given to submarine commanders that no recurrence of incidents similar to that of the *Arabic* was considered possible; that in that case the commander thought the *Arabic* intended to ram him; that he undertook to attack against his instructions; that his government disavowed his act; and that it would pay an indemnity for American lives. This was noticed with satisfaction by Mr. Lansing, who said that he was ready to negotiate for the amount of the indemnity.

Then followed the sinking of the *Ancona* in the Mediterranean by an Austrian submarine on November 7th; our protest to Austria, and her unsatisfactory reply. Finally, Austria announced that the commander of the submarine had been punished.

The next incident to demand even more serious attention, in view of the pledge of the German Government, was the sinking of the Channel steamer, the *Sussex*, on March 24, 1916. This followed the receipt of several more notes from Germany explaining her submarine operations and policy. Mr. Gerard was instructed by the State Department on March 27th to ask Germany whether the *Sussex* was sunk by a German submarine or by one belonging to her Allies. Later, he was instructed to make a similar inquiry as to the Dominion horse ship, the *Englishman*, the *Manchester Engineer*, the *Eagle Point*, and the *Berwindale*, having Americans on board and having been torpedoed without warning between March 16th and March 28th.

The answer came dated April 10, 1916. It was not convincing as to any of the cases. In respect to the *Sussex*, the most important, it was singularly unsatisfactory. It was even trivial. The German commander, it was stated, had made a sketch of the vessel sunk near where it was claimed that the *Sussex* went down. This had been compared with a picture of the *Sussex* in the *Graphic* and the two were found not to be identical! The German Government was forced to assume that the damage to the *Sussex* was to be attributed to another cause. If the United States had facts which seemed to conflict, it should communicate them to her and, if then there was still a difference of opinion, it could be submitted to a mixed committee of investigation.

The United States had the facts. It gave them in its reply of April 18th. The *Sussex* had never been armed. It was known to be habitually used only to carry passengers. It did not follow the route taken by troop or supply ships. A careful investigation by United States naval and military officers conclusively established the fact that the *Sussex* was torpedoed without warning or summons to surrender, and that the torpedo was of German manufacture.

The German Government, the note stated, apparently failed to appreciate the gravity of the situation which had resulted, not alone from the attack on the *Sussex*, but from the whole method and character of submarine warfare as disclosed from the unrestrained practice of her submarine commanders for twelve months and in the indiscriminate destruction of merchant vessels of all sorts, nationalities, and destinations.

The German Government had again and again given its solemn assurances that passenger ships would not be dealt with in such fashion; but no limit of any kind had been set. The roll of Americans who had lost their lives

[154]

had grown month by month. The government of the United States had been very patient. It had accepted the assurances of Germany in good faith. It had made every allowance for unprecedented conditions and had been willing to wait till the facts were susceptible of only one interpretation.

"It now owes it to a just regard for its own rights to say to the Imperial Government that that time has come. It has become painfully evident to it that the position which it took at the very outset is inevitable, namely, the use of submarines for the destruction of an enemy's commerce is, of necessity, because of the very character of the vessels employed and the very methods of attack which their employment of course involves, utterly incompatible with the principles of humanity, the long established and incontrovertible rights of neutrals, and the sacred immunities of non-combatants."

If it was still the purpose of Germany to prosecute relentless and indiscriminate warfare against merchant vessels by the use of submarines, this government would be forced to conclude that there was only one course it could pursue. "Unless the Imperial Government should not immediately declare and effect an abandonment of its present methods of submarine warfare against passenger and freight-carrying vessels, the Government of the United States can have no other choice but to sever diplomatic relations with the German Empire altogether."

The following day, April 19th, the President appeared before Congress to inform it fully and frankly concerning the situation and its seriousness. He had taken this course before, when the Mexican situation became acute. He was anxious to omit nothing which might make Con-

[155]

gress feel that he was more than willing to let it know formally everything he knew and which might win its support and that of the people for any necessary course of action. He outlined the history of the controversy and closed with a statement of the decision he had reached and had communicated to Germany.

The note, the President's appearance before Congress, and the cordial support evidenced by it and the press of the country produced results. On May 4th, the German Foreign Office handed to Mr. Gerard a long note. It denied that there was any incident which demonstrated that German submarines were waging indiscriminate warfare, insisted that their commanders had orders to conduct operations in accordance with the general principles of visit and search, but pointed out that no assurances had been given with reference to enemy trade carried on in enemy ships in the war zone, and that it could not dispense with the use of submarines against enemy trade. Great Britain had forced her to resort to her present practices. The government of the United States should extend her principles of humanity to the millions of German women and children whom the British by their course were starving. But Germany, in the interest of peace and friendship, would make further concessions. It had therefore given orders to its commanders as follows: "In accordance with the general principles of visit and search and destruction of merchant vessels recognized by international law, such vessels, both within and without the area declared as naval war zone, shall not be sunk without warning and without saving human lives unless these ships attempt to escape or offer resistance."

However, neutrals could not except Germany, fighting

for her life, to restrict the use of her effective weapon if her enemy is permitted to apply at will methods of warfare violating the rules of international law. Accordingly, the German Government was confident that the United States would now demand that the British Government forthwith observe the rules of international law as laid down in her note to Great Britain on December 28, 1914. If this object should not be attained, "the German Government would then be facing a new situation in which it must reserve to itself complete liberty of decision."

And thus again Germany made a promise in one breath and took it back in the next, promised as usual nothing absolute, but promised everything, if an impossible condition were satisfied. Great Britain was starving Germans, if anybody. She was neither starving nor killing Americans, while Germany was killing Americans. It was up to Germany to deal with Britain for starving Germans, that was something she ought to have foreseen as a possibility when she defied Britain in 1914 and violated her pledge to Belgium. It was up to us to deal with Germany for killing Americans. The note did not unqualifiedly promise anything.

The President replied along these lines on May 8th. He notified Germany that we would rely upon a scrupulous execution of her altered policy and that it could not be made contingent upon the course of our diplomatic negotiations with Great Britain. The respect for the rights of Americans by Germany could not in any way be made contingent upon the conduct of any other government. "Responsibility in such matters is single, not joint; absolute, not relative."

And thus this controversy for the time being rested.

[157]

As the war progressed in Europe, and as the situation became more acute, particularly in respect to our relations with Germany, the thought of leaders throughout the nation was directed more and more to our inadequate military and naval preparedness.

When the war began, our regular army consisted of 4,701 officers and 87,781 men, including about 8,000 officers and men in the Hospital and Quartermaster's Corps. Our mobile army was on a peace footing and had 2,935 officers and 51,444 men; our coast artillery had 758 officers and 17,901 men; and our mobile army in the United States had 1,498 officers and 29,405 men. Our regular reserve consisted of 26 men. Our only other organized force consisted of 8,323 officers and 119,087 men in the militia who were required to attend twenty-four drills a year and to spend five days in the field.

The War Department, in 1914, recommended that the existing organization be filled up by adding 1,000 officers and 25,000 men, that the army be used as a school, turning out men after twelve months who would constitute a reserve, and that a reserve for the militia be constituted.

In December, the President, in his Annual Address, as has been pointed out, took a stand against a large regular army and advised reliance upon "a citizenry trained and accustomed to arms," who would volunteer, upon a strengthened National Guard, and upon a strong navy. We should not alter our attitude "because some amongst us are nervous and excited. We shall wisely and sensibly agree upon a policy of defence. . . . We shall learn and profit by the lesson of every experience and every new circumstance; and what is needed will be adequately done."

Provision was made by Congress along the line of the War Department's suggestions of 1914 and the additions were made to the army. In 1915, the total force consisted of 5,023 officers and 102,985 men. Of this number 67,000 belonged to the mobile army and 20,000 to the coast artillery, and 29,000 of these were on duty outside the United States.

The War Department came forward with a carefully considered plan for additional preparedness which was strongly presented to the public for the first time by the President on November 4, 1915, before the Manhattan Club of New York City and in more detail by the Secretary of War in his Annual Report. The President, in his Annual Address to Congress, December 7, 1917, formally approved and recommended the programme advocated by Secretary Garrison. In his address before the Manhattan Club, he adverted to the European conflict, to the facts that many of the greatest nations of the world were involved, that the influences of the war were everywhere in the air, and that our people everywhere were asking how far we were prepared to maintain ourselves against interference. "Our mission," he said, "is a mission of peace, and we have it in mind to be prepared for defence, to protect our security." In his message to Congress, he said that we would not maintain a standing army except for uses which are as necessary in times of peace as in times of war, and that it was no larger than was actually needed in peace times; but we should have citizens know how modern fighting is done, and therefore they must be adequately trained and equipped. Our confidence had been that our safety would lie in the rising of the nation to take care of itself, "but war has never been a mere matter of men and guns. It is a thing of disciplined might."

The programme contemplated an increase in the regular army from 5,023 officers and 102,985 men to 7,136 officers and 134,700 men, a total of 141,836; the creation of a continental army of 400,000 men, raised in three equal increments, who would serve for three years with the colours and then three years with the reserve; and a strengthening of the National Guard. The raising of the continental army would depend upon the patriotic feeling of the young men and upon their willingness to volunteer. In addition, a comprehensive plan for enlarging the navy was suggested. Proposals were also incorporated looking to the training of more officers through increased provision for West Point and through cadet companies recruited from the National Guard to be attached to regular regiments and trained with them, or through plans to strengthen the military training in educational institutions throughout the Union. The National Guard was to be developed, but it was not to be regarded as a first line of defence. It could not satisfactorily be trained and officered in time of peace by the Federal Government and could be used in war only as provided in the Constitution.

Secretary Garrison, following the guidance of the regular army staff, was very pronounced in his views on this point, and was equally strong in his opposition to the suggestion that the Swiss system be introduced into this country. It was objectionable because it would require compulsory service, because it started with the public schools and was dependent upon them, because it required a great number of local officials controlled by a central authority which we did not and should not have, and because the Federal Government had no power over schools. The system would not be suited to his country.

The programme, when in complete operation at the end of three years, would give us a force of 670,836 officers and men, composed of a regular army of 141,832, a continental force of 400,000, and a National Guard of 129,000, to cost annually $182,234,500. It was proposed to spend in four years $104,326,000 for material.

The acceptance of this programme by the President involved a very marked change of mind on his part. This he frankly avowed in the course of a trip through the country beginning January 27th which he felt it necessary to make to arouse the country and to get it to back up his proposals in a reluctant Congress. At this time, Congress had been in session nearly two months. The preparedness measures were having hard sledding. There was much opposition to them in that body, and the people seemed to be apathetic. There were those even who preferred to surrender to Germany by warning American citizens off the sea except in ships following routes prescribed by Germany.

In his first speech to the Manhattan Club of New York City, January 27, 1916, the President referred to his change of mind in this way: "Perhaps when you learned, as I dare say you did learn beforehand, that I was expecting to address you on the subject of preparedness, you recalled the address which I made to Congress something more than a year ago, in which I said that this question of military preparedness was not a pressing question. But more than a year has gone by since then, and I would be ashamed if I had not learned something in fourteen months.

The minute I stop changing my mind with the change of all the circumstances of the world, I will be a back number." He advocated the programme as the War Department had drawn it and particularly pointed out that, while he believed in making the National Guard stronger, he recognized that it could not be a direct resource as a national reserve under national authority. What we ought to insist on, he added, is a body of at least a half a million trained men who will be immediately available. But, he interjected: "I am not a partisan of any one plan. I have had too much experience to think that it is right to say that the plan I propose is the only plan that will work, because I have a shrewd suspicion that there may be other plans that will work."

There was another plan which was being very aggressively pushed, while a large faction was demanding insistently that there be no plan at all. The State Guard advocates did not want the Continental force. Many regarded this force with no compulsion back of it as even less satisfactory than the federalized National Guard would be.

It became clear that the whole programme of the President would not go through, but that one could be passed providing a larger regular army, 186,000 in place of 142,000, to be increased in time of war, a federalized National Guard of 425,000, the members of which were to take an oath both to the United States and to the state, a reserve corps of men discharged from the army and the National Guard, and an officers reserve corps and an officers' training corps at colleges and universities. The National Guard was to be uniformed, equipped, and disciplined like the regulars, and its training period to be increased. Of particular importance was the provision that when Congress authorized the use of the land forces, the President could draft all the members of the National Guard and its reserve to serve through the war.

CHAPTER XI

GARRISON RESIGNS

Correspondence Between Garrison and the President—Mobilization on the Border—Creation of Council of National Defence—War-time Revenues

WHEN the President finally assented to the Hay bill as a means of getting action, Secretary Garrison resigned doubtless still being in general out of sympathy with the Administration and conceiving that the President and he differed sharply at this time on fundamental principles of national defence. In view of the great advance in preparedness made in this compromise measure, I could not understand why he could not see his way clear to remain in his position. Which plan, as an abstract proposition, was preferable, I shall have to leave to military experts, but that the President was wise in acting as he did I do not doubt.

It is debatable, certainly, whether, all things considered, the plan adopted was not a better one than that proposed. It provided for a larger regular army and made available by draft a very large already organized force. At any rate, the Secretary's quarrel was more with the people and with Congress than with the President. The President evidently preferred the plan of the army staff. Otherwise, he would not have advocated before Congress and the people, but he was not so stubborn and cocksure as to be willing to say that he would take that or nothing. If

[164]

he had done so, he might have failed to secure any satisfactory legislation and have more widely split his party.

The correspondence which passed between Garrison and the President makes their positions very clear. One cannot fail to admire the President's patience and courtesy. These were the letters exchanged:

War Department, Washington.
January 12, 1916.

MY DEAR MR. PRESIDENT:

In my judgment, we are facing a critical juncture with respect to the military part of the national defence programme.

I am convinced that unless the situation is dealt with promptly and effectively we can indulge in no reasonable expectation of any acceptable result.

So far as the military part of national defence is concerned, there can be no honest or worthy solution which does not result in national forces under the exclusive control and authority of the national government. Any other solution is illusory and not real, is apparent and not substantial.

There is a perfectly legitimate field of discussion and debate as to the means of obtaining these national forces. The proportion thereof that should be the regular standing army; that should be reserves of the regular standing army, or should be drawn from the body of citizens for shorter periods of national service than those in the regular standing army, are all legitimate and proper matters for consideration, analysis, and discussion.

But there is absolutely no dissent from the military standpoint from the conclusion that the only measure

[165]

of national defence that possesses any virtue is one which produces national forces. From the beginning of the government to this time, excepting during periods of actual war, the acknowledged weakness and defect of the situation arose out of the lack of any system producing these Federal forces. The situation was rendered worse by the presence of state troops, raised, officered, trained, and governed by the states, that were assumed to be a military reliance for the nation, when, in fact, they are not, and can never be made to be. Under the Constitution of the United States, these state troops must always be governed, officered, and trained by the respective states.

The very first line of cleavage, therefore, which must be encountered and dealt with by the student of the situation is between reliance upon a system of state troops, for ever subject to constitutional limitations which render them absolutely insecure as a reliance for the nation, or reliance upon national forces raised, officered, trained, and controlled by the national authorities. Upon this subject there does not exist, and there cannot legitimately exist, any difference of opinion among those who are unbiassed and who believe in real national security and defence.

The policy recommended to you and adopted by you squarely placed the nation upon the sure foundation of national forces. If that policy is made effective by legislation, there will be secured to this country for the first time a real, stable foundation for the military part of its national defence. If, however, instead thereof a policy is adopted based upon the state troops as the main reliance of this country for its military arm, not only has no advance been made from the deplorable and inexcusable situ-

[166]

ation in which we have so long been, but an effective block has been placed across the pathway toward a proper settlement.

The adoption of such a policy would serve to delude the people into believing that the subject had been settled, and therefore required no further consideration upon their part. It would, therefore, in my judgment, be infinitely worse than an entire failure of all legislative enactment upon the subject. The latter would at least leave it open for future settlement.

I of course am not advised as to the statements of intention made by Mr. Hay to you in the conversation held with you prior to your message to Congress at the opening of the present session. I have always felt, and have so expressed myself to you, that the situation in the Congress was such that unless you personally exerted the power of your leadership you would not obtain any worthy results in this matter.

Mr. Hay has not made the declaration of his intention. He announces that he does not intend to press for the enactment of the military policy advocated in your message. With respect to the regular army he does not purpose giving us the organizations asked for and imperatively necessary if the Federal volunteers (so-called continental army) are to be properly trained; he purposes adding a few thousand men to the enlisted strength of the army in its present organization, the adding of a few regiments of field artillery to the existing organizations of the regular army, the entire abandonment of the idea of a Federal force of national volunteers, and the passing of a bill granting direct Federal pay to the enlisted men and officers of the state troops.

[167]

In my judgment, the effect of the enactment of Mr. Hay's programme would be to set back the whole cause of legitimate, honest national defence in an entirely unjustifiable and inexcusable way.   It would be, in my judgment, a betrayal of the trust of the people in this regard.   It would be illusory and apparent, without any reality or substance.

There is, unfortunately, very little knowledge and very little intense personal interest in any of the members of the House concerning military affairs.   Apart from the power that always resides in every chairman of committee, Mr. Hay has the additional power of dealing with a subject concerning which the rest of the House has no knowledge, and about which it has never concerned itself.   In this particular instance, his proposal of settling this matter by voting money to the interested men and officers of the state troops appeals to the direct personal political interests of the members.

In these circumstances it seems to me to be perfectly clear that, unless you interpose your position as leader of the country on this great subject, the result will be the lamentable one which I have just described.

It seems to be equally imperative that this interposition should be immediate.   If this proposed programme by Mr. Hay is accepted by the Committee and by public opinion and by the House as a solution of this vital matter any position subsequently taken will be negligible, so far as substantial, actual results are concerned.

The issue must be plainly and clearly drawn.   It has nothing whatever to do with the number of men to be raised or with the means of raising them, as Mr. Hay would have it appear that it has.   It is between two absolutely different systems, one of which is based upon the nation undertaking upon its own responsibility the raising and management of the national troops, and the other of which leaves us in the position that we have always been in since the institution of the government, to rely upon the states doing this thing for the nation, a situation in which the nation is relying upon a military force that it does not raise, that it does not officer, that it does not train, and that it does not control.

A mere statement of the situation shows that the two different proposals are as wide apart as any two proposals upon any subject possibly can be.

Mr. Hay's proposal to include a draft or compulsory provision so that at the outbreak of war the nation could bring under its control these state troops utterly fails to meet the essential objections to the perpetuation of the militia system. The difficulty to be dealt with does not arise out of the government not being able to take over these troops in the event of war, but arises out of its inability under the Constitution to have the essential unity of responsibility, authority, and control in the raising, officering, training, and governing of its military forces.

If the public obtains the impression that Mr. Hay's solution is merely another means of accomplishing the same end as your proposed policy, they will accept the same and rest content that their desires have been properly met. If, on the other hand, they are clearly and unmistakably advised that to adopt the policy submitted by Mr. Hay is to make a mockery of all that was worthy and virtuous in the proposal of a proper military policy, and that it is a delusion to consider such a solution as a real reliance or security, then there is hope that we can obtain

[169]

results commensurate with the necessities of the case, and with a self-respecting consideration and treatment thereof.

I cannot, therefore, too strongly urge upon you my view of the imperative necessity of your seeking an occasion at the earliest possible moment to declare yourself with respect to the matter and in doing so to make it clear beyond peradventure that nothing excepting national forces, raised by the nation and subject to its exclusive authority, responsibility, and control, is any real settlement of this issue.

Sincerely yours,
LINDLEY M. GARRISON.

War Department
Washington, January 14, 1916.

MY DEAR MR. PRESIDENT:

What you said to-day by way of response to my letter of the 12th requires me to make my position perfectly clear to you.

You stated that Mr. Hay told you that your proposal of Federal volunteers could not be procured and that the same end for which you were striving could be procured by other means—by utilizing the procured by other means—by utilizing the state troops as the basis of the policy, and making appropriations of pay to the states conditioned on Federal control of state troops.

You stated to him that you were not interested in any particular programme or means of accomplishing the purpose of securing the men and would accept his proposal if it accomplished that purpose.

Since the policy that was recommended to you and adopted by you discarded as absolutely impossible a military system based upon state troops and asserted that the only possible basis for a military policy was national forces, it is entirely clear that the proposals are diametrically opposed to each other and are irreconcilable.

Those who are conscientiously convinced that nothing but national forces can properly be the basis of a policy of national defence cannot possibly accept a policy based upon state forces. It not only does not in itself offer an acceptable solution, but acts to prevent any proper solution.

If those who are thus convinced are faced with the necessity of declaring their position on the matter, they can only show their sincerity and good faith by declining to admit the possibility of compromise with respect to this essential fundamental principle.

I am thus convinced; I feel that we are challenged by the existing situation to declare ourselves promptly, openly, and unequivocally, or be charged properly with lack of sincerity and good faith.

We cannot hope to see our programme, based on this essential principle, succeed if we admit the possibility of compromise with respect to it.

Yours is the ultimate responsibility; yours is the final determination as to the manner in which the situation shall be faced and treated. I fully realize this, and I do not desire to cause you the slightest embarrassment on my account; if, therefore, my withdrawal from the situation would relieve you, you should not hesitate for a moment on that account.

Sincerely yours,
LINDLEY M. GARRISON.

The President

The President's reply was:

The White House,
Washington, January 17, 1916.

MY DEAR MR. SECRETARY:

I am very much obliged to you for your letters of January 12th and January 14th. They make your views with regard to adequate measures of preparation for national defence sharply clear. I am sure that I already understood just what your views were, but I am glad to have them restated in this succinct and striking way. You believe, as I do, that the chief thing necessary is that we should have a trained citizen reserve and that the training, organization, and control of that reserve should be under immediate Federal direction.

But apparently I have not succeeded in making my own position equally clear to you, though I feel sure that I have made it perfectly clear to Mr. Hay. It is that I am not irrevocably or dogmatically committed to any one plan of providing the nation with such a reserve, and am cordially willing to discuss alternative proposals.

Any other position on my part would indicate an attitude toward the Committee on Military Affairs of the House of Representatives which I should in no circumstances feel at liberty to assume. It would never be proper or possible for me to say to any committee of the House of Representatives that, so far as my participation in legislation was concerned, they would have to take my plan or none.

I do not share your opinion that the members of the House who are charged with the duty of dealing with military affairs are ignorant of them, or of the military

[172]

necessities of the nation. On the contrary, I have found them well informed, and actuated by a most intelligent appreciation of the grave responsibilities imposed upon them.

I am sure that Mr. Hay and his colleagues are ready to act with a full sense of all that is involved in this great matter, both for the country and for the national parties which they represent.

My own duty toward them is perfectly plain. I must welcome a frank interchange of views and a patient and thorough comparison of all the methods proposed for obtaining the objects we all have in view. So far as my own participation in final legislative action is concerned, no one will expect me to acquiesce in any proposal that I regard as inadequate or illusory.

If, as the outcome of a free interchange of views, my own judgment and that of the Committee should prove to be irreconcilably different, and a bill should be presented to me which I could not accept as accomplishing the essential things sought, it would manifestly be my duty to veto it and go to the country on the merits. But there is no reason to anticipate or fear such a result, unless we should ourselves take at the outset the position that only the plans of the Department are to be considered; and that position, it seems to me, would be wholly unjustifiable.

The Committee and the Congress will expect me to be as frank with them as I hope they will be with me, and will, of course, hold me justified in fighting for my own matured opinion.

I have had a delightfully frank conference with Mr. Hay. I have said to him that I was perfectly willing to consider any plan that would give us a national reserve

[173]

under unmistakable national control and would support any such scheme if convinced of its adequacy and wise policy. More he has not asked or desired.

Cordially and sincerely yours,

WOODROW WILSON.

Hon. Lindley M. Garrison,
Secretary of War.

Garrison on Wednesday wrote the President as follows:

War Department, Washington,

February 9, 1916.

MY DEAR MR. PRESIDENT:

Two matters within the jurisdiction of this department are now of immediate and pressing importance, and I am constrained to declare my position definitely and unmistakably thereon. I refer, of course to the Philippine question and the matter of national defence.

You know my convictions with respect to each of them. I consider the principle embodied in the Clarke amendment an abandonment of the duty of this nation and a breach of trust toward the Filipinos; so believing, I cannot accept it or acquiesce in its acceptance.

I consider the reliance upon the militia for national defence an unjustifiable imperilling of the nation's safety. It would not only be a sham in itself, but its enactment into law would prevent, if not destroy, the opportunity to procure measures of real, genuine national defence. I could not accept it or acquiesce in its acceptance.

I am obliged to make my position known immediately upon each of these questions—in a speech on Thursday afternoon upon the national defence question and in a communication to the House committee having charge of the Philippine question. If, with respect to either matter, we are not in agreement upon these fundamental principles, then I could not, with propriety, remain your seeming representative in respect thereto. Our convictions would be manifestly not only divergent, but utterly irreconcilable.

You will appreciate the necessity of timely knowledge upon my part of the determination reached by you with respect to each of these matters, so that I may act advisedly in the premises.

Sincerely yours,
LINDLEY M. GARRISON.

The President.

To this letter the President replied as follows:

The White House,
Washington, February 10, 1916.

MY DEAR MR. SECRETARY:

In reply to your letter of to-day, let me say:

(1) That it is my own judgment that the action embodied in the Clarke amendment to the bill extending further self-government to the Philippines is unwise at this time, but it would clearly be most inadvisable for me to take the position that I must dissent from that action should both houses of Congress concur in a bill embodying that amendment. That is a matter upon which I must, of course, withhold judgment until the joint action of the two houses reaches me in definite form.

What the final action of the houses will be, no one can

[175]

at this time certainly forecast. I am now, of course, engaged in conference with Mr. Jones and others with regard to the probable action of the House of Representatives in this matter, and do not yet know what it is likely to be. The one obvious thing, it seems to me, is the necessity for calm and deliberate action on our part at this time, when matters of such gravity are to be determined, and not only calm and deliberate action, but action which takes into very serious consideration views differing from our own.

(2) As I have had occasion to say to you, I am not yet convinced that the measure of preparation for national defence which we deem necessary can be obtained through the instrumentality of the National Guard under Federal control and training, but I feel in duty bound to keep my mind open to conviction on that side, and think that it would be most unwise and most unfair to the Committee of the House which has such a plan in mind to say that it cannot be done. The bill in which it will be embodied has not yet been drawn, as I learned to-day from Mr. Hay. I should deem it a very serious mistake to shut the door against this attempt on the part of the Committee in perfect good faith to meet the essentials of the programme set forth in my message, but in a way of their own choosing.

As you know, I do not at all agree with you in favouring compulsory enlistment for training, and I fear the advocacy of compulsion before the Committee of the House on the part of the representatives of the Department of War has greatly prejudiced the House against the proposal for a continental army, little necessary connection as there is between the plan and the opinion of the Chief of Staff in favour of compulsory enlistment.

[176]

I owe you this frank repetition of my views and policy in this matter, which we have discussed on previous occasions in the letters which we have exchanged and in conversation. I am very much obliged to you for your own frank avowal of your convictions. I trust that you will feel no hesitation about expressing your personal views on both these subjects on the two occasions to which you refer, but I hope that you will be kind enough to draw very carefully the distinction between your own individual views and the views of the Administration.

You will, of course, understand that I am devoting my energy and attention unsparingly in conference with members of the various committees of Congress to an effort to procure an agreement upon a workable and practicable programme. This is a time when it seems to me patience on the part of all of us is of the essence in bringing about a consummation of the purpose we all have in mind.

Very sincerely yours,
WOODROW WILSON.

Hon. Lindley M. Garrison,
　Secretary of War.

Upon receiving this letter, Mr. Garrison replied, tendering his resignation:

War Department,
Washington, February 10, 1916.

MY DEAR MR. PRESIDENT:

I am just in receipt of yours of February 10th in reply to mine of February 9th. It is evident that we hopelessly disagree upon what I conceive to be fundamental princi-

[177]

ples. This makes manifest the impropriety of my longer remaining your seeming representative with respect to those matters.

I hereby tender my resignation as Secretary of War, to take effect at your convenience.

Sincerely yours,
LINDLEY M. GARRISON.

The President.

The President's letter accepting the resignation follows:

The White House,
Washington, February 10, 1916.

MY DEAR MR. SECRETARY:

I must confess to feeling a very great surprise at your letter of to-day offering your resignation as Secretary of War. There has been no definite action taken yet in either of the matters to which your letter of yesterday referred. The whole matter is under debate, and all the influences that work for clarity and judgment ought to be available at this time.

But since you have felt obliged to take this action, and since it is evident that your feeling in the matter is very great indeed, I feel that I would be only imposing a burden upon you should I urge you to retain the Secretaryship of War while I am endeavouring to find a successor. I ought to relieve you at once, and do hereby accept your resignation, because it is so evidently your desire that I should do so.

I cannot take this important step, however, without expressing to you my very warm appreciation of the distinguished service you have rendered as Secretary of War, and I am sure that in expressing this appreciation I am only putting into words the judgment of our fellow citizens far and wide.

With sincere regret at the action you have felt constrained to take,

Sincerely yours,
WOODROW WILSON.

Hon. Lindley M. Garrison,
  Secretary of War.

Assistant Secretary Breckinridge, following his chief's lead, tendered his resignation:

War Department, Office of the Assistant Secretary,
  Washington, D. C., February 10, 1916.
MY DEAR MR. PRESIDENT:

The Secretary of War, Mr. Garrison, has just informed me of the fact that he has submitted his resignation, to take effect at your convenience.

I have been cognizant of each detail of the correspondence between yourself and him leading up to this action on his part. I have subscribed to each statement of principle made by him throughout this correspondence. I share without exception his conviction, and, therefore, have tendered my resignation to take effect at your convenience.

Very respectfully,
HENRY BRECKINRIDGE.

The President.

In accepting the resignation of Mr. Breckinridge, the President wrote:

[179]

The White House,
Washington, February 10, 1916.

MY DEAR BRECKINRIDGE:

I can quite understand why you deem it incumbent upon you in loyalty to your chief to follow his example in tendering your resignation, and, since I have accepted his resignation, I am sure it will be your desire that I accept yours also. I do so with genuine regret, because you have in every way fulfilled the highest expectations and rendered the country the most conscientious and efficient service.

It is with genuine sorrow that I see this official relationship between us brought to an end.

Cordially and sincerely yours,
WOODROW WILSON.

Henry Breckinridge,
Assistant Secretary of War.

The Act embodying the compromise provisions was approved June 3, 1916. Within a few days, the feature whose effectiveness was most questioned was subjected to a severe test. Partly because of the Mexican situation, the entire National Guard was called out on June 8th and by the 30th of that month, this force in the service of the United States numbered 143,702 officers and men, of whom 108,018 were on duty on the Mexican border and 35,684 in state camps.

Thus there had been secured the enactment of the most important peace-time military legislation in our history. The foundations which could be extended had been laid, and the way was open for the development of the necessary machinery. Furthermore, the weakest part of the force was in the course of receiving rigid training and dis-

[180]

cipline and the most valuable experience under trying conditions.

At the same time the navy was being put on a much
stronger footing. Even more striking measures for its
development were enacted by Congress. The Naval
Appropriation Bill for 1915 had provided for 2 battleships,
6 destroyers, 2 fleet submarines, 16 coast-defence submarines, and 1 fuel ship. It also allowed $1,000,000 for
an aviation corps and provided for a chief of operations
and a naval reserve.

The following year, much more liberal authorization
was given. A naval expenditure of $315,000,000 was
made available for the following programme: 10 battleships, 6 battle cruisers, 10 scout cruisers, 50 torpedo boats,
destroyers of the greatest practicable speed and radius of
action, 9 fleet submarines, 58 coast submarines, 1 specially
equipped submarine, 3 fuel ships, 1 repair ship, 2 destroyer
tenders, 1 fleet submarine tender, 2 ammunition ships, and
2 gunboats. It created an important Naval Reserve, a
Naval War Staff, and a Naval Flying Corps. It allowed
$705,611 toward the construction of a projectile plant,
$11,000,000 for armour plant, $18,223,523 for ammunition,
$480,000 for torpedo nets, $1,000,000 to begin new dry
docks, $1,600,000 to extend old ones, $500,000 for coal and
oil, $1,500,000 for research, $3,500,000 for aviation, and
about $1,500,000 for a naval militia.

But this was not all. The President, in his message of
December 7, 1915, spoke of "the creation of the right
instrumentalities by which to mobilize our economic resources in time of national necessity." He took it for
granted that he did not need additional authority to call
into consultation "men of recognized leadership and

ability from among our citizens who are thoroughly familiar, for example, with the transportation facilities of the country and therefore competent to advise how they may be coördinated when the need arises, those who can suggest the best way in which to bring about coöperation among the manufacturers of the country, should it be necessary, and those who could assist to bring the technical skill of the country to the aid of the government in the solution of particular problems of defence. I only hope that, if I should find it feasible to constitute such an advisory body, the Congress would be willing to make available the small sum of money that would be needed to defray the expenses that would probably be necessary to give it the clerical and administrative machinery with which to do serviceable work.

"What is more important is that the industries and resources of the country should be available and ready for mobilization."

There was suggested in these expressions a need which received formal recognition in the Army Appropriation Bill of August 29, 1916, nearly two months after the passage of the National Defence Act. The Appropriation Bill authorized the establishment of a Council of National Defence, which should consist of the Secretaries of War, Navy, Interior, Agriculture, and Labour. This body was directed to nominate for appointment an Advisory Commission consisting of not more than seven persons, each having special knowledge in some industrial field or being otherwise qualified, and to serve without compensation.

It was made the duty of the Council to supervise and direct investigations and make recommendations to the

President and the heads of executive departments as to the locating of railroads with reference to the frontier of the United States, so as to render possible expeditious concentration of troops and supplies to points of defence; the coördination of military, industrial, and commercial purposes in the location of extensive highways and branch lines of railroad; the utilization of waterways; the mobilization of military and naval resources for defence; the increase of domestic production of articles and materials essential to the support of armies and of the people during the interruption of foreign commerce; the development of sea-going transportation; data as to amounts, location, method, and means of production and availability of military supplies; the giving of information to producers and manufacturers as to the class of supplies needed by the military and other services of the government, the requirements relating thereto, and the creation of relations which will render possible in time of need the immediate concentration and utilization of the resources of the nation.   A large order, without doubt!

The first duty of the Council was to select men to be appointed to the Advisory Commission by the President. Many were canvassed and were discussed informally with the President at Cabinet meetings.   It happened that all the men who were seriously discussed at one of the conferences were Republicans, so far as anybody knew, and someone remarked jokingly that we had better be careful or we would be accused of being too partisan.   The men finally selected, as it turned out, were, with one exception, Republicans, though nobody at this or any later time gave much thought to the political affiliations of any one considered, and the President accepted the recommendations of the Council. The Commission was constituted as follows: Chairman, Daniel Willard, President of the Baltimore and Ohio Railroad, Transportation and Communication; Howard E. Coffin, Vice-president of the Hudson Motor Company, Munitions and Manufacturing and Industrial Relations; Julius Rosenwald, President of Sears, Roebuck and Company, Supplies, such as clothing; Bernard M. Baruch, Banker, Raw Materials, Minerals, and Metals; Hollis Godfrey, President of the Drexel Institute, Engineering and Education; Samuel Gompers, President of the American Federation of Labour, Labour, including the Conservation of the Health and the Welfare of Workers; and Franklin Martin, Secretary of the American College of Surgeons of Chicago, Medicine and Surgery. Each of these members was authorized to select staffs to take immediate charge of the various subdivisions of the work under his direction.

The most important officer provided for was that of Director. He was to be the central administrative head and the coördinator of all the forces and activities of the organization. In December, this position was filled by the appointment of Walter S. Gifford, of the American Telephone and Telegraph Company, a man of exceptional organizing and administrative ability, keen intelligence, and great energy.

Thus were securely laid the foundations of military preparedness.

But another important further step remained to be taken. What was in mind and what had been decided upon involved large expenditures. It was recognized that, if war came, further stupendous burdens would have to be borne and that a sound fiscal structure was essential to the national security. The nation had never faced a great emergency financially prepared. It had always promptly suspended specie payments and laboured under the disabilities imposed by an inadequate and unwise fiscal policy. This was true in the Revolutionary War, the War of 1812, and the Civil War.

A necessary vital step had been taken by the organization of the Federal Reserve System to safeguard our banking structure, and an important fiscal advance had been made by the adoption of a direct income tax in the Tariff Act of 1913. This law imposed a normal tax of 1 per cent. on personal and corporation net incomes up to $20,000, and supertaxes of from 1 per cent. to 6 per cent. on net incomes in six classifications of amounts in excess of $20,000, $50,000, $75,000, $100,000, $250,000, and $500,000.

As has been stated, the President, on September 4, 1914, appeared before Congress and urged it to make provision for additional revenues through internal taxes instead of through tariff increases or loans. He suggested the need of raising $100,000,000 by such levies. Congress responded by passing the emergency measure which the President approved on October 22d. This act increased the taxes on beer, wines, ales, tobacco, cosmetics, and chewing gum, imposed special taxes on bankers, brokers, theatres, and other amusements, and provided a schedule of stamp taxes.

Again, in 1915, the President returned to the subject of revenues in connection with his preparedness programme. In his message to Congress, December 7, 1915, he pointed out that that programme for the fiscal year 1916–17 would require additional revenues of $93,800,000 and that, if the Emergency Revenue Act of 1914 and the existing sugar duty were discontinued, the total estimated deficit June 30, 1917, would be $235,000,000; or, if the Treasury was to have a safe working balance of $50,000,000 and the usual deficiency estimates were included of $12,000,000 for 1917, the total amount needed would be $297,000,000. "The obvious moral of the figures," he insisted, "is that it is a plain counsel of prudence to continue all of the present taxes or their equivalents, and confine ourselves to the problem of providing $112,000,000 of new revenues rather than $297,000,000."

"How shall we obtain the new revenue?" he asked. It had been suggested that certain bonds already authorized to reimburse the Treasury for expenditures on the Panama Canal be sold. This he rejected. "Borrowing money is a short-sighted policy. . . . It seems to me a clear dictate of prudent statesmanship and frank finance that in what we are now, I hope, about to undertake, we should pay as we go. . . . We should be following an almost universal example of modern governments if we were to draw the greater part or even the whole of the revenues we need from the income taxes. . . . What is clear is that the industry of this generation should pay the bills of this generation."

I was delighted to see the President persist in his course of having the nation safeguard itself from financial chaos by reliance in full measure upon taxation. It was obvious that the belligerents on the Continent of Europe were not taking a wise course in this matter and that they were heading for trouble. Great Britain alone had taken the necessary steps.

Congress by resolution in December continued the Emergency Act of 1914 and proceeded to devise further measures which were embodied in the Act of September 8, 1916. This law doubled the normal income rate, increased the supertax classes from 6 to 13, the rate rising from 1 per cent. to 13 per cent. on amounts in excess of $20,000, $40,000, $60,000, $80,000, $100,000, $150,000, $200,000, $250,000, $300,000, $500,000, $1,000,000, $1,500,000, and $2,000,000, levied an estate tax of 1 per cent. on amounts up to $50,000 and of from 2 per cent. to 10 per cent. on amounts in excess of $50,000 to those in excess of $5,000,000, placed a tax of $12\frac{1}{2}$ per cent. on the net profits of munition manufacturers, and fixed the normal income rate on corporations at 2 per cent. and added 50 cents on each $1,000 of fair valuation of capital stock.

The effects of these various revenue measures may be indicated by the statement that, in spite of a decline in tariff receipts, mainly on account of the war, from $292,000,000 in the fiscal year 1913–14 to $226,000,000 in the year 1916–17, the total ordinary revenues increased from $735,000,000 to $1,118,000,000. In 1914, the corporation and individual income-tax yield of the Act of 1913 was $61,000,000; the emergency tax of 1914 gave $52,000,000 in 1915, and the income taxes $80,000,000; in 1916, their total was $209,000,000; and in 1917, the Act of 1916 and the emergency measure yielded $454,000,000; and what is of even greater importance, a sound policy had been fixed and the machinery was in operation and was developing.

CHAPTER XII

*The Conventions of 1916—Mr. Hughes as a Candidate—The
Record of the Democratic Party*

AS THE time for the nomination conventions approached (1916), there was much speculation
as to whom the Republicans would select as
their candidate for the Presidency. It was a
foregone conclusion that the Democrats would name Mr.
Wilson. It was, of course, understood that Mr. Roosevelt
would like to be the candidate either of the Progressive
party or of the Republican, if he could not command the
support of both. It was equally clear that the Old Guard,
while it would manœuvre to induce the Progressives not
to place a candidate in the field, would have nothing to
do with Roosevelt.

Mr. Justice Hughes's name was being frequently mentioned, but I personally felt that he would not be the
candidate. In the first place, I doubted if he would take
a course which might permit it to be said by anybody that
members of the Supreme Court might have political aspirations and that the Court was a stepping stone to the
Presidency. In the second place, I was influenced by
what he had said to me several months before when I sat
by him at a public dinner. In the course of our conversation, I spoke of his career as Governor of New York and
particularly of his political addresses in his campaign for

the governorship and during the Presidential campaign in 1912. I said: "I imagine you must find the bench very tame after what you have been through, and that you really enjoyed much more the activity and excitement of political life." He replied, as I recall, that I could not be much more mistaken about anything than I was about him and his inclinations; that he had never enjoyed his political activities, especially the speaking part; that he hated political speech-making; that he was perfectly happy on the Supreme Court and that he knew of nothing which could induce him to abandon it and return to political life.

Never having attended a national political convention, I decided to attend, not only the Democratic Convention in St. Louis, but also the Progressive and Republican conventions in Chicago. In Chicago, I made the Chicago Club my headquarters in daytime and spent part of each day at the conventions. At the Club I frequently saw members of the Old Guard, which, it was asserted, was really steering the Republican Convention. This convention was uninteresting. Its main concern seemed to be to keep the Progressives from nominating a candidate and therefore to select some satisfactory person whom they would support. I listened to the keynote speech of Senator Harding. It was long, conventional, and dull; but he seemed to be very much pleased with it and with himself. He showed it by his manner and bearing.

The Progressive body seemed to be very much at sea. The members were earnest and enthusiastic, but their leaders, including Roosevelt, who was not present, appeared to be playing a game, which was to frighten the Republicans into taking Roosevelt, if possible; or, if this could not be done and the Republicans were willing to

[189]

take a reasonably good man, to dissolve the Progressive organization and try to take the members over to the Republicans. One incident in the game interested me and caused me to place big question marks after the names of some of the Progressive leaders.

A friend of mine came to me one day in the Chicago Club and suggested that we go to the Progressive Convention. He said he thought that there might be an interesting development; that a message had come from Roosevelt which a Progressive leader had, and that it would be read during the afternoon. We went early and took our places in a box which had been put at our disposal. After a few minutes, the chairman came forward and announced that they were waiting for a message from their great leader; that it would come at any moment; and that while they were waiting they would listen to some speeches. After each speech, he would announce that the message would probably soon arrive and that another short speech would be heard. Then he shifted and announced that, while they were waiting for the message from their great leader, they would take up a collection for expenses. After a considerable sum had been subscribed, he came forward and said that the message had come and that he would read it. It stated that the great leader would not be a candidate and asked the body to give its support to that great Progressive, Henry Cabot Lodge! A more stunned, whipped crowd, I had never looked upon. It was a pitiful spectacle. It had been hoaxed.

When the Republicans nominated Mr. Hughes, I felt that they had put up their strongest candidate and that he would make an able and aggressive fight. He was not hampered by any commitments in his party platform.

[190]

It was little more than a string of platitudes. It knew "no allegiance except to the Constitution, to the government, and to the flag of the United States." It believed "in American policies at home and abroad." This was very informing! It might have been interesting if it had professed allegiance to Germany or Ireland and expressed belief in Italian policies at home and Japanese policies abroad. It, of course, demanded just as much protection as was necessary, and announced something which it could not possibly know—that the Underwood Tariff of 1913 would have ruined industry and labour. It cried for national preparedness, which many of its members opposed during the spring, and informed the world that the Administration had "destroyed our influence abroad and humiliated us in our own eyes." It also favoured the extension of woman suffrage, but preferred to let "George" do it.

The task of the Democrats in St. Louis was simple. They had only to name Wilson and Marshall and to adopt with minor modifications the platform outlined by the President and carried to St. Louis by Newton Baker under his vest, so careful was he of it. The platform, as adopted, after setting out the record of the Administration, condemned groups of all kinds which had as their object to advance foreign interests, favoured the bill to create a merchant marine, the enactment of a Child Labour Law, a Budget System, Suffrage for Women on the same terms as for men, and the granting of self-government to the Philippines and territorial government to Alaska, Hawaii, and Porto Rico.

I came away from these conventions with a feeling of depression. They are not edifying spectacles, and they

[191]

are an offence to the ear and to reason. They seem to indicate that the nation is still in the boyhood stage of its development. They are distinctly inartistic, not to say common and vulgar. The speeches delivered before the audiences are full of the same sort of "bunk" which characterizes and mars most of our political meetings. The conventions are, in fact, the fountain sources of "bunk." The demonstrations as a rule are forced, childish, and trivial, and the extravagant utterances do not arouse the partisan and they do repel the independent.

In all our party activities we are too partisan, too prone to resort to sharp practices, and too much addicted to personalities. The "fiery orator" is still accorded an honour which is not his due. As a rule, he is a person whose physical energy and lung power are out of all proportion to his mental power and to the number and soundness of his ideas. Apparently, the masses like a good deal of bunk and enjoy being fooled a large part of the time.

It would be a great relief if our conventions would adopt a more decent and seemly procedure, one more in keeping with their high purpose. It would be a greater relief if the public would force party leaders to show a higher regard for facts, to evidence a desire and demonstrate a capacity to get the pertinent facts, to interpret them reasonably, and to follow their conclusions regardless of consequences. This would, of course, retire many of our leaders to the shades of private life, but the public could survive their disappearance. If nothing but the facts were set out and fair interpretations of them were given, there would still be sufficient differences of opinion to sustain at least two parties. With increase in the number of independent-minded men and women, it may be that a change will be witnessed and that the right and sound course will come to be regarded as the best politics. The party which can see and will most frequently do the right thing undoubtedly stands the best chance of commanding the support of the American people and of perpetuating itself in power. Unless our leaders, including the press, more fully realize their responsibility and change their tactics, our experiment in democracy is likely to have hard sledding as our population increases and our problems become more complex; and it may fail. It will be interesting to discover whether or not women will stand for "bunk" as men have.

As the campaign opened, I felt that the Administration faced the people with a record, in both foreign and domestic matters, made in a time of exceptional difficulty and delicacy, which on the whole was highly creditable. The course of the government in respect to Japan, Mexico, and Germany had seemed to satisfy most reasonable requirements and to meet the views of the great majority of the people and of fair-minded and intelligent leaders of thought. In the field of military and financial preparedness, the President had pressed matters about as far as it was possible to carry them with any hope of having a majority in Congress and the public back of him. Of course, he had not satisfied the extremists and could not hope to meet the demands of those who were making them merely for partisan purposes and party gain. He had "sought to maintain peace against very great and sometimes very unfair odds."

He had nothing but disgust and anger for those citizens who were "born under other flags but welcomed under our generous naturalization laws to the full freedom and opportunity of America, who have poured the poison of

[193]

disloyalty into the very arteries of our national life; who have sought to bring the authority and good name of our government into contempt, to destroy our industries wherever they thought it effective for their vindictive purposes to strike at them, and to debase our policies to the uses of foreign intrigue. . . . It is possible to deal with these things very effectually. I need not suggest the terms in which they may be dealt with." The President had even greater contempt for native-born citizens who "had been guilty of disturbing the self-possession and misrepresenting the temper and principles of the country during these days of terrible war, when it would seem that every man who was truly American would instinctively make it his duty and his pride to keep the scales of judgment even and prove himself a partisan of no nation but his own." He wished he might say that there were only a few such men. But he could not. "There are some men among us, and many resident abroad who, though born and bred in the United States and calling themselves Americans, have so forgotten themselves and their honour as citizens as to put their passionate sympathy with one or the other side in the great European conflict above their regard for the peace and the dignity of the United States. They also preach and practise disloyalty. No laws, I suppose, can reach corruptions of the mind and heart; but I should not speak of others without also speaking of these and expressing the even deeper humiliation and scorn which every self-possessed and thoughtfully patriotic American must feel when he thinks of them and of the discredit they are daily bringing upon us."

On such people, the President and the Cabinet did not waste much thought. The attitude of the great mass of

[194]

the American people was the thing which concerned them,
and they had a feeling of confidence that if the people
were fully informed they would lend their support and
stand any test to which they might be subjected. The
President did not want "the question of peace and war
entrusted too entirely to our government." He wanted
war, if it had to come, "to be something that springs out
of the sentiments and principles and actions of the people
themselves."

But there was much more than the foreign policy and
preparedness issues on which the Administration could go
before the nation.

The Administration had a domestic record "of extraordinary length and variety, rich in elements of many
kinds, but consistent in principle throughout and susceptible of brief recital," as the President said in his speech of
acceptance.

It had kept its promises. It had dispersed the Lobby,
overthrown the "Invisible Government" against which
Roosevelt and more than four million Republicans apparently had protested, and had again established a free
and untrammelled government of the people.

It had set aside the Payne-Aldrich bill against which,
likewise, four millions of Republicans had risen in revolt,
had kept its pledge to the people to revise the tariff downward, and had enacted the Simmons-Underwood measure.

It had placed upon the statute books a national income
tax, long demanded by the country and approved at least
in principle by the best economic thought of the day.

The law providing for the Federal Trade Commission
whose creation the President had urged in January, 1914,
had been passed. Business had demanded that the

[195]

government let it alone or tell it what were to be the "rules of the game." It was hampered by uncertainty and needed a more explicit definition of the anti-trust laws. But it needed something more than that the menace of legal process be made explicit. Regulation by judicial process was impossible. There was need of a piece of machinery which might give legitimate and honest business advice and guidance and protect it from the unfair competition and practices of dishonest enterprises; and this need was met by the establishment of the Trade Commission.

More important still was the passage of the Federal Reserve law and the organization of the Reserve System which had already been subjected to a severe and unexpected strain and had saved the nation's banking system from a breakdown.

Another commission of great potential usefulness had been added or was about to be added: the Tariff Commission. An experiment in the direction of a tariff board had been tried under a provision of the Tariff Act of 1909, but it had not demonstrated its usefulness and had raised doubts as to the desirability of such a piece of machinery. The President, himself, when it was first suggested that a tariff commission be created, was emphatically opposed to it. Several of us had brought the matter up early in the history of the Administration. The President said that the thing had already been tried and had failed. Again we urged the idea, and again he resisted it. A third time I suggested it. I stated that I was not foolish enough to think that the tariff or any other form of taxation could be taken out of politics, that I recognized clearly that taxation was the sort of thing that constituted the very

[196]

essence of political difference, around which politics always had revolved and always would turn, and that I was not so innocent as to believe that any Congress would ever fully accept the conclusions of any administrative or investigating commission on any matter of taxation, but that I was convinced that such a body could be of great service by gathering reliable data for the information of the President, of Congress, and, above all, of the public. I insisted that the matter was essentially one of public sentiment, that the public was ignorant both of the principles and of the facts, and that, if it was informed, it could no longer be imposed upon, and that tariffs could no longer be framed in the dark and secret chamber of conference committees in the interest of special groups. When I finished, the President said: "Well, if you feel so strongly about it and are so fully convinced that a commission will serve a useful purpose, why don't you send me a memorandum and try your hand at a tentative draft of a bill?" I told him that I would gladly do so. The President soon wholly committed himself to the idea and wrote a letter to Mr. Kitchin suggesting that his committee take up the matter. In it he set out at some length the purpose of such a body and the scope of its duties along the lines of my statement, and in due course the committee presented a measure which received the sanction of Congress and of the President.

The President, himself, on at least one occasion referred to his position in this matter and indicated that he had changed his mind about it. In speaking before the Railway Business Association of New York, January 27, 1916, he said:

"There is another thing about which I have changed

my mind. A year ago, I was not in favour of a tariff board, and I will tell you why. Then the only purpose of a tariff board was to keep alive an unprofitable controversy. . . . But the circumstances of the present time are these: There is going on in the world under our eyes an economic revolution. No man understands that revolution; no man has the elements of it clearly in his mind. No part of the business of legislation with regard to international trade can be undertaken until we do understand it; and the members of Congress are too busy, their duties are too multifarious and distracting, to make it possible within a sufficiently short space of time for them to master the change that is coming. . . . There is so much to understand that we have not the data to comprehend that I for one would not dare, so far as my advice is concerned, to leave the government without the adequate means of inquiry."

In addition to this legislation, which for the most part directly affected every interest and individual in the nation, there had been enacted into law measures for the improvement of agriculture and the betterment of rural conditions which in number and importance exceeded the record made in the preceding twenty or thirty years; and these had been supplemented by an unusual body of administrative improvements and extensions.

CHAPTER XIII

Dr. Knapp's Farm Demonstration Method Made National policy—Reorganizing the Department—The Farm Loan Act— The Federal Aid Road Act—A Political Speaking Tour

THIS programme, formulated during my first year in the Department of Agriculture, was the result of the best thought of men in the Department, in Congress, and in private life. It had been executed, with one exception, substantially as planned and in terms satisfactory to me and to the agricultural leaders of the nation. The one exception was a measure for the improvement of rural sanitation and health through the coöperation and joint support of Federal and state authorities.

The programme was not suddenly or hastily conceived. Members of the Agricultural Committees in both Houses of Congress had been giving much thought to its leading features and had been securing the views of experts in the Department of Agriculture and in the Land Grant College. For many years I had been in touch with rural problems and had developed very definite views as to the needs of agriculture and the course which should be taken. I was keenly aware of the fact that much could be done to improve the processes and methods of production, but I was still more alive to the fact that greater problems presented themselves in the fields of marketing and finance and that

[199]

in no small measure further profitable production waited on the correct solutions of problems in those fields. There was no question as to the ability of the nation to produce a much greater volume of agricultural commodities. Less than 60 per cent. of our arable land was under cultivation, and of the land under cultivation not more than 12 per cent. of it was yielding reasonably full returns. Two important questions were whether or not the farmers could secure credit on terms suited to their needs and as favourable as those obtained by others with equally good security, and whether they could distribute their products more economically and at fair prices, at prices which paid them to produce their crops.

Farming must pay. It is a hazardous undertaking at best. It is important, not only to the farmer, but also to the nation, that on the average his accounts show a balance on the right side. But something more is necessary. Rural life must not only be profitable: it must also be comfortable, healthful, and attractive. It is not sufficient that farming be profitable. In Illinois, for instance, many farmers have made money, but the result in too large measure has been that they have moved to town to enjoy educational and social advantages, have held on to their farms, refusing to sell, and have operated them through tenants. The tenants have been given little or no incentive to improve the farm or themselves, and the landlords have taken too little effective interest in them and have not contributed enough to the building up of rural communities. As a consequence, Illinois is one of the tenancy plague spots of the country.

The remedy involved better methods of production through the use of good cultural practices, soil improvement, plant and animal breeding according to the best known principles, the control and eradication of plant and animal diseases, the standardization of products, the development of standard grain and cotton grades for use in trading, more economical methods and processes of marketing including the effective coöperation among producers, credit on more reasonable terms, good roads, and modern schools.

The programme involved a conception of rural life as a whole and its proper relation to the industry of the nation. Up to 1913, attention had been directed almost exclusively to one side of agriculture, that is, to production. The other great half, including finance and distribution, had, relatively speaking, been ignored.

The time was ripe for action. The notion that a departure should be made had become fixed; and, very fortunately, there was available for leadership of the forces in Congress interested in agriculture, one of the best real friends the farmers have ever had and one of the ablest and most satisfactory legislators it has been my fortune to know, A. F. Lever, of South Carolina. He was alive to the needs of the farmer and was unwilling to play the demagogue. He was skilful in handling measures in committee and on the floor of the House, was willing and anxious to get the best thought of the most competent experts, and had the faculty in high degree of coöperating with departmental and other leaders, including the forces of the Land Grant colleges, in developing and framing measures.

The Department of Agriculture, by reason of its great number of able and loyal practical experts, was in position to furnish guidance in matters of substance, and by reason of its excellent legal staff, headed by one of the best and soundest lawyers in the country, Francis Gordon Caffey, was able to provide the requisite legal advice in drafting measures. The following outline will give a sufficient hint of what was accomplished in less than four years.

(1) Appropriations for the support of the regular activities of the Department increased 50 per cent., or from $24,100,000 to $36,130,000. Particular pains were being taken to foster production through every promising approach, and, especially, to increase the meat supply of the nation.

(2) Realizing that the Department had in its possession a vast store of information that should be conveyed to the farmers and conveyed in such manner as to induce them to apply it, that it had a constituency of nearly fifty million people, that it did one of the largest printing businesses in the world, and that much of its matter was badly organized and written, I took steps to place the information activities on a new footing.

The first thing I did was to invite Walter H. Page to come to Washington to talk to the heads of services about the need of writing bulletins in good plain simple English —in fact, to translate their technical language into English. He accepted and gave the group one of his characteristic talks. He began by telling the members that they could not write; and to soften the blow, he added that very few people in this country could write, that he had to have at least 50 per cent. of the manuscripts submitted to him by professors of English in leading universities rewritten, and that he, in despair, had had to train a staff of his own in order to carry on this business. Then he very vigorously outlined what should be done.

Subsequently, the Department took three helpful steps. It created the Office of Information; segregated the scientific matter for the scientists from the popular matter for the farmers, and simplified its farmers' bulletins, using the briefest forms and the simplest and clearest English. The Office of Information undertook to supervise the preparation of printed matter and particularly to facilitate the securing of news items by all interested parties, including the daily and weekly newspapers and the agricultural journals. It was ascertained that the press would use much material if it were furnished in readily available form and that much of the timely matter bearing on urgent situations would be sent by telegraph.

(3) Furthermore, it was recognized that the printed page was not the most efficient educational medium, but needed to be supplemented by personal effort of sensible, trained leaders in intimate contact with farmers and their families and more particularly through the means of demonstrations of good agricultural methods on the farms themselves.

Experiments with the farm demonstration method had been tried successfully on a small scale by the Department about ten years before, and under the direction of a very unusual man, Seaman A. Knapp, of Louisiana and Texas, formerly of Iowa. About 1905, another very valiant citizen, Dr. Wallace Buttrick, of the General Education Board, came in contact with Doctor Knapp at my home at the Texas State College of Agriculture and was much impressed by him and his methods and results. In a short time, the General Education Board made a substantial appropriation for the support of the work to be administered through the Department and this was increased from time to time till, in 1913, it was spending for the support of the coöperative undertaking a very large amount. The funds of the Board and of the Department were supplemented by contributions from the state and the localities, which was a wise feature of the plan, since self-help in such matters is of the greatest value The Board's disinterested efforts were appreciated by the people and helped to bring the work to the point where it was possible to induce Congress to make a sufficient appropriation to enable the undertaking to be taken over and supported entirely out of Federal, state, and local funds, and to receive the sanction of Congress in the most significant and far-reaching single educational extension laws ever enacted by any government. On May 8, 1914, the Agricultural Educational Extension Act was approved by the President.

This measure did much more than to make an appropriation. It incorporated a very helpful principle bearing on the relation between the Federal and state governments. It provided for close coöperation between the two jurisdictions, and thus removed the jealousy, friction, and wasteful duplication of effort, which had been growing as the activities expanded. The Act provided that no expenditure should be made out of Federal funds except to execute plans previously mutually agreed upon by the Secretary of Agriculture and the State College of Agriculture. This, therefore, meant more than coöperation. It meant that careful joint planning would supplant impulsive and ill-considered action. It also meant the reduction to the minimum of the pressure of local politics and the development of a great piece of nation-wide machinery under the direction of non-political Federal and state agencies which would be of great assistance in time

[204]

of emergency as well as in normal times. It was contemplated that ultimately there would be placed in each of the 2,850 rural counties of the Union two agents, at least, perhaps a man and a woman, and, in each state, district specialists who would give advice in the more complex and difficult problems. Every state in the Union acted quickly and accepted the measure.

(4) Before the measure just outlined was passed, the Department had created a piece of new machinery intended to supervise investigational work in rural finance and marketing. This was the Office of Markets and Rural Organization. It began work with the modest sum of $50,000, which by 1916 had increased to $1,200,000, including the items authorized for the enforcement of new marketing laws which were assigned to this agency. It was the only organization of its kind in the world.

(5) It soon became evident that, in the interest of efficiency, the work of the Department needed rearranging. Certain changes were made quickly, but more radical steps had to await Congressional authorization, and this I asked for in the estimates submitted in 1913. It was granted, and action followed promptly. The services did not need any revolutionary alterations, but they were susceptible of much improvement. The Office of Farm Management and the Farm Demonstration work were taken out of the Bureau of Plant Industry. The first was attached to the Office of the Secretary and the second to the Office of Experiment Stations, the name of which was changed to the States Relations Service. It was the intention to expand the work in farm management, redirecting it more along economic lines, and to assign to the States Relations Service the administration of the Agricul-

[205]

tural Extension Act.　Certain transfers of special activities were made in the interest of better coördination.

(6) Three pieces of legislation of great importance bearing on marketing were enacted into law.　Two of them, the Cotton Futures Act and the Grain Standards Act, had as their main object to enable the producer to sell his product as nearly as possible for what it was, to get a fair price for each part of it according to its character and quality and to control the exchange transactions in such manner as to eliminate certain abuses which had developed.

The situation had been very unsatisfactory.　Different standards for cotton were used in the markets of the South, and there existed nowhere definite uniform grain grades.　The local buyers knew the standards in use and understood them; the producers did not, and it was impossible to educate them to the use of a variety of standards.　There was not only no incentive to the farmer to place a better product on the market; he was actually penalized if he took pains to do so.　Simple justice to the producer and the welfare of the consumer as well dictated that the situation be changed.

The third measure, the permissive Warehouse Act, was intended to facilitate the safe storage of agricultural commodities, the better distribution of satisfactory warehouses throughout the nation, the financing of crop movement, and the orderly marketing of products.　It was expected that, by the better business handling of storages under license from the Department, warehouse receipts would be issued which would be accepted by banks more readily as collateral for loans.

(7) Two steps were taken bearing more directly on the

problem of enabling farmers to secure credit on more satisfactory terms. The first was a provision in the Federal
Reserve Act. The Federal Reserve Board was given
power to define the paper which would be eligible for discount, to make agricultural paper eligible, and to give it a
maturity of six months as against ninety days for ordinary
commercial paper. This difference was justified by the
fact that the farmers' operations are seasonal, involving a
long turnover. As the President had aptly said: "The
farmer is the servant of the seasons."

The second step was taken by the passage of the Farm
Loan Act. The existing banking machinery was suited
to the needs of urban producers and dealers but not to
those of farmers. There was need of institutions, man-
aged by men who understood and were sympathetic with
the farmers' plans and needs, reaching out into the rural
districts and operating on terms demanded by the seasonal
character of their activities. It was apparent that farmers in many sections were being compelled to pay higher
rates of interest than were justified. On long-time loans,
they varied from about $5\frac{1}{2}$ per cent. in older states like
Illinois, to $8\frac{1}{2}$ per cent. or more in such states as Florida,
Oklahoma, and Montana, and on short-time loans from
7 per cent. to $14\frac{1}{2}$ per cent. Furthermore, there was no
satisfactory arrangement for obtaining loans on the
amortization basis. The need of stimulating agriculture
by enabling farmers to obtain loans for productive purposes at reasonable rates under intelligent and safe direction was manifest. This need the new system, organized
on the model of the Federal Reserve System, was designed
to meet.

(8) The other measure which completed the programme

to the close of 1916 was the Federal Aid Road Act. Since its beginning, the nation had had enlightened leaders who recognized the imperative need of better highways and of their development under expert central bodies. Washington and Jefferson had spoken for the cause and had used their best efforts to secure action, but with little effect. In 1913, Virginia was still in the mud. It was impossible in wet weather to go from Washington, the capital of the nation, to Richmond, the former capital of the Confederacy, safely or at all in an automobile. Only a few Eastern states had either a rational highway organization or many decent roads. In most of the states, road building was under the jurisdiction of local bodies who called out road gangs at convenient seasons and succeeded in many instances in marring the roads by throwing up a little dirt on them which the next rain converted into mud or washed off.

It was estimated that, on the average road, it was costing about twenty-three cents a ton a mile to haul a load, while on a good road it would cost only about eleven cents. And there was this further waste. Under the conditions as they existed, the farmers had to haul when they should have been ploughing or harvesting, while, under changed conditions, they could haul when they could not get into the fields. Good roads were a prerequisite, not only for better distribution, but also for good schools, and for a more healthful, comfortable, and attractive rural life. They were as necessary for the city as for the rural districts; and yet there were people so short-sighted that they raised strong objections because of the cost which would be entailed.

Some of them, in particular in the older states like

[208]

Massachusetts and New York, opposed the legislation because money would be taken from them to build up the
newer states. They were as irrational as are the people of
cities who object to expenditure of their funds in the
country surrounding them for schools and roads. They
do not see that their prosperity is dependent on that of
the back country, that, in fact, the back country makes
them possible and makes them prosperous as it prospers.
New England and New York are made by the rest of the
nation in large measure, and such of their funds as go into
the newer sections for such things as roads economically
planned and constructed are a direct investment for them
yielding them immense returns. It is likewise true that
the cost of good roads is negligible in comparison with that
of bad roads.

Of course, it takes much money to make good roads in
America, but it costs immeasurably more to have bad
roads; and good roads are part of a necessary programme
to retain in rural districts a sufficient number of contented
and efficient farmers to produce what the nation must have
if it is to grow and be strong. In view of the fact that the
Federal expenditure for roads is relatively small in comparison with the amounts the states have been induced
to spend or to make available, and that the amount of
Federal funds which would be taken out of the older states
in excess of what they receive under their allotment is not
very great, the attitude of those who resist the highway
policy seems to be all the more petty and shortsighted.

The Act, like the Agricultural Extension measure, contained a provision intended to lessen the difficulties of
double jurisdiction and to minimize friction, waste, and
duplication. It made available a large sum of money,

but stipulated that none of it should be expended except upon plans, specifications, and contracts submitted by a central highway body in each state and approved by the Secretary of Agriculture, who would act through the Bureau of Roads. It required that the work, as it proceeded, should be inspected by the Federal agents, and made it necessary for the state to make available for road construction a sum at least equal to the Federal apportionment, and placed on the state the burden of maintenance. The requirements that the work be done through the Federal department, with its Bureau of Roads, the best organization of its kind in the world, in coöperation with a central state highway body, and that plans be carefully worked out, were of peculiar importance and of far-reaching consequence. All the states accepted the Act within a very short time; and the first and most significant result was that central administrative agencies were created in all the states under legislation which also met all the other requirements of the law, including the financial arrangements.

Such were the main achievements in the foreign and domestic fields on which the Administration could go before the country in its appeal for support.

The last week in September, I received a letter from the Chairman of the Speakers' Committee of the National Democratic Executive Committee indicating that the Committee expected me to give my entire time from the first of October to the close of the day before the election to the making of campaign speeches. In fact, he sent me a schedule covering a considerable section of the country which would have taken all my time for five weeks and would have involved my absence from Washington for that period. I replied that I would be glad to be of service, but that I had my estimates to prepare and my Annual Report to write, that I could not leave Washington except for very short trips till after the fifteenth of October but that from that time till the day of the election I would be glad to speak wherever the Committee wished to send me. In the meantime, I told him, I would speak at places in such states as Ohio, Maryland, Pennsylvania, and West Virginia, which I could reach overnight or at week-ends. During the longer period, I told him that I would prefer the parts of the country where independents were numerous and where, therefore, there was a possibility of making converts. I had no desire to speak merely to Democratic partisans. They were already converted and needed only to be aroused. I felt that somebody else could more effectively serve that purpose.

I was convinced that the Democratic party could not win the election unless it could command the support of a large percentage of the independents, and that, if I could do any good at all, it would be through an appeal to them. I said this to the Chairman of the Committee. I told him also that I doubted the wisdom of the members of the Cabinet absenting themselves from Washington for long periods and of their making very partisan speeches. They would, of course, make party or administration speeches; but, as it was very desirable that they secure the attention and support of the independents, they would more certainly accomplish the purpose by the exercise of restraint and by a sound appeal to the public's intelligence. I learned later that these suggestions did not appeal to the Chairman. In fact, I was informed, when I called at headquarters in New York City after I had spoken for a week in Connecticut, that he was irritated over the contents of my letter and had thrown it aside. This accounted for my delay in getting from the Committee a list of speaking dates for the period after October 15th and the imperfect arrangements which had been made for my first four or five meetings.

It was finally arranged that I was to speak in Connecticut, New York at central and northwestern points, Ohio, and Indiana.

By the time I left Washington, the character of the campaign had been pretty well defined. The Republicans, true to their platform, were presenting nothing constructive. They were indulging in blanket criticisms and in generalities as to what they would do if they won the election. I was greatly surprised at the failure of Mr. Hughes at the outset to make a strong appeal. I had expected that he would be aggressive, keen, and skillful, and I hoped that he would pitch his campaign on a moderate and broad plane. I could not see how he could offer a very constructive programme, but I assumed that he would at least be concrete and courageous. But his whole programme, like that of the other Republican leaders, seemed simply to be this: Anything to beat Wilson and to get the Republican party back into power, and therefore to pursue the course of least danger, avoiding offence to anybody or to any element.

As a matter of fact, it was very difficult for Mr. Hughes to take a concrete, definite line. He had a very unruly team to drive. He had to steer between the views of men like Penrose, Smoot, and Lodge, on the one hand, and Progressives like William Allen White and Pinchot on the other, and between the pro-Ally and the pro-German. He had the impossible task of attempting "to coördinate the incongruous." He had too many mental and emotional patterns to match, and, like the chameleon which tried at the same instant to match all the colours of a "crazy" quilt, he blew up.

Others had a similar awakening. Mr. Richard Olney, Cleveland's Secretary of State, writing about Mr. Hughes, had this to say: "Why did not the Republican Senators resort to it (the filibuster against the eight-hour bill) and get all the time for deliberation they wanted? What was candidate Hughes doing that he did not make the wires hot with messages to Washington, warning against the law the seventy-four Republican Representatives who voted for it, and urging the twenty-eight Republican Senators to filibuster to the last ditch?

"But neither he nor the Republican leaders generally had the nerve to face the situation. With ample means in their hands to prevent legislation until after due consideration, they elected that it should appear to be enacted under coercion in order that after the great national deliverance had been effected, they might object to the mode of its accomplishment. A pettier and more ignoble game of politics was never conceived. In comparison, and in view of the sudden and extraordinary exigency sprung upon the country, President Wilson's course was characterized by both courage and common sense."

Finding the Administration's record of domestic affairs uncommonly difficult to criticize, the opposition concentrated its attacks upon the conduct of foreign affairs. That field being largely in charge of the President himself, the ordinary opposing political speaker naturally resorted to personalities and found such epithets as "weak," "vacillating," "fatuous," "insincere," "inconsistent," and "un-American" only too feeble to do justice to his real sentiments.

Mr. Hughes, in his campaign, made the impression on me that he was lacking in imagination and in high constructive ability; and I concluded that he was being badly advised.

President Eliot felt the same sense of disappointment in Mr. Hughes. In the *Atlantic Monthly* he wrote:

"The most thorough search in the long essay in which Mr. Hughes accepts the nomination will fail to find a specific recommendation on any controversial matter. The paper is filled with universally accepted statements concerning the proper national policies and general description of what ought to be done and ought not to be done by national administration.

"From the comparatively short passage on protection and the proper regulation of industries it is impossible to derive any exact information as to what measures Mr. Hughes would support if he were elected.

"Mr. Hughes's most distinct announcement relates to woman suffrage. Believing that inevitable, he declares in favour of it now, but assigns as his reasons the bitterness of women's struggle for the suffrage and his apprehension that a long-continued feminist agitation will obscure normal issues. For a brave man, this seems a strange submission to what he thinks destiny and an intemperate agitation."

President Eliot advised the voter to seek guidance in the deeds of the Administration in comparison with those of the four preceding administrations. He commended its foreign policy and its preparedness programme, saying of the latter that, in measures of preparedness, President Wilson had gone further than any other American President. He added: "In regard to the provision of adequate military and naval forces at whatever cost, President Wilson is far in advance of the average American voter. President Roosevelt's martial temperament and emphatic language brought little to pass."

President Wilson, favoured by extraordinary circumstances which he thoroughly understood, had brought much to pass. He concluded with this striking statement: "The Democratic party has done such an extraordinary amount of good work during the present Administration that the period from 1912 to 1916 will be memorable in the history of the United States."

In my speeches, I summarized the achievements of the Democratic party, particularly in the field of rural life, pointed out the lack of constructive criticism and programme of the opposition, and touched upon a number of topics which were being stressed by Republican speakers. Some of the points I made are indicated in the extracts, which I have inserted in Appendix I, to help give a picture of the time.

Immediately after my return to Washington from Indiana, where I spent the last week of the campaign, two days before the election, Tuesday, November 7th, I took pains to get in touch with a high officer of the National Democratic Committee to give him my impressions. In substance, I said this to him:

"The President will be reëlected. The people know that he has done a good job and they will not turn him down; but the outcome will not be due to any excellence of the Democratic organization as a whole or to the efficiency of the Democrats as publicity experts. He will be reëlected in spite of the imperfection of the organization locally and of the indifference of leading Democrats, especially in Congress, in keeping the achievements of the party before the public. The Republicans have the support of the majority of the publicity organs and have much larger campaign funds than the Democrats, and the Democrats cannot hope to compete with them in general publicity; but they do not even compete with them in directions where funds are not required. They could very effectively use the *Congressional Record*, but they do not do so. Their opponents miss no opportunity to do so. They are on the job every minute and make very effective use of a free medium.

"Furthermore, they do not rely so exclusively on intensive work during the few weeks preceding the election. In my judgment, the Republicans will begin work the day after the election. They will incessantly spread misrepresentations as well as truth. They will organize every precinct in America, and they will have the elections of 1918 and 1920 won long before the nominations are made. I apprehend that as usual the Democrats will wait till it is too late and then depend on a whirlwind drive. It is also a question how long they can stand prosperity and continue to do team work and whether they can stand much longer the strain of trying to follow a leader who thinks as straight and objectively, who has so little patience with personal politics and aspirations, and who acts as courageously as Wilson does. I am not optimistic that they can or will, or that they will have the foresight and energy to organize or the money to perfect and support an organization."

[216]

CHAPTER XIV

DRIFTING TOWARD WAR

The President's Peace Note—Disagreement with It—Unrestricted Submarine Warfare—Sending Bernstorff Home

WHEN we assembled in the Cabinet room at half-past two, Friday, December 15, 1916, the President promptly joined us. He had a document in his hand which he said he desired to present to us for our criticism. He very pointedly asked us to be very careful to say nothing about the note to anybody. "Forget it," he said, "after you have heard it. If necessary, say that there never was such a paper." I knew that he still had in mind what he had complained of months before, namely, that certain members of the Cabinet kept none of the Cabinet proceedings secret, and that their heedlessness caused him no little embarrassment. In fact, it was this singular conduct which caused him to refrain from bringing matters to the Cabinet which otherwise he would have been glad to present; and yet, these very men with whom nothing was confidential were the very ones who complained that he did not bring more things before us.

The President referred to the German note of December 12th, in which Germany made a formal proposal "to enter forthwith into peace negotiations." There had been rumours of such a note, but there was nothing definite. It turned out that the Central Allies desired neutrals to

[217]

transmit to the Entente Allies the information that they desired peace and wished to know whether or not they were desirous of entering into negotiations. The note was thoroughly characteristic. It had an obvious self-assured tone, and was so worded that, if the Allies had responded favourably, Germany could have said to her people that, since she was waging a defensive war, she had accomplished her purpose and had come off victor.

The note which the President had prepared he proposed to send, not in reply or in response to this note of the Central Allies, but in spite of it. For a long time he had had in mind the matter of asking all the belligerents if they wished to state or would state the terms on which they might make peace. When he prepared his paper, he was not thinking about this particular document of the Central Allies. He was really embarrassed, apparently, by its appearance, but he was not to be turned aside from his course. Others had had in mind some such plan as the President proposed. More than a year before, Senator Newlands had several times, in conversation with me, very emphatically suggested that the Allies be sounded. I assume that he took the matter up with the President, but I do not know that he did so.

The President said that he had come to the conclusion that it was desirable to ask the nations to indicate their views as to the terms on which the war might be concluded, and that he was fully conscious of the fact that many people would represent that he was playing into Germany's hands. He read the note in full. In it he took "the liberty of calling attention to the fact that the objects which the statesmen of the belligerents on both sides have in mind in this war are virtually the same, *as*

[218]

stated in general terms to their own people and to the world."
He pointed out that, in measures to secure the future
peace of the world, the United States was as vitally interested as the belligerents, that it desired to coöperate
in the attainment of right ends when the war was over with
every resource, and that the war should be brought to a
speedy conclusion if civilization was to be saved a deadly
blow.   The concrete objects for which the nations were
fighting had never been definitely stated.   It was possible
that the warring nations were nearer together than was
supposed, and that a comparison of views might clear the
way for a conference, and that a permanent concord and
concert of nations might be immediately practicable.

It is to be noted that the President did not say in the
final note that the nations were fighting for the same things
but that the objects as stated by the leaders on both sides
to their people were in general terms the same, which is
a very different thing.

There was much discussion of the note.   McAdoo and
I expressed strong doubts as to the wisdom of sending it.
We said that, in any event, it should not appear so soon
after the German note of the twelfth.   McAdoo reiterated
his opposition to sending it.   I urged that it be deferred
at least.   I suggested that it would be resented and might
be regarded as an act of friendship toward Germany and
possibly as a threat, and that, if anything was to be done,
the Entente Allies should merely be sounded to ascertain
whether or not such an inquiry would be agreeable to
them.   The President said: "It may be wise to send nothing, but I will send this note or nothing."   With that I
sat back and said nothing further.

I had it in mind to suggest modifications of certain

[219]

statements, but the matter seemed to be closed. I had intended to suggest that if the note was to go forward he should make it absolutely clear that he was not asserting that he thought the belligerents were fighting for identical things, but merely that the leaders on both sides appeared to profess the same objects. This, I recognized, was what the note did say, but I thought it should be brought out more emphatically.

We adjourned without certain knowledge as to whether or not the President would send the statement. I left the city for New York, to spend the week-end. Of course, I did not refer to the matter. The note appeared in the papers Wednesday morning.

Soon after the note was published, when I returned to Washington, I saw Maurice Low, correspondent of the London *Morning Post*. He was very much disturbed and angry about the note. He said to me that it would be resented by the Allies; that it was a peace move, that the President had played into the hands of the Germans, and that he had created a very delicate situation which might become serious. I replied that he was unduly excited. I protested that I could not speak for the President, that I did not know all that was in his mind or that lay behind the note, but that I presumed he had a faint hope that, if the Allies and the Central Powers stated to the world what they were fighting for, it might be discovered that they were not far apart in what they would be willing to set forth, and that a basis for a conference and peace might be reached. I added that I had no such hope, but that I was confident that the note would place the Allies in a favourable tactical position. They would be able to make a statement of their purposes, one which would appeal to our own people and to the conscience of the world. The Germans could not make any statement whatever, or, at any rate, one which would not cause world-wide resentment. The further result would be the education or enlightenment of the American people. They would be brought to a fuller realization of the fact that the Allies were waging a just war and fighting for a higher civilization. As we were profoundly affected, it was not inappropriate that both sides should tell us directly and concretely what they stood for in their own way. Each evidently valued our good opinion and wanted at least our moral support. Low assented to this last statement but asserted that we knew what each was fighting for and that the Allies had stated their terms—"full reparations, complete restitution, and adequate guaranties." I agreed that they were fighting for these things and that they ought to have them. "Certainly," I said, "the Allies are in the right—that is, Great Britain, France, and Belgium are. I have been on their side since the first day the Germans moved. They ought to win, and I believe they will win, in the end; but I am not so blind as not to know that they are not fighting merely for the three things they proclaim. Their motives and purposes are very complex. The British for a long time have been very jealous of the growing commercial as well as of the growing naval power of the Germans. Not unnaturally, they have watched with apprehension the development of German colonies. They are anxious about the Dardanelles, Asia Minor, Egypt, and India. Great Britain intervened in 1878 to prevent the Turks from being driven out of Constantinople by the Russians. Great Britain, France, and Belgium have acted nobly, but they have not acted from

[221]

single or simple motives, and when the war is over we shall see evidence of the truth of it. If they win, we shall see a great scramble. There have been other wars, and in all of them there were complex motives and loud protestations of unselfish aims."

It will do the Allies no harm to state their purposes again and more fully. Their terms will be approved by most of our people. They will include the evacuation and restitution of Belgium and France, the return of Alsace-Lorraine, a new Poland, an enlarged Serbia, a weakened Austria, the disappearance of the Turks from Europe, and of Germany from Africa, the overthrow of Prussian militarism, the safeguarding of backward nations, and some sort of international concert.

"I believe that our people can be brought to join in some concert of action based on just principles." Low interrupted me to say that our people would not join in such an enterprise because they were too isolated and too uninformed in international matters. I replied that they could be educated; that they could be brought to support a sound plan to underwrite a prevention of war; that they would be willing to put the power of the nation back of such a plan; but that they would have no enthusiasm for larger military preparedness, for piling battalion on battalion or squadron on squadron, in a mad race for military supremacy; and that they would not support the Allies in a scramble for power or territory or aid in making it possible for any one of them later to lord it over Europe or over any other part of the world. The American people, I added, would not welcome dictation even from one of the Allies, and this nation itself did not wish to dominate anybody. It was sick of all that sort of mad business. It merely wanted a clean national house for itself, peace and law everywhere in the world, so that people everywhere might prosper and nations might live together in neighbourly fashion.

Low thought that it was more than doubtful whether or not our people would ever coöperate with Europe in any such fashion. A treaty would have to be made, and the assent of the Senate would be required. The Senate would not assent. Our Constitution stood in the way. I expressed the belief that a plan could be worked out which would not run counter to the Constitution, which would still leave the ultimate determination of peace or war in the hands of Congress, and which the people would support. I asserted that it was a question of wise and courageous leadership, a question whether the people in such a matter would follow the leadership of the President, Hughes, Taft, and Root, who seemed to be together on essentials. I added that, unless something of the sort came out of the world tragedy, the sacrifices would have been largely in vain and that I should be pessimistic about the future.

Low left me, saying that he thought he would send to his paper a statement giving the substance of what I had said without in any way involving me.

He went to the British Ambassador and reported our conversation; for when I got home the next afternoon, Lady Spring-Rice was with Mrs. Houston. She said that Low had spoken to her husband about our interview and that the Ambassador was doing everything in his power to place the note in a favourable light.

The reply of Germany, as well as that of the Allies, confirmed my view. Germany stated no terms: She

[223]

merely offered to appoint delegates to a conference, which was not at all what the President had suggested. The joint note of the Allies, after protesting against the "assimilation" established in the American note between the two groups of powers and saying that their objects would not be given in detail until the hour of negotiations outlined a number of adjustments which would be insisted upon, including the reorganization of Europe upon a stable basis. Mr. Balfour himself wrote that a stable peace could not be made till Germany was defeated, and that three things were necessary for safety in the future: plotting such as Germany had engaged in must end; the Germans themselves must be brought to see that their former unscrupulous, aggressive methods were wrong and intolerable; and some international force must be created to give sanction to law and treaties.

Apparently, Germany hoped to trap the Allies into a peace which would spell victory for her, or failing that, she proposed to resume unrestricted submarine warfare without running grave risk of drawing the United States into the war. She was laying a predicate for such a course.

On January 16, 1917, I went to Cheyenne, Wyoming. On my return trip, Tuesday the 23d, I picked up a paper and found in it the President's address to the Senate on the duty of our government in the days when peace should come and its terms should be fixed. The President had said nothing before I left Washington about his purpose to make this address to the Senate. His main points were familiar. They had been made by him before in various ways at different times, and had been a part of his thought for many months.

It was not an easy note to interpret and it did not surprise me that there was much criticism both of its substance and of its phraseology. I could not presume to know fully just what was back of it, but certain things were clear. In guarded terms, he intimated his satisfaction with the reply of the Allies and his disappointment over that of Germany. He then projected his thought to the period of adjustment following the end of the war and the conclusion of treaties by the belligerents at its close. We would have no voice at the time in determining the terms of the peace, but something more, something larger would be required to make the peace lasting and permanent, something to be done by the nations in coöperation later. We must indicate that we propose to use our influence for such a concert of action, for a covenant of peace, an underwriting to prevent another upheaval. This nation must be educated and prepared in mind and resources. He had outlined part of this address in his talk before the League to Enforce Peace in May, 1916. The process of education must continue. And further, if permanency of peace was to be secured, the terms made by the belligerents must be just, and by speaking our view now we might influence action in the direction of moderation and justice.

The New World must be considered by the belligerents when they come to act. Mere terms of peace will not suffice. Peace must be "made secure by the organized major force of mankind. It must not involve merely a new balance of power. It must not be a mere crushing of antagonists, a humiliating, hate-breeding peace. The rights of small nations must be recognized and peoples must not be handed about as so many cattle. There must be freedom of intercourse among nations by land and sea. Armament must be reduced and limited.

[225]

"We must join the other civilized nations of the world in this guarantee of peace; and, in doing so, we shall not break with our traditions. We advocate extending our Monroe Doctrine to all the world. This will be no entangling alliance or balance of power. It will be a common concert of power for the welfare of the whole world."

This was a logical sequence to the note asking the belligerents to state their terms. The major aim as I saw it was, if possible, to commit them in advance of the outcome to a programme of moderation, to make it difficult for either side later to think of new and extreme things to demand, and in the second place, to win the people over to the support of a just international concert of power after the war. There was also, I imagine, in the President's mind, the possibility that we might be drawn into the struggle; and he wished to warn the world and to have our people informed as to what we would fight for.

So considered, I thought the address was noble and timely, but I regretted the use of the phrase "peace without victory" and the reference to the freedom of the seas. I did not want to see a stalemate. I wanted to see Germany vanquished. I wanted to see terms forced upon the Central Powers by the Allies, but I wanted, of course, to see the terms just, reasonable, and designed to perpetuate peace. I realized the danger that the victor would not be moderate and the value of cautions; and this I supposed was what the President really meant to give.

I felt that the reference to the freedom of the seas was unfortunate, because I had never heard any one even suggest how in time of war they could be free. They can be free only when there is peace; and the only method I have any knowledge of for keeping the seas free is to prevent war among the great powers. No great nation in time of war will fail to use its navy to prevent its enemy from getting supplies or to protect its own. Free movement of all commerce in time of war is inconceivable. The only remedy is to have no war.

On Friday, February 2, 1917, when I went to Cabinet meeting, I realized that we might be facing the most momentous issue in our experience and in the history of the nation. I had heard a rumour that a German note had come or was on the way, renouncing all her partial pledges and recent practices and declaring her intention to engage in unrestricted submarine warfare.

The note announced that beginning February 1st, a new war zone would be established around Great Britain and along the coast of France and Italy, and that any ship found within it would be sunk without regard to life or property. This zone extended 400 miles west of Ireland and ran south to a point 900 miles west of Bordeaux. The eastern half of the North Sea, a narrow strip on the north coast of Spain, a space on Spain's east coast in the Mediterranean, and a lane to the coast of Greece were exempt. For Americans who wished to visit England, a ship bearing a certificate from the government of the United States that she carried no contraband, striped on each side with three alternate red and white stripes a meter wide, flying at each mast a large flag in white and red, might sail along the fiftieth parallel to Falmouth in Cornwall, provided she arrived on Sunday and departed on Wednesday!!

This was the last word of a mad war lord—the farthest limit of dictation. If we accepted it, we surrendered our sovereignty and self-respect. When I heard its terms, I

[227]

knew that Uncle Sam would begin to take off his coat and roll up his sleeves.

This note could have just one meaning for us. It meant war and meant the beginning of the end for Germany. There had been rumours for some time that she might pursue this course, but I could not believe that she would be so stupid. There was no ground for believing, in any event, that she would take such a course before the beginning of spring. March 1st was the date suggested. Why did she set February 1st as the date, or why did she make the decision at all?

Either she had really desired peace and thought she could induce the Allies to make one largely on her own terms and had been baulked, or she had made an insincere bid for peace to lay a predicate for a barbarous method of warfare, or she had made up her mind that, by the use of the submarine, she could crush England quickly and then deal with France before this country could make her power felt. She could say to the neutrals: "We wanted peace. We tried to get it. Our adversaries are stubborn and blind. They persist in their mad course. They are trying to starve us. Two can play at this game. We are driven to desperation. We must resort to extreme measures. It is not our fault. Let the Allies take the consequences. What else can we do? We cannot hold our hands and tamely drift to destruction." Or she was bluffing, which was unlikely, or else she wanted by drawing us and perhaps other nations into the war to save her face, to say to her people: "It is no use. The world is against us. What can we do? We must give in."

The chances are that Germany's leaders have made up their minds that by using the submarine ruthlessly they

[228]

can starve England, get a quick decision, and dictate terms. There are rumours that Germany has at last got ready a large number of improved submarines, that she feels that she can now do the job, and defy the world. It is not unlikely that she was temporizing with us up to this time because she was not ready, and that she is now prepared to practise what she before was afraid to do, that she had no real intention of complying with our demands.

As we sat down, the President asked what we thought should be done. "Shall I break off diplomatic relations with Germany?" He immediately followed this question with a somewhat startling statement. He would say frankly that, if he felt that, in order to keep the white race or part of it strong to meet the yellow race—Japan, for instance, in alliance with Russia, dominating China— it was wise to do nothing, he would do nothing, and would submit to anything and any imputation of weakness or cowardice. This was a novel and unexpected angle.

Several of us immediately began to speak. McAdoo did much talking. He was for prompt action. We must act or swallow our brave words. Baker was much impressed with the President's long look ahead, as was Daniels. Redfield favoured action. Burleson, while reminding us that the Allies were violating international law, thought we should make good our warning to Germany and our implied pledge to our people. The President observed that all these expressions were the result of a natural impulse, but that they did not aid him greatly.

When it came to my turn to speak, I began by saying that I was not apprehensive in the least about Japan, or about Japan, Russia, and China combined; that they were relatively weak intellectually, industrially, and morally;

[229]

and that at best, the danger from them was remote. I continued:

"We are now confronting a grave pressing menace. Civilization is at stake. Justice and fundamental national rights are involved. We must start from where we are and take the next right step. Nothing worse can ever befall us than what Germany proposes, and no greater insult can be offered to any people. If we acquiesce, we ought not to pose as a nation or as a free people. We ought to invite the Kaiser to set up as our permanent dictator. I have heard of nothing which Japan stands for which I would not prefer. If we are capable of submitting, Japan or anybody else who would take us ought to have us. We would not be worth saving. Granting that the Allies have violated law and are not free from selfishness, normally, essentially they stand for law and order. I am for asserting our rights, for standing with the Allies, for doing our part for our sake and for humanity."

The President said: "Very well. That does not reach far enough. What is the proposal? What is the concrete suggestion? What shall I propose? I must go to Congress. What shall I say?"

I replied: "Do not wait to set out a full programme. Immediately sever diplomatic relations and let come what will. Tell Congress what you have done. Say that you propose to protect American lives and rights. If necessary, ask for additional authority. Let our merchant vessels arm. Let Allied vessels come freely into our harbours. Aid the Allies with money, and, if necessary, with the army and navy. These things would, of course, involve action by Congress, including a declaration that a state of war exists, but such action is not necessary for a

[230]

severance of diplomatic relations and the arming of our merchantment for defence." After a little more discussion, we adjourned.

Saturday morning, I received a telephone message from the White House that the President would address Congress. I hurried up to the Capitol and listened with interest to his address announcing the severance of diplomatic relations.

And thus Bernstorff and his objectionable and perniciously active aids were set upon their way; and I thought that the former went with no misgiving as to what his walking papers meant. I believe he had warned his government against dragging us into the struggle. He knew the power of this country and I think he realized that what the submarine might do to England would be negligible compared to what we would do to Germany. He apparently was confident that Germany would win if this country was not drawn in.

In fact, Bernstorff tried to convince himself and others that Germany had already won. About two weeks before he was sent home, I went to a luncheon given by a friend of mine at his home and, much to my surprise, I found Bernstorff among the guests. After we went into the smoking room, I was sitting a few feet from Bernstorff and overheard him say to his companion, who seemed to be quite sympathetic: "Of course, you know that Germany has won the war." This was a trifle too much for me, and so I quickly interposed and said: "That is very interesting. How do you figure it out?" "Why, can't you see," he replied, "that Germany's armies are on foreign soil everywhere and cannot be driven back? If they move, it will be forward. At worst, it can only be a stale-

[231]

mate." "No," I said, "I cannot see it. Military history has been my hobby for thirty years. I seem to recall that more than one army has surrendered on foreign soil. Two British armies surrendered in this country. I remember, too, that Robert E. Lee, for four years, almost, marched back and forth from the Rappahannock to the Potomac and beyond, and then suddenly surrendered. There are strange parallels in history. And then you must not forget what Napoleon said about the English." "What did he say?" he asked, with much show of interest. "He said," I told him, "that the English never had sense enough to know when they were beaten." Bernstorff showed no resentment over what I said. He made no reply. We separated and I left the party.

CHAPTER XV

THE CABINET'S VIEWS ON THE WAR

McAdoo Strong for Action—Burleson: "We Are at War"—Baker for Universal Service—Letter of President Alderman of the University of Virginia

ON TUESDAY, February 6th, at Cabinet meeting, the situation of our American merchantmen occupied attention. Of course, they had a right to go to sea, but would they exercise it, or would they tie up in our ports? Would it be right to allow them to take risks if they wished to do so? Should we require ships to observe their mail contracts? It was suggested that the Postmaster General tell such ships to use their discretion. I said that, if this was done, they should be told that they might arm for defence and that the government should advise them of their rights—that it was necessary that they be told the policy of the government. Some said that the government ought not to give any advice. Others insisted that the situation was highly abnormal and that to the shipowners should not be left the responsibility of deciding the course of action. It was decided that they be told that their rights were just the same as if Germany had said nothing, and that they could arm for defence.

At the meeting on Friday, the 9th, it was clear that the shipping situation had not been cleared up. The ships were not sailing. They were showing every sign of in-

[233]

terning. They wanted further assurances and protection. They wanted the United States to furnish arms and gun crews. They could not otherwise get satisfactory guns or efficient marksmen. It was suggested that we had power to sell, lend, or give guns to them and to furnish crews. The question of convoy was raised. Baker said that inoffensive merchantmen should not be exposed to danger. It would be better to send naval vessels along and have a clear test. It was customary to convoy and to guarantee the safety of goods. We had to adjourn without arriving at a final decision.

On Tuesday, the 13th, the shipping matter was again immediately taken up. McAdoo was strong for action. It would be folly to play into Germany's hands by permitting our ships to tie up in ports. It was urgent that they sail, and therefore that they be armed and provided with trained gun crews without delay, and, if wise, be convoyed. The question was raised as to the adequacy of arming or convoying or both. It was asserted that speed and manœuvring would be the best protection, but it was recognized that guns and crews were also desirable. The President said that Governor McCall of Massachusetts had called and had advised that the government go slow. The people would approve delay for careful consideration. They did not wish precipitate action.

McAdoo was insistent. The President said that he could not act as suggested, using a government instrumentality, without going to Congress. Action might precipitate war, and he did not wish to force the hand of Congress. It was its province to determine the matter of peace and war. McAdoo contended that the President had power to take the course indicated, that delay would be dangerous, and that if trouble came from exercising our plain rights in the face of Germany's illegal and offensive dictation, the people would gladly face the consequences. I agreed that action was necessary, and that the first step was for the President to go to Congress and to go as soon as possible. Several supported this view, and the President assented.

On Friday, the 16th, the question was once more discussed. The situation was more embarrassing and critical but no determination was reached.

The following day, at the meeting of the Council of National Defence, I had a talk with Lane. We agreed that it was necessary that the President do something. I discussed the situation with Baker. I said that the time for action had come. We could no longer play into Germany's hands. "It is obvious that the freedom of our nation and of the world is at stake. We should side with the Allies promptly and wholly. They are not unselfish, but their brand of selfishness is much better than that of Germany. I would rather see this nation side with the Allies, go down to destruction with them if necessary, and disappear from the map as a nation, than to see it exist and prosper subject in the slightest degree to the dictation of an arrogant mediæval tyrant and his supporters." Baker assented.

On the 23d, we again brought up the matter of arming ships and the necessity of the President's going to Congress. McAdoo was emphatic in expressing his opinion that ships ought to be armed. The President ought to go ahead, Congress or no Congress. Action, prompt action, was demanded. It was no time for hesitation and slow courses. The President seemed to be somewhat nettled by Mc-

[235]

Adoo's insistence and emphatic manner and language. He said that things were being suggested which he had no right or power to do as a constitutional executive and some were apparently willing for him to assume the rôle of a dictator. He added that, no matter what happened, he would do nothing which savoured of dictatorship—that the government would continue to be one of law.

I supported the view that there should be no further delay, that the ships should be armed, and that the President should go immediately to Congress and ask its support.

The President inquired what I thought he should say to Congress and what form of support he should seek. I replied that he should lay the situation before that body, point out how, on account of the uncertainty and danger, our commerce was being destroyed, and say that since Germany had plainly warned us that she would sink our ships if they went about their business in lawful manner, it was not right that we should ask them to sail unprotected, and that Congress should authorize him to furnish them with guns and crews and any other necessary safeguards.

There was much discussion. I insisted that it was time to act. We had to face facts. We could not afford to let Germany dominate us or cut England off and then crush France. We would be next on her list. If she starved England, we alone would stand for law and order in the world. Germany would demand an abject surrender from England. She would demand her fleet and would take her colonies and a huge indemnity. She would be the mistress of the world, and her arrogance and ruthlessness would know no bounds.

[236]

The President, I felt, agreed with everything we said, but appeared to take an attitude of resistance to make us prove the case; and it was natural and wise that he should do so, seeing that the final responsibility was his and that it was a terrible thing to lead a great nation into such a war. I felt confident that he held the same views that we did.

Monday morning, the 26th, word was sent to me at my office that the President would address Congress and that it would be best to say little about it. After reviewing the situation, the President remarked that the tying up of our ships was complete so far as we were concerned and was what the Germans desired, but that no overt act had occurred. It was clear, however, that if our ships were spared it would be because of restraint unexpectedly exercised by German commanders and not because of their instructions. The situation was fraught with the gravest dangers. Necessity for action might come at any moment, if we were to defend our elementary rights. "It would be most imprudent to be unprepared."

The session and term of Congress were about to expire. He desired its "full and immediate assurance of the authority" which he might need at any moment to exercise. "No doubt," he said, "I already possess that authority without special warrant of law, by the plain implication of my constitutional duties and powers; but I prefer, in the present circumstances, not to act upon general implication. I wish to feel that the authority and the power of Congress are behind me in whatever it may be necessary for me to do. We are jointly the servants of the people and must act together and in their spirit, so far as we can divine and interpret it.

[237]

"No one doubts what it is our duty to do. We must defend our commerce and the lives of our people in the midst of the present trying circumstances with discretion but with clear and steadfast purpose. Only the method and the extent remain to be chosen, upon the occasion, if occasion should indeed arise."

It was devoutly to be hoped that it would not be necessary to put armed forces into action anywhere. The American people did not desire it. They would understand the spirit in which he was now acting. He desired that the belligerents also should understand it. He was the friend of peace and meant to preserve it for America as long as he was able. He was not proposing war or steps leading to it. War could come only from the wilful acts and aggressions of others. He could not forecast the form or method of action. The people would trust him to act with restraint. He desired that Congress authorize him "to supply our merchant ships with defensive arms, should that become necessary, and with the means of using them, and to employ any other instrumentalities and methods that may be necessary and adequate to protect our ships and our people in their legitimate pursuits on the seas." He was not thinking merely of material interests. He was thinking also of rights of humanity without which there was no civilization. "I cannot imagine any man with American principles at his heart hesitating to defend these things."

And yet, when the bill embodying his views was presented, there was so much objection that its failure seemed likely. There were two factions in temporary or permanent opposition. The regular Republicans led by Lodge criticized the President on the one hand for pursuing a vacillating policy, and on the other for usurping power. The pacifists, headed by La Follette, were opposed to any resistance. Nothing could induce them to yield. I asked Captain Bill McDonald, the Texan Ranger, who happened to be in Washington at this time, what he thought ought to be done. He said: "I would give La Follette a swift, hard kick where it would do most good and take his tobacco away from him."

The opponents, led by La Follette, filibustered till the end of the session and defeated the measures; and during this time an amendment was proposed by Cooper, the ranking Republican member of the House Committee on Foreign Affairs, to prohibit the arming of munitions ships. It received 124 votes in its favour to 295 against it. This was not the unanimity which the President so much desired or the spirit which he had a right to expect from American citizens, particularly from those who held positions of power. The regular Republican leaders themselves had held a caucus on February 23d and had decided to filibuster to defeat necessary measures in order to force the President to call an extra session of Congress after the Inauguration, another disturbing and petty exhibition of partisan spirit in the face of a grave national crisis.

The action of the opposing forces ought to have been a sufficient answer to those who complained that the President was not moving fast enough; and his frequent appearance before Congress to take the members into his confidence should have been a complete refutation of the assertion that he had usurped or desired to usurp power and to make himself something of a dictator—a stupid partisan misrepresentation.

[239]

The President properly characterized the action of the filibuster group in the Senate. He stated that while 500 of the 531 members of the House were ready to act, the Senate could not act because a group of 11 Senators said it should not. "The Senate of the United States is the only legislative body in the world which cannot act when the majority is ready for action. A little group of wilful men, representing no opinion but their own, have rendered the great government of the United States helpless and contemptible. The only remedy is that the rules of the Senate shall be so altered that it can act."

On Inauguration Day, March 5th, I saw the President in his room in the Capitol and talked with him about the Senatorial filibuster. I asked him whether he was about to be inaugurated President of the United States or Poland. He knew what I meant and instantly answered: "Poland." He commented on the vanity of La Follette and the slipperiness of Stone.

In his Inaugural Address, the President devoted his attention almost exclusively to the foreign problems. The chief thoughts in his mind were the part that this nation should be ready to play when the war ended, the possibility of our being drawn into the struggle, and the high need of unity and genuine patriotic spirit.

"We are making our spirits ready for those things," he declared. "They will follow in the immediate wake of the war itself and will set civilization up again. We are provincials no longer. The tragical events of the thirty months of vital turmoil through which we have just passed have made us citizens of the world. There can be no turning back. Our own fortunes as a nation are involved, whether we would have it so or not." He pointed out

[240]

again the things we would stand for in peace or in war. Upon such a platform we could stand together.

"And it is imperative that we should stand together. We are being forged into a new unity amidst the fires that now blaze throughout the world. In their ardent heat we shall, in God's providence, let us hope, be purged of faction and division, purified of the errant humours of party and of private interest, and shall stand forth in the days to come with a new dignity of national pride and spirit. Let each man see to it that the dedication is in his own heart, the high purpose of the nation is in his own mind, ruler of his own will and desire. . . . The thing I shall count upon, the thing without which neither counsel nor action will avail, is the unity of America, an America united in feeling, in purpose, and in its vision of duty, of opportunity, and of service. . . . For myself, I beg your tolerance, your countenance, and your united aid. The shadows that now lie dark upon our path will soon be dispelled, and we shall walk with the light all about us if we be but true to ourselves—to ourselves as we have wished to be known in the counsels of the world and in the thought of all those who love liberty and justice and the right exalted."

The Congress having failed to take action on the request of the President that it lend its support directly to the arming of our ships, the President, after asking for an opinion from the Attorney General as to his powers in the matter and receiving one to the effect that he had the power to act, directed that guns and gunners be placed on merchant ships, and an announcement was made on March 9th that this would be done.

At Cabinet meeting, Tuesday, March 20th, the President said that he had two matters or questions on which he wanted our advice. Should he call Congress in extra session before April 16th, the date set? What should he say to it? He reviewed the situation and remarked that it might look as if he were calling the body together to tell it what he had done. Doubtless, he had power to do more. Unquestionably, Germany had committed a number of overt acts. He had directed that the ships be armed. He could spend and was spending $115,000,000. The War and Navy departments are very active. What is the next step? He paused. No one else seemed inclined to say anything, so I began:

"To answer both questions, it is necessary to decide whether we wish to do more than has been done and what it should be. I think we should do much more. Germany is now making war on us. She has been making war on us for some time, sinking our ships, even our empty ships homeward bound, and killing our citizens. We see what she is trying to do against us in Mexico. We ought to recognize that a state of war exists. What can we do? We can get a big army and navy started. We can further prepare financially. We are organizing industrially. First of all, find out from the Allies just what aid we can most quickly and effectively give. The quickest way to hit Germany is to help the Allies. The thinking of many of our people is crude. They are discussing only a large army, and that as if it were part of a permanent policy. That is one thing—a long way off. We shall need a large army quickly, but in the meantime, we must give other help. Get supplies to the Allies. Help with our navy. Hurry up with submarines and submarine destroyers. Build ships, multitudes of ships for freight, very fast ships, not necessarily big ones. Extend liberal credits to the Allies. Send to France regulars who can be spared from training our new army. Send them 'to return the visit of Rochambeau.'" I said that I was quoting the French Ambassador with whom I had dined Sunday. He had said to me: "I do not know whether you will enter the war or not, but if you do, we shall not expect you—and I am sure that I am speaking the sentiments of my government—to send any men to France except a detachment, for sentimental reasons, to return the visit of Rochambeau. We shall want you to aid us mainly on the sea and with credits and supplies."

Baker said he thought that immediate steps should be taken, or that the country would demand that immediate steps be taken, to raise a great army and that universal training be inaugurated. I added that I was in favour of both, but that in the meantime other things could be done. I suggested that Congressional sanction would be required for the things I thought should be done. It should first of all recognize that a state of war existed. Even if that step was not to be taken, it was desirable to have the Legislative branch in thorough understanding and accord with the Executive. We were drifting. Why delay two weeks? Call Congress and ask it to declare that a state of war existed, to pass the necessary legislation, and to vote the needed appropriations or authorizations. There could be no halfway measures. War could not be waged mildly.

McAdoo spoke to the same effect, indicating many domestic matters which would need immediate attention. Lansing said little or nothing, as usual. Wilson, Secretary of Labour, said that he had reluctantly made up his mind

[243]

that action had to be taken. We were at war. Congress should be called to declare that it existed. Gregory and Baker and Redfield expressed the same opinion. Lane said nothing. Burleson and Daniels had not spoken.

The President said: "Burleson, you and Daniels have said nothing."

Burleson replied quietly: "We are at war. I am in favour of calling Congress at the earliest moment."

Daniels gave us the views of the naval experts.

The President said that the principal things which had occurred since he had last addressed Congress which differed, except in degree, from what had been discussed, were the Russian Revolution, the talk of more liberal institutions in Germany, and the continued reluctance of our ships to sail. If our entering the war would hasten and fix the movements in Russia and Germany, it would be a marked gain to the world and would tend to give additional justification for the whole struggle, but he could not assign these things as reasons for calling Congress at an earlier date. The justification would have to rest on the conduct of Germany, the clear need of protecting our rights, of getting ready, and of safeguarding civilization against the domination of Prussian militarism.

I remarked that he would not have to determine the details of his address or his exact recommendations till a few days later, but that what he had said was sufficient. The entire Cabinet was definitely in favour of going to the mat with Germany and of going immediately and with all the nation's power.

Events moved very rapidly. In a few days, the Russian Revolution was under way; the British were advancing up the Tigris; and the railroad strike was called for Saturday but was postponed for forty-eight hours, when concessions were made.

Of these things, the Russian Revolution was the most important, dramatic, and far reaching. The question is whether it will stick and whether the new government can and will wage war effectively against the Germans. Another question is whether or not the revolutionary spirit may not extend to Austria and Germany and assist in undermining the morale of the people in those countries. Certainly, it will abate their fear of the Russians. The Russians ought to be able to carry on. The Church is with the Revolution. Russia got rid of serfdom peaceably. Her people have experience, especially in local coöperation. She ought to be able to push the war. France waged war successfully, after her revolution, against a large part of Europe. But France had to fight for her freedom. The Russians may say that they have won their freedom and that there is nothing to be gained by fighting longer.

On Wednesday, the 21st, the President called Congress to meet on April 2d. At the Cabinet meeting, Friday, March the 23d, the time was consumed in discussing routine matters of preparation, particularly with legislation which it would be necessary for Congress to pass.

Next day, March 24th, there was an important meeting of the Council of National Defence. Much excellent work had been done by the various agencies of this body, and reports of progress were received and considered. The Advisory Committee said that it desired to go on record in favour of getting ready an army of 1,000,000 men and of universal military training. It was stated that the President's thought seemed to be that the regular army should be raised immediately to its full quota, that the militia should be thoroughly prepared, and that we should have 500,000 volunteers. If volunteering failed, we should resort to conscription. We were not in position to waste time debating a permanent policy. It might be a waste not only of time now, but of time after the war closed, because the nations might be induced to disarm in large measure.

The majority of the members of the Council strongly objected to the volunteer idea and advocated the draft. One member questioned the wisdom of resorting to the draft and another emphatically opposed it.

I advocated compulsory training. I strongly objected to volunteering on the ground that it was undemocratic and wasteful. It is unjust to allow those to fight our battles who have the vision to see and appreciate the issues, and the character and patriotism to offer their lives; and to permit those who are slow to remain in security. We cannot afford to have our most eager men swept away as England did. Volunteering is unjust. It is also inadequate and unsafe in modern war, especially where great numbers have to be raised and trained quickly. It has been ruinous in every other war in which we have engaged. It is likewise much more costly in dollars and cents. Compulsion alone permits the requisite selection of men and their designation for tasks which are essential and for which they are best fitted.

The Chairman, Secretary Baker, said that he would present our views strongly to the President.

At Cabinet meeting, Friday, March 30th, we had a long discussion of the handling of the interned German ships. The opinion was unanimous that their crews ought to be taken off and that the vessels should be requisitioned. The discussion turned on the method of taking the crews off quietly and suddenly. Any other nation but this and England would have taken them off directly by the use of soldiers or marines. But we had to do the thing legally or under the guise of legality. It was suggested that the Department of Labour could act under the Immigration Laws on the assumption that the aliens were in our ports, that they could be admitted to the United States, and could then be interned!! This seemed to be a feasible course, and it was agreed that the army and navy might coöperate with the immigration authorities in the task.

The President raised the question of the sentiment of the country. It was our view that the country would be back of the government in a declaration that a state of war existed. I made a report as to the state of mind in the Middle West. On Tuesday, I had read to the Cabinet this letter from President Alderman of the University of Virginia:

> University of Virginia, Charlottesville,
> Office of the President,
> March 22, 1917.

Hon. D. F. Houston,
   Department of Agriculture,
   Washington, D. C.
MY DEAR HOUSTON:

I quite appreciate your position, and we will simply hope that you can come. With all your burdens, no one should expect much from you.

I do wish I could talk with you about the world situation. I think about it all the time. I believe it to be our duty, as a nation now, as a matter of self-interest, as a matter of national honour, as a matter of future world influence, and as a matter of keeping quick and vital the national spirit and the national conscience, to go to war with Germany, unless the present control of the German Government sees fit to cease its methods of crime and aggression.

Of course, we are at war with Germany, or rather, they are at war with us. You know my admiration and confidence and affection for the President. In the first place, his knowledge of the real facts goes far beyond anything we outsiders can appreciate; and, in the second place, he has great power of analysis, calmness of judgment, coolness of mind, and a great background of knowledge and understanding. I never permit myself to criticize him, even as a friend, because I have a feeling that in the end it will be shown that he is right. I can understand his aversion to carrying a nation into war that does not want to be carried into war. But he never said a truer thing than when he said that no great war could hereafter occur without our participation. In my judgment that applies to 1917 as well as to some future date.

The President has been patient; he has been reasonable; he has preserved our dignity and honour; but I do not think it can be done longer without a frank resort to force. Personally, of course, I have never drawn a neutral breath since August 1, 1914. I believe that the victory of the present German system would mean the deadliest blow that democracy has ever received in its splendid progress in human society. I believe our destiny is not to serve the world at this juncture by a soft mediation, but by the use of righteous force at the decisive moment to help turn the tide as between the ideals of democratic society and the ideals of autocratic society; and if we do go to war, I pray we shall go at it like practical people, seeing war as war, and using every weapon and forming every alliance, temporary though they may be, and taking every step that can in honour be taken to achieve a victory for democracy and end the present mad condition of affairs in the world. If it means expeditionary force, large numbers of destroyers, participation in the active fighting in the war zone, we should go to it under the best advice our experts can give. If it means credit and food and all sorts of economic aid, then that is the direction to take. Delicacy and dallying do not go down with the Prussian. Force and fear are his controlling motives, and he understands no psychology that is not tied up with these impulses. I confess it is the situation after the war, no matter which way the tide turns, that makes me feel that we should go in for thoroughgoing reorganization of our life on a basis of defensive preparation. This, of course, is against all of my predilections and traditions, but I have been driven to it by the unfolding of events.

I thought these people might be bluffing, as they are great bluffers, until the sinking of the last three ships. I am in favour of universal service, and I believe the country wants action now. The country trusts the President. They know that he is a patriot with a vision and with a heart, but if he should now act simply, directly, forcefully, the heart and pride and spirit of this whole nation will rise to his leadership and to his call in a way that might astound him in its devotion and purpose.

It is time now, I believe, to sound the tocsin, and no man can sound it, if he so wills, so effectively as the President.

[249]

I wish I could talk with you about this matter. One cannot dictate without consciousness that he is speaking ineffectually about such a great matter.

Give my love to Mrs. Houston and to Charlie Crane, if he is in reach.

Faithfully yours,
(*Signed*) E. A. Alderman.
President.

I added that it was unnecessary for me to say again that I thought the time for debate had passed and the time for strong, vigorous action had come—that I fully agreed with Alderman.

It was recognized that there would be a great many disaffected individuals, and that precautions which had already been discussed and taken, such as the guarding of railways, tunnels, ports, and important buildings, should be followed up and strengthened. It was also, however, confidently believed that no situation would develop which could not be readily handled.

We adjourned, feeling confident that the President would recommend the declaration of the existence of a state of war, and that the nation would pledge all its resources to the prosecution of the struggle to a speedy end. As we were leaving the Cabinet meeting, someone asked me what I would do if the President should decide not to take up Germany's challenge or to go before Congress. I replied that I was not in the least apprehensive about the course he would take, and that there was no use in wasting time speculating about the matter. I added that, if by any chance he should not act, there would be such a fundamental difference of attitude on a vital issue that the only decent course open to me would be to resign and let the President put somebody in my place whose views accorded with his. I suggested that it would be very unfortunate even to raise such a question or to refer to it on the outside, as rumours would quickly spread that there had been or was any doubt whatever.

In the afternoon, when I got back to my office, feeling that the President in the hour of his great trial and responsibility would not object to a word of sympathy and support, and to comply with my promise to send him a copy of Alderman's letter, I wrote the following note, enclosing the letter:

March 30, 1917.

DEAR MR. PRESIDENT:

I am sending you Alderman's letter. I promised to leave it with you but neglected to do so.

Alderman, as usual, expresses himself very admirably. He says many things that we here think and feel. I think it is strikingly true that the great mass of the American people trust you. They trust you so completely that they have not thought it necessary to advise you. They have assumed that you know the situation and the facts better than they do. I think that the overwhelming sentiment is in favour of going forward and of taking a strong course. The only alternative to a strong forward course is to recede from our former position, to shut ourselves off from international affairs, and to confine ourselves within our own borders. This is impossible. One result would be to run the risk of leaving democracy to the tender mercies of the Central autocracies. I do not believe that we can morally longer throw the responsibility for safeguarding

[251]

civilization on England and France. The time for debate, as it seems to me, has passed. I believe that the course of action you wish the country to follow should be outlined not in passionate, but yet in very strong and forceful terms. "It is time now, I believe, to sound the tocsin." I know the case is difficult to state, and yet I believe it is a very strong one.

Faithfully yours,
D. F. HOUSTON.

The President,
    The White House.

CHAPTER XVI

THE WAR MESSAGE

Its Dramatic Setting—Chief Justice White's Approval—Methods of Meeting Crisis—Organization of the Food Supplies of the Country

MONDAY evening, April 2d, will stand out in my mind as the date of the most dramatic scene I ever witnessed and of the most historic episode in which I ever had any part. That evening, the President, at half-past eight o'clock, appeared before the Joint Session of Congress to advise that body to declare that the recent course of Germany was nothing less than war against the government and the people of the United States.

The Hall of the House of Representatives was crowded. The floor was occupied by the members of the House and the Senate, the Diplomatic Corps, the Supreme Court, and the Cabinet. The Cabinet was seated as usual in the front seats at the left side of the Speaker's desk and the diplomats were placed immediately back of the Cabinet. Seats for the Supreme Court had been placed in the pit in a half circle just in front of the Speaker; and the members of that body were in their places on either side of the Chief Justice. The galleries were packed. There was an air of tenseness and expectancy. The President had been escorted to the Capitol by a body of cavalry to protect him from possible annoyance by pacifists who had tried to bank themselves around the approaches to the Capitol. This was a very unusual incident and added to the tenseness of the occasion.

As the President entered, he was given an ovation. As I was standing with the others while the demonstration lasted, I glanced around and bowed to Spring-Rice and Jusserand, who were expectant and happy.

The President began reading as soon as quiet prevailed; and, as he proceeded, I found myself watching Chief Justice White, who sat a very short distance in front and to the left of me. I knew what his reaction would be, but I did not anticipate that he would show his emotions so strikingly. Several times I had talked to him about the war. Shortly after England entered the war, he came up to me one evening at a social gathering, put his hand on my shoulder, and said in a low voice: "I wish I were thirty years younger. I would go to Canada and volunteer." He listened with interest to the President's review of the submarine controversy. When the President said: "The present German submarine warfare against commerce is a warfare against mankind," he gave a vigorous nod. He repeated it when the President added: "It is a war against all nations. . . . The challenge is to all mankind." He listened with evident satisfaction to the statement characterizing armed neutrality as ineffectual, as "likely only to produce what it was meant to prevent," and as practically certain to draw us into the war without either the rights or the effectiveness of belligerents. But when the President said: "There is one choice we cannot make, we are incapable of making: We will not choose the path of submission," he did not wait to hear the rest of the sentence. He was on his feet instantly leading the Supreme

Court and the entire assembly. His face was a study. It worked almost convulsively and great tears began to roll down his cheeks. From that moment to the end he was vigorously applauding everything. He had a profound realization of the issues at stake and particularly of the part England had played in the world, of the meaning of her institutions, and of the menace to the world of her overthrow by Germany. He knew what war meant, having been a soldier in the Civil War, and he was willing and anxious to stand the horrors of war again for vital principles.

From time to time, also, I looked at the next most interesting figure in the audience, John Sharp Williams. He, too, was a study. He sat, huddled up, listening attentively and approvingly, with one hand to his ear, removing it frequently for an instant, just long enough to give a single clap, for fear of missing something. And he was well advised, for no other address to a legislative body was ever better worth listening to. Its words rang then and they will continue ringing for many years to come.

The President did not omit to indicate methods and measures. In particular he approved the "principle of universal liability to service" and the meeting of the expenses so far as was equitable "by the present generation, by well-conceived taxation. . . . It is our duty, I most respectfully urge, to protect our people so far as we may against the very serious hardships and evils which would be likely to arise out of inflation which would be produced by vast loans." He drew a distinction between the German people and their government just as he had between the Mexicans and theirs; and he found added hope

[255]

for future peace in the heartening things that had happened in Russia in the few preceding weeks.

It was particularly interesting to me to hear him say that his own thought had not "been driven from its habitual and normal course by the unhappy events of the last two months" and that he "had exactly the same things in mind" that he had when he addressed the Senate in January. He had been preparing to meet the change in circumstances and had systematically indulged in a campaign of education of this nation and of the world.

This message was striking in its boldness and completeness. It was obvious that it would greatly impress and stimulate our people and hearten the Allies. It was worth many battalions.

As I passed the President, after the session had adjourned, I congratulated and thanked him and remarked that if it was any comfort to him I could tell him that I had been watching the Supreme Court, that it had on the spot unanimously given him a favourable verdict as to the constitutionality of his proposal and as to the righteousness of his cause, and that it would give a favourable verdict on any proposal necessary and designed to beat the Germans. He smiled, thanked me, and passed on.

When, on April 6, 1917, the existence of a state of war with Germany was declared by Congress, this country was facing an unsatisfactory situation in respect to its supply of foods and feedstuffs. The production in 1916 of the leading cereals, corn, wheat, oats, barley, rye, buckwheat, rice, and kafir was comparatively low, aggregating 4,806,000,000 bushels, as against 6,010,000,000 for 1915, 4,983,000,000 for 1914, and 4,884,000,000, the annual average for 1910–1914. The wheat crop of 1916 especially was strikingly small. It was only 639,886,000 bushels as compared with the record production for 1915 of 1,026,000,000, with 891,000,000 for 1914, and with the average for the five years 1910–1914 of 728,000,000. It was certain, too, that on account of adverse weather conditions, the output of winter wheat for 1917 would be greatly curtailed. The world production of wheat for 1916 also was unsatisfactory, and the prospects for the ensuing year were not good. The situation was no better in respect to another conspicuously important food product, the Irish potato. The yield of this crop for 1916 in the United States was only 285,437,000 bushels, while for 1915 and 1914, respectively, it was 359,721,000 and 409,921,000. For the period 1910–1914 it averaged 360,772,000.

Even in normal times public attention fixes itself particularly on the supply of wheat. In time of war it does so much more intensely. Wheat is peculiarly important from a military point of view. Because of the wheat shortage here and elsewhere and of the large foreign demand, apprehension and, in some quarters, hysteria developed. The supply of meats and of poultry and dairy products was somewhat larger than in the years immediately preceding, but the foreign demand was great and increasing, and exports were steadily rising. It was obvious that the supply of feedstuffs would not be normally abundant, and that it would be difficult to maintain the usual number of live stock and practically impossible within a reasonable time to increase it. Then, too, competitive purchasing by foreign agencies on a large scale of all food products was prevalent, and speculation was rife. Prices were mounting rapidly and conditions of living were becoming more difficult.

It was recognized, even before we entered the war, that the food problem was serious and that constructive action was necessary. The Department of Agriculture accordingly had taken steps to allay unnecessary apprehension, to promote economy and thrift, to secure fuller conservation of farm products and of foods, and to insure increased production of all essential agricultural commodities. The many agricultural agencies of the nation began to direct attention to these problems and to coöperate effectively with the Department. The increased need of this nation and of the world for food from our farms and the importance of greatly increasing production were emphasized. In the South, in particular, where effective work had been done for years to secure a diversified agriculture and greatly to increase yields of staple commodities, and where unusual opportunities to increase food products were presented, a special campaign was conducted by the Department in coöperation with agricultural colleges and other agencies, with the effective aid of the daily press, agricultural journals, farmers' associations, bankers, and other business men. Many pertinent bulletins and circulars were distributed. The farm-demonstration machinery was fully utilized. More energetic action everywhere was taken to combat plant and animal diseases.

In January, 1917, appeals were sent to the South to help feed the nation, to supply its own necessities so far as possible, and to produce a surplus of foodstuffs. It was urged especially that each farm family make a home garden, plant enough corn to last the family and the live stock for a year, raise sufficient oats and other small grain

[258]

to supplement the corn, as well as the necessary hay and forage crops for the live stock, produce the meat, poultry, and dairy products required by the family, and at the same time devote adequate attention to cotton as the main money crop.

In February, special emphasis was laid on the necessity of raising beet seed on a large scale to make certain a larger supply of sugar beets. It was pointed out that, before the war, the beet-sugar industry had been almost wholly dependent on Europe for its seed supply, and that superior seed could be produced in this country, which could be further improved by selection and breeding. About the same time, a warning was issued to cattle owners to make arrangements for the proper feeding of their cattle until spring, in order to prevent heavy losses in breeding animals. In each instance suggestions as to the methods to be followed were offered.

In March, it became certain that a large percentage of wheat in the West and Pacific Northwest had been winter killed. Information as to the course to be pursued was issued to the farmers of the winter-wheat section. It was suggested that, where the crop had been not more than half killed, it might be advisable to let the remainder grow, but that some other food crop should be started without delay.

In the meantime, I had appointed a committee of specialists of the Department to study the whole agricultural situation and to make recommendations. On March 27th, an appeal was made to farmers to adopt measures to secure maximum returns from the farms. Special attention was directed to the necessity of careful seed selection, of controlling plant and animal diseases,

[259]

and of conserving farm products through proper storage, canning, drying, and preserving. On April 5th a special plea was made for an increased production of corn and hogs, and on April 7th the farmers were urged to increase the output of staple commodities as well as of perishables.

On April 4th, two days before a state of war with Germany was declared, I telegraphed to the state commissioners of agriculture and presidents of the Land Grant colleges—the official agricultural representatives of the several states—inviting them to a conference in St. Louis on April 9 and 10, 1917. Editors of farm journals were asked to meet at the same place on April 11th. It was thought to be highly desirable to secure the views of the official agricultural representatives of the states and of other leaders of agricultural opinion. There was a generous response to the invitation. Very many of the state commissioners of agriculture and representatives of nearly all the agricultural colleges east of the Rocky Mountains were present at the two-days' meeting. Sixty-five officials represented thirty-two states. On the third day, about seventy-five representatives of the agricultural press were present. A similar conference for the states west of the Rocky Mountains was held at my request at Berkeley, California, on April 13th, under the leadership of President Benjamin Ide Wheeler of the University of California.

At the St. Louis conference, the entire agricultural situation presented by the emergency was thoroughly discussed. The major problems considered were the production of sufficient foods and feedstuffs, not only for this country, but also for the nations of Europe with which we were associated in the war, the conservation of farm products and of foods, the mobilization of farm labour, the regulation of storage and distributing agencies, and the further organization of all the nation's agricultural instrumentalities—national, state, and local. A comprehensive programme for execution under existing law and for additional legislation was unanimously adopted. This programme was communicated to the Berkeley conference, which concurred in it. It is noteworthy that, in two days, the agricultural leaders of the country drew up a programme the wisdom of the essential features of which has not been successfully questioned and the substantial part of which was embodied in two bills. The prompt and effective handling of the situation was made possible by reason of the fact that the American people, generations before, had wisely laid the foundations of many agricultural institutions and had increasingly liberally supported them. The nation was fortunate in having had in existence for many years, for the purpose of promoting scientific and practical agriculture, its Federal Department of Agriculture, and a department of agriculture and a Land-Grant college in each state, as well as great farmers' organizations. It is further interesting to note that two of these agencies, the Federal Department and the Land-Grant colleges, had their national official recognition and their real origin in another period of stress—in 1862—in two acts of Congress approved by Abraham Lincoln.

It was recognized as of special importance that the views and coöperation of the great farmers' organizations of the nation and of leading individual farmers be secured. Representative farmers were therefore invited to come to Washington on April 23d to give advice and to make rec-

[261]

ommendations. They included mainly officials of the National Grange, the Farmers' Educational and Coöperative Union, the Gleaners, and the Farmers' National Congress. The American Society of Equity was invited to send a representative. It was unable to do so, but proffered its coöperation.

In the meantime, pending action by Congress, the Federal Department of Agriculture, the state departments, the Land-Grant colleges, and other agencies actively devoted their attention to the immediate task in hand. Working in close coöperation with one another and with the farmers' organizations throughout the nation, they immediately took steps to execute that part of the plan which had reference to a more perfect organization and coördination of the nation's agricultural activities. The task was promptly undertaken of promoting in each state, in connection with the state council of safety, the organization of a small central division of food production and conservation composed of representatives of the State Board of Agriculture, of the Land-Grant College, of farmers' organizations, and of business agencies. It was suggested, also, that similar bodies should be created in each local subdivision, and all were requested to devote their energies to the problem of increasing the production and conservation of food supplies and of promoting more orderly and economical marketing. Copies of the recommendations of the St. Louis conference and of those made to the Senate on April 18th were sent to the Governor of each state. It was urged that attention be given immediately to the perfecting of agricultural organizations along the lines indicated.

As a further step in organization, the Council of National Defence on April 5th invited Mr. Herbert Hoover to return to this country to advise with the Council in reference to the domestic handling of food supplies and the most effective ways of assisting the European nations with which we are coöperating to satisfy their food necessities.

At the Cabinet meeting, Friday, April 13th, immediately after my return from St. Louis, I asked the President to make an appeal through the agricultural press to the farmers of the nation to increase their production and to practise conservation. He said that it was a good suggestion, but that perhaps it would be better to make a broad appeal to all classes, that he would draw up one, that if I would furnish him agricultural material, he would incorporate it, and that I might segregate the parts bearing on agriculture and send the matter to the farm papers. I decided to telegraph the entire appeal to such papers, and when an advance copy reached me before its appearance on April 16th, it was wired to all the leading agricultural journals. The paragraphs addressed to the farmers were as follows:

"These, then, are the things we must do, and do well, besides fighting—the things without which mere fighting would be fruitless.

"We must supply abundant food for ourselves and for our armies and our seamen not only, but also for a large part of the nations with whom we have now made common cause, in whose support and by whose sides we shall be fighting. . . .

"I take the liberty, therefore, of addressing this word to the farmers of the country and to all who work on the farms: The supreme need of our own nation and of the nations with which we are coöperating is due abundance of supplies, and especially of foodstuffs. The importance of an adequate food supply, especially for the present year, is superlative. Without abundant food, alike for the armies and the peoples now at war, the whole great enterprise upon which we have embarked will break down and fail. The world's food reserves are low. Not only during the present emergency, but for some time after peace shall have come, both our own people and a large proportion of the people of Europe must rely upon the harvests in America. Upon the farmers of this country, therefore, in large measure, rests the fate of the war and the fate of the nations. May the nation not count upon them to omit no step that will increase the production of their land or that will bring about the most effectual coöperation in the sale and distribution of their products? The time is short. It is of the most imperative importance that everything possible be done and done immediately to make sure of large harvests. I call upon young and old alike and upon the able-bodied boys of the land to accept and act upon this duty—to turn in hosts to the farms and make certain that no pains and no labour are lacking in this great matter.

"I particularly appeal to the farmers of the South to plant abundant foodstuffs as well as cotton. They can show their patriotism in no better or more convincing way than by resisting the great temptation of the present price of cotton and helping, helping upon a great scale, to feed the nation and the peoples everywhere who are fighting for their liberties and our own.

"The Government of the United States and the governments of the several states stand ready to coöperate.

They will do everything possible to assist farmers in securing an adequate supply of seed, an adequate force of labourers when they are most needed, at harvest time, and the means of expediting shipments of fertilizers and farm machinery, as well as of crops themselves when harvested. The course of trade shall be as unhampered as it is possible to make it, and there shall be no unwarranted manipulation of the nation's food supply by those who handle it on its way to the consumer. This is our opportunity to demonstrate the efficiency of a great Democracy and we shall not fall short of it!

"This let me say to the middlemen of every sort, whether they are handling our foodstuffs, or our raw materials of manufacture, or the products of our mills and factories: The eyes of the country will be especially upon you. This is your opportunity for signal service, efficient and disinterested. The country expects you, as it expects all others, to forego unusual profits, to organize and expedite shipments of supplies of every kind, but especially of food, with an eye to the service you are rendering and in the spirit of those who enlist in the ranks, for their people, not for themselves. I shall confidently expect you to deserve and win the confidence of people of every sort and station. . . .

"Let me suggest, also, that everyone who creates or cultivates a garden helps, and helps greatly, to solve the problem of the feeding of the nations; and that every housewife who practises strict economy puts herself in the ranks of those who serve the nation. This is the time for America to correct her unpardonable fault of wastefulness and extravagance. Let every man and every woman assume the duty of careful, provident use and ex-

[265]

penditure as a public duty, as a dictate of patriotism which no one can now expect ever to be excused or forgiven for ignoring. . . .

"The supreme test of the nation has come. We must all speak, act, and serve together!"²

CHAPTER XVII

THE ALLIED WAR MISSION

Balfour's Tennis at Sixty-Nine—Joffre's Account of the Battle of the Marne—Balfour's Estimate of Washington—Secretary Baker's Task and Abilities

ON SUNDAY, the 22d of April, the English Mission, headed by the Right Honourable Arthur James Balfour, arrived in Washington. It had been expected as early as Tuesday, the 17th, but nothing was known about its movements by the public till the night of its safe arrival in an American port. The day was beautiful, fresh, clear, and sparkling. Crowds began early to line the streets along which the Mission was to pass from the station to the McVeagh house on Sixteenth Street. I was deeply moved as I thought of what was back of it and of its significance. I was particularly glad to have another opportunity to see Mr. Balfour, and to see him in this country.

Mrs. Houston and I decided to walk up Sixteenth Street with our two younger children, Helen and Lawrence, to see the procession and to witness from the sidewalk the reception of the Mission by the people. As we passed the French Embassy, however, Madame Jusserand, who was in the balcony of the Embassy, saw us and asked us to join her. We did so and viewed the procession from the balcony. We waved our handkerchiefs as Balfour passed, and Lansing, who was in the carriage with him, seeing us, called his attention to our little group, and both he and Balfour bowed.

I had my first meeting with the members of the Mission at the President's dinner to them at the White House. When I was introduced to Balfour, I told him that I had the advantage of him in at least one respect—that I had seen him a number of times and had heard him speak day after day in the House of Commons in the summer of 1909 during the Budget debate. He asked quickly: "What Budget debate?" I answered: "The debate on the Lloyd George Budget in 1909." At first he seemed to have difficulty in turning his thoughts to anything so far removed from the war, so far back in the ancient days before the war, but after a few seconds he said: "Oh, yes, I remember. How things have changed in a few years! That seemed like a very important measure then. We were much stirred over it. But England has passed far beyond it. England has proceeded very far on the way toward Socialism since 1914." I told him that I remembered very clearly one passage between him and Asquith on an interesting and difficult question. It was this: Balfour, who was sitting, or rather lounging, on the front opposition bench, slowly unfolded himself, stood up, and said in substance: It fills me with amazement that the Chancellor of the Exchequer should entertain the stupid notion that land is the sole source of the unearned increment. There are many sources of the unearned increment. There was, we may say, a struggling village and in it, on a corner where the principal streets crossed, a chemist's shop. There was also in the village a struggling country physician. The village has become a great manufacturing

[268]

city. The chemist's shop has become a great and prosperous establishment and the physician, through no particular effort of his own or increase of skill, has become a specialist with a greatly increased income. Would the Right Honourable Gentleman undertake to say that the increased profits of the proprietor of the establishment and the much larger income of the physician were earned? He then gave a number of other instances of a similar nature; and in all of them I thought he was apt and right. I was curious to hear what the government would say. Lloyd George was absent and Asquith replied. He said: "I desire to thank the Right Honourable Gentleman for calling the attention of the House to the wide applicability of a sound principle. It so happens that the government do not now need all the revenues which would accrue from attaching the tax to all the sources of the unearned increment, but I desire to assure the Right Honourable Gentleman that when the government need the revenue they will spread the tax." That was all. How different it would have been if the same question had been raised in our House of Representatives! Either the matter would not have been followed up or it would have given rise to long-winded speeches which would have greatly clouded the issue. Mr. Balfour had forgotten all about the matter. I told him that I was much impressed by the fact that, while I spent parts of nearly every day for more than two weeks in the House of Commons, I had not heard a speech—I had heard only brief talks by members, or conversations between members, who seemed to know what they were talking about and how to express their views in a few words. I told him that I knew that then the House was sitting in committee of the whole and that the same sort of interchange occurred in our small House committees but not in the whole House.

Another incident I mentioned as we continued to discuss the matter. I gave it as an illustration of the same thing. It was when a member got up and criticized the government for proposing to lay a tax on "ungotten" minerals. He argued that it would or might result in a dead loss to the owners or force the premature or undue exploitation of the nation's mineral resources. I thought he was right and wondered what the government would say. They said nothing then, but next day they came in with an amendment to levy a tax on royalties.

I told him that for several days I had had great difficulty in getting access to the House on account of the limited number of seats in the gallery but that, through a friend, I had met the Secretary of the Budget League, who was very civil to me and gave me a card of introduction to Lloyd George, who very kindly sent me two tickets of admission to the House, one of which I gave to Colonel House. These tickets admitted us to the floor immediately back of the members, separated from them only by a rod which runs across one end of the hall. I had an excellent opportunity to hear the debates. I could not take Mrs. Houston, as the suffragettes were then picketing the House and were indulging in rowdyism, and no ladies were allowed.

Mr. Balfour had forgotten all about such matters, including the suffragettes.

He asked me if I was impressed with any of the members. I replied that I had been particularly impressed by Lloyd George's agility, by Ure and Cecil, and by Asquith. I said that I had heard Austen Chamberlain several times, and that, while he seemed to know his subject, he had great difficulty in expressing himself, that he was not fluent. I told him this: "Mr. Asquith was speaking. Suddenly I turned to Colonel House, who was with me, and said: 'Shut your eyes a moment and listen!' He did so. I asked: 'What American is speaking?' He replied, after an instant's hesitation, 'President Eliot,' who was the one I had in mind. Their tone, accent, and phraseology were strikingly alike."

Before we separated I said: "You are an Englishman. I know you want to take exercise every day. I should like to organize a conspiracy to see that you have an opportunity to do so. It would give me pleasure to take you to Chevy Chase every afternoon for a round of golf." "Would you play tennis?" he asked with some eagerness. I replied that I was a trifle old for such sport, but that I would do my best to interest him. Mr. Balfour was then only sixty-nine years old, nearly twenty years older than I was. But he was youthful compared with the veteran who had caused me to take up tennis after I had stopped playing it for several years. In August, 1914, at Woods Hole, Massachusetts, I played a number of games of golf with Richard Olney, Cleveland's distinguished Secretary of State. He played a very good game and, notwithstanding the fact that I walked fast, he kept up with me and did not delay the game. Still, I was feeling some concern for him till, at the end of a round of eighteen holes, he turned to me and said: "This is all very well, but I much prefer tennis. Will you play tennis with me?" He was then only seventy-nine years old, and he played a very good game in doubles. Mr. Balfour, when I told him about Mr. Olney, seemed to be cheered up and remarked that when he got to be seventy-nine he would challenge Mr. Olney.

In passing, I may say that, at the time I was playing with Mr. Olney in 1914, I expressed my regret that he had not accepted President Wilson's tender of the Ambassadorship to the Court of St. James's in 1913. Mr. Olney replied that if he had known that the war would break out and that the job would be a man's job, he would have accepted, but that, at the time the tender was received, it looked as if the position would mean little except a round of social functions and the exchange of diplomatic platitudes and that he had no stomach for such things.

The French Mission, headed by Viviani, reached the United States Tuesday, April 24th, and proceeded to Washington. There was much excitement and enthusiasm in the city over its appearance, and an intense eagerness to see the Hero of the Marne, General Joffre. The streets were lined. I watched the procession from the sidewalk near the Cosmos Club.

The people gave Viviani a friendly greeting but its attention was centred on Joffre. They gave him an ovation. A mighty roar announced his approach. As he passed where I was standing, he was on his feet in the automobile with his hand at salute.

I met the party in the evening at the President's dinner. I had a very distinct thrill as I walked forward to shake hands with the man who had won the greatest battle of modern times. I realized that I was about to greet a man about whom historians would write for centuries as others had greeted Cæsar and Napoleon. He did not look like a conqueror or a military hero. He looked like an amiable, placid, stolid grandfather. His bulk and poise were the

[272]

outstanding things. I made up my mind to ask him about the Marne. There was one great military figure whom I would question about his achievement. I had often wanted to stand face to face with one. In the next world I hope to confront in similar fashion Alexander, Hannibal, Cæsar, Marlborough, Cromwell, Napoleon, Washington, and Lee and Grant.

I began by saying that military tactics and strategy had been my hobby for thirty years, and that I hoped he would forgive my presumption in asking him about his great victory. He replied that he would gladly answer any question I wished to ask him.

I said: "Where did you get Manoury's army?"

He replied: "I quickly assembled it by calling up widely dispersed units."

"How widely dispersed? From what parts of the line?"

"From below Nancy to Amiens," he replied.

"The reporters," I remarked, "said that his army went out from Paris in motors."

"That made a good headline," he answered. "Only about 5,000 men went out of Paris in motors, and it would have been much better if they had marched. The motors, many of them, broke down, and there was much confusion, and some of them got to the front too soon. It was not well."

I asked him to tell me if I had a correct notion about Foch's movements in the centre. He inquired what my conception of them was. I gave it as quickly as I could, and he told me that it was substantially accurate. I then said:

"What was the most critical point or position in your line?"

[273]

He answered: "Every position.   If any point had been broken, there might have been serious trouble.   If the Germans had gone through below Nancy there would have been trouble.   If Foch had not held, there would have been serious trouble.   Every point in a battle line is critical."

McAdoo, who was listening, said: "What is your feeling about the fighting which is now raging in the west?   Do you think Haig and Nivelle will make headway?   Are you optimistic?"

He replied simply: "I am not there," meaning that he would express no opinion about movements he was not in touch with.

At dinner at the French Embassy, I met the Mission again.   I talked at some length to Colonel Requin, who seemed to be an expert on strategy.   I asked him more particularly about Foch's tactics.   I told him I understood that his right had been pushed back, that his centre was giving ground or was threatened, and that then certain gaps in the Prussian line (due to the leaching of the line to the right to protect positions weakened by Von Kluck's turning movement) were reported, and that Foch had ordered the 42d and Moroccan divisions on his left to attack.

He replied: "That is correct.   I conveyed the order. I was on staff duty."   This was getting pretty close to headquarters.

Saturday afternoon, I had my first game of tennis with Mr. Balfour.   Malcolm, one of his aids, and Frank Polk completed the doubles.   We played five sets.   Mr. Balfour had a good stroke and a long reach and got very good results when he could reach the ball, but he had trouble when he had to run for it.   When he had to make anything of a run, he usually failed to make a return, and then invariably he exclaimed: "Too old—idiot. I am very angry. I must keep my temper." After the game, Mrs. Houston and Mrs. Hamlin joined us, and we had tea at the clubhouse. We gave Mr. Balfour a big comfortable chair. He was the picture of content and was very reluctant to drag himself away and return to town and the business of getting on with the war.

The following day, Sunday, April 29th, was a beautiful, crisp spring day. It had been set aside for a trip on the *Mayflower* to Mount Vernon, where both missions were to pay homage to Washington. Mount Vernon was exquisite. The trees and flowers were at their best. The dogwood trees were particularly beautiful and greatly impressed Mr. Balfour, who told me that he would plant some of them in England if he found that they would probably live there. Washington's Tomb was especially beautiful, covered with wistaria at its best, with the American, British, and French flags flying above it.

The scene and ceremonies at the Tomb were most impressive. Viviani delivered a brief but eloquent oration. Then Balfour read a brief statement which was to be left with the British wreath. When he finished, Joffre said that he saluted a great soldier. He and Viviani stepped inside the Tomb and he stood rigidly at salute while Viviani placed the artistic French wreath. Then followed Balfour and General Bridges and a similar affecting ceremony.

When this function was over, the whole party went up to the House and made a thorough inspection. As we returned, walking down the slope with Balfour, I said, pointing to the Tomb: "You cannot imagine what an

[275]

appeal it made to me—I have long studied English and American history and institutions—to see you, the last of the English conservatives, stand reverently before the tomb of Washington and to hear you pay a tribute to a successful rebel."

"Why," he quickly replied, "he did more for us than he did for you."

"Meaning——?" I said.

"Yes, meaning," he said, interrupting me, "that he taught us how to deal with colonies."

And I added: "The fruits are the loyalty and sacrifices to-day for the Empire of all the Colonies; and there could be no finer testimony to the essential justice and wisdom of Britain's rule." He assented to this and thanked me, and said that he hoped that our two great nations would always be friends and work together to promote the true and highest interest of humanity.

I had the good fortune to see much of Mr. Balfour during his stay in Washington. I saw him a number of times on business matters, particularly on matters pertaining to food supplies, but I came to know him better through our contacts on the tennis court, where I met him many afternoons with Malcolm, or Sir Eric Drummond, and Frank Polk. I had the pleasure also of meeting him a number of times at official or social functions, and he was always interesting and sometimes unexpected. At a dinner at Frank Polk's I was sitting on his right. As the dinner ended, he pushed back his chair, looked at me a moment, and said:

"Am I dreaming?"

I replied: "You have the reputation of being a dreamer at times. What is troubling you now?"

He answered: "Am I dreaming or is it true? They tell me that you have already passed a draft act. We have not after three years. Canada has not. They tell me that you have already registered nine millions of men, that you have organized a number of officers' training camps, and that Congress has authorized or is about to authorize an expenditure of $21,000,000,000. Is it true or am I dreaming?"

I replied: "Unless I am dreaming, it is true."

"I must, of course, accept what you say," he answered, "but I do not believe it."

It was not strange that he could not take it in. The draft was enough, and the figures for particular items of expenditures were startling: For ships, $1,900,000,000; for aviation, $640,000,000; for torpedo-boat destroyers, $350,000,000; for army subsistence and supplies, $860,000,000; for clothing, camp, and garrison equipment, $581,000,000; for transportation, $597,000,000; for medicine, $100,000,000; for mobile artillery, $158,000,000; for ordnance stores and supplies, $717,000,000; for heavy guns, $850,000,000; and for ammunition for the same, $1,807,000,000!! This was part of what the President meant by pledging our fortunes, and it was a source of comfort to Mr. Balfour and his associates; and they greatly needed comfort, for things were looking exceedingly black for the Allies at the time, in spite of our entry into the war. Mr. Balfour and his colleagues reflected in their appearance, manner, and conversation the gloom that hung over their country and the Allies: the submarines were playing havoc with shipping, and it did not seem impossible that Great Britain might be cut off—horrible thought; Russia was going to pieces; and things were going badly with

Nivelle and Haig. America must hurry and she was hurrying, so much so, in fact, that she was getting in her own way.

From the time of our entry into the war, every regular and every emergency agency in Washington was ceaselessly active in the task of organization and of preparation; and this task, which was incredibly difficult, was prosecuted with zeal and, on the whole, with intelligence. There was, of course, much annoying gossip and hurtful criticism in Washington, and particularly in the Senate. Some Senators, as usual, wished to get in the limelight and did no little harm by insisting upon senseless investigations. Efforts were made to get the President to create a non-partisan Cabinet. This failed, and then proposals were made to constitute a Congressional committee on the conduct of the war. There was nothing new in this. It was the same old story. It had been tried in the Civil War and had miserably failed. Congressional committees on the conduct of war have been and always would be nuisances, pure and simple. A change to a non-partisan regular Cabinet would have served no good purpose; and, as a matter of fact, the scheme which was developed was far better, namely, that of creating special services to deal more freely with emergency war activities, such as the War Industries Board, the Railroad Administration, the Shipping Board, the Food Administration, the War Trade Board, and the Fuel Administration. The heads of these agencies constituted a sort of second Cabinet, and the President wisely adopted the practice of meeting the regular Cabinet one day in the week instead of two, and of holding conferences with this emergency Cabinet at least one day in the week.

The heads of these emergency bodies were selected, like all other individuals who served the nation during the war, with reference solely to their fitness and without any thought of their political connections. Many, if not most of them, as it happened, and most of their assistants, as it chanced, were Republicans, such as Brookings, Willard, Rosenwald, Gifford, Hoover, Stettinius, and Schwab. And, for the first time in our history, the civil part of the government did not hamper or attempt to control military and naval operations. The chief military and naval officers, like Pershing and Sims, were selected on expert recommendation for their ability in their particular fields and were given a free hand so far as their particular tasks were concerned. In France, in military matters, Pershing was supreme. What he decreed and recommended was accepted, so far as circumstances permitted, and officers whom he desired were given him and none others. The civil government made it its duty to try to see that the army and navy got what they needed.

Of course, mistakes were made, many of them. It was singular that more were not made; but, as a high French officer, with characteristic wit, said to Mrs. Houston, when she remarked that we seemed to be making many mistakes, we did not invent any: the Allies had anticipated us.

One source of difficulty was the rapid shifting of events and conditions and the changing demands of the Allies. These changed week by week and almost day by day. At first, the Allies did not seem to expect us to send any considerable number of men to Europe. I have already referred to the statement of the French Ambassador to me made just before we entered the war, to the effect that

[279]

his government would not expect us, if we entered the struggle, to send men to France, except a detachment to return the visit of Rochambeau. I understand that Joffre, himself, when he came over, did not at first make any urgent request that a large number of men be sent across, and that it was not till after the breakdown of Russia became apparent and things were going less satisfactorily on the Western Front that he made an appeal for men, and then for only 500,000.

Later, the cry came for more men and still more men, and for ships and still more ships. And then demands would come for certain sorts of guns and supplies, and almost immediately an appeal that we do not bother about these and instead send something else. The Allies would supply big guns, or machine guns, or airplanes, or something else. Do not stop for these. Hurry up with something else—come on!

Many men—in fact, everybody in a responsible position—had difficult tasks, but next to the President, the man in Washington who seemed to me to have the most difficult one was Secretary Baker.

His is really an impossible task, but I believe that he is meeting it with rare courage and intelligence. I have had a good opportunity to see him in action. The Council of National Defence meets in his office three or four times a week for from one to three hours. Many problems are raised and discussed. No member of the Council shows more alertness, or better judgment, or more courage than he does. And then, his military advisers as well as his civil aids are constantly coming in—the military through one door, the civil through another—that is the game—with matters for him to decide; and I am impressed with the quickness and soundness of his decisions. If Baker were six feet high and weighed 200 pounds, he would now be regarded as a great Secretary of War. Whether he can get away with it with his short, slender, boyish stature, I do not know. He will in time. Incidentally, the last thing he thinks about is himself.

In June, 1917, thinking that there was need of a more concrete statement of what the German menace meant to us and to the world, that those who were attempting to enlighten the public were as a rule ignorant of what was behind the German mind and were indulging too much in platitudes, I prepared and published two statements summarizing the history of the submarine controversy and explaining the Prussian autocracy and its mediæval foundations and political philosophy. They were used by the Committee on Public Information and are given in Appendix II as part of the story of the period.

On the evening of December 6th, in response to an invitation from the Economic Club of New York City, I delivered an address on "Steps to Victory." I made this address partly because of the vast ignorance of the public of what the government was doing and had done, and the consequent apparent success which was attending the efforts of mean partisans and malicious obstructionists to misrepresent those who were fighting the war and to hamper their efforts. The address, which is inserted as Appendix III, may serve to give a hint of the situation at the time and to indicate in part the progress which had been made. I would direct attention particularly to my insistence at the time on the need of a unified command as a prerequisite to victory, and the necessity of a resort to drastic taxation as a means of preventing inflation with

all its attendant evils, and the hardships which would otherwise be encountered in the period of peace following the
victory over the Germans which I felt sure was not very
far off. I had insisted on both these in our councils from
the moment I knew we were going into the war and, for
that matter, had from the outset wondered why the Allies
could not recognize the supreme necessity of both.

On the eleventh of March, at the request of the Committee on Public Information, I left Washington on a
speaking trip through the Southwest and the South. I
was informed that I would be joined in the Southwest by
a French officer who would speak for France. Our first
joint meeting was held in Dallas, Texas. We spoke also
in Houston, Texas; Shreveport and New Orleans, Louisiana; Jackson, Mississippi; Birmingham, Alabama; Atlanta,
Georgia; Tampa and Jacksonville, Florida; and Columbia,
South Carolina. Each of us had a set speech. We varied
it just enough to meet local situations and developments.
Neither had had time to prepare anything. We had to
do the best we could under extreme pressure.

I had asked a stenographer to go with us to look out
for our tickets and railroad and hotel accommodations and
to take down what each of us said at the first two or three
meetings. His name was McPherson. He was, perhaps,
the best stenographer in the Department of Agriculture
and had been exempted from the draft because he was
needed in Washington. He was invaluable to us on the
trip. When we returned, he came to my office, gave me
a copy of what each of us had said during the trip, and
handed me his resignation. I said: "What does this
mean?" He replied: "I must get into the trenches
at the front." "But," I said, "you are needed here."

"That may be," he answered, "but I must get to the front. I am going to Denver to say good-bye to my mother, and then I am going to make an effort to get to France immediately."

I accepted his resignation and wished him good luck. The day after he left, I had a telephone message from the State Department to the effect that a first-class stenographer was needed at once in London to work for a special mission, that it was understood that we had a few excellent men, and it would be a service if we would let one be sent across at once. "Could I suggest one?" I suggested McPherson. "Would I get in touch with him immediately and ask him to report?" I did so and got this reply by wire: "Greatly appreciate opportunity. Regret cannot accept. Must get into the trenches." I told the State Department it would have to look elsewhere.

The address which I made at Fort Worth, Texas, and which contains substantially what I said at each other place, will be found in Appendix IV.

The French officer who accompanied me was Lieutenant Paul Périgord, one of the rarest characters I have ever known. He had come to this country a number of years before the war, and as Professor of Christian Ethics had taught in the St. Paul Seminary under the administration of Archbishop Ireland. Being of an inquiring turn of mind, he had taken leave and had studied language and sociology first at Minnesota, later at Chicago and Columbia, and then at Harvard, where he was about to take his Doctor's degree when France entered the war. He took the first ship home and volunteered as a chaplain in the French Army. There were no vacancies, and he immediately enlisted as a private in an infantry regiment

[283]

and was in time to fight at the battle of the Marne. Later he fought at Vimy Ridge, Ypres, and at other places, and finally at Verdun. He was gassed, wounded, temporarily blinded, buried under earth torn up by shell explosions, and was rescued and restored to health. After we entered the war, he was sent over to assist in training troops, but one day he made a speech to the boys in camp. One of the men connected with the Committee on Public Information heard him and, recognizing that he would be a greater asset as a speaker than as a trainer of troops, suggested that he be drafted for this service.

I have never heard a more effective speaker. He made no attempt at oratory. He always stood erect at the front of the platform with his hands on the hilt of his sword which stood straight in front of him resting on its point on the floor. He had a most winning manner and sympathetic voice, and spoke in quiet conversational tones, using good simple English with just enough accent to give it piquancy and charm. He had his audience under his control, making it laugh or cry at will. I heard him more than a dozen times. I am not usually accused of wearing my feelings on my sleeve, but I could not keep my face straight the last time any more than I did the first. I shall let these excerpts from his address speak for themselves:

"Now, my friends, before I begin my little talk I must comply with the request of your Secretary of War. When I left Washington a short time ago, he told me that he had quite a little trouble with this young American Army. It seems that in this army every boy wishes to be an officer. They are all asking for commissions. Nobody wants to be a private. As the Secretary made this remark, a well-known Irishman who was present, Hon. T. P. O'Connor, of the British House of Commons, wittily remarked, 'Why, Mr. Secretary, we have always had the same trouble with the Irish people. We have never been able to get up a band, because they all want to be leaders.' So it is with this young American Army. But the Secretary, knowing how I got my commission, said to me, 'Lieutenant, wherever you go I want you to tell the boys how you became an officer.' So, not in the spirit of vainglory, but merely to comply with the Secretary's request, I shall tell you how I got my commission. For you know a soldier cannot be proud. If I were anything, I would be ashamed, that is, ashamed of being alive. Most of my friends are dead. Of the sixty officers who were promoted with me at the beginning of the war in my regiment, there are two to-day doing active duty. Forty-one have been killed and the others are crippled for life. So, whenever I speak of the war I am not proud of my own achievements, for I have before me the vision of thousands of boys, all much braver than I ever was or ever will be, who have laid down their lives in defence of our cause. I do not tell this in a boastful spirit, but merely to comply with the request of a superior. When I went to France I intended to serve in the army, of course, as a chaplain. But when I arrived there I found all the vacancies filled. At the same time, I realized that the provision made for the spiritual and moral welfare of the army was not sufficient. The boys needed comfort and help most where they suffer and where they die, and that is in the infantry and in the trenches, for the infantry in the trenches is doing most of the suffering and most of the

[285]

dying. So I enlisted as a private in the infantry so that I could be with the boys when they suffered and when they died. I would gladly have remained a private, but circumstances imposed upon me greater responsibilities. One day in February, 1915, we were in the region which the Canadians have made famous by their bravery and which is called the Vimy Ridge. You remember that the Canadians have distinguished themselves there. You remember, perhaps, that gas, that infamous weapon used by the Germans, was first tried on the Canadians. At that time they had no masks and, of course, the only thing they could do was to run away, and so they did when they saw their comrades falling and dying in agony. We teased them about it, but they very cleverly answered: 'That's all right. The Germans beat the French, and they beat the English, but when they tried to beat the Canadians they had to give them gas first.'

"At any rate, we were in the region of Vimy Ridge, and one day a unit of the Imperial Guard broke through our line. My battalion was billeted in a small town near by, and as the Imperial Guard advanced, we were called out to meet it and, of course, to stop it. My company was that day the leading company of the battalion. You no doubt recall that the French officers, at the beginning of the war, were not dressed as I am to-night. This is a war uniform, which has been chosen because it blends best with the landscape. At the beginning of the war, we had a uniform which was black and red and which made the officers very conspicuous. The German soldiers had received orders to shoot the officers first and so, as we came out of the small wood, each officer leading his platoon, our officers fell deadly wounded. I was standing

[286]

by the side of my captain when he received a bullet through his right lung. Taking his sword, the sword I still carry with me, and which he had himself received from his dying captain at the battle of the Marne, he gave it to me, saying, 'Now, my friend, you must lead the company, for I see all the officers have fallen.' So I led the company and, thanks to the bravery of the boys more than to any great military knowledge of mine, in a brilliant charge they reëstablished the French line, and even did a little better than that, for they brought back with them whatever was left of that Imperial Guard unit when they got through with it. The next day, when the general came to look us over, he came to my company and asked me where my officers were. I told him they were all dead. He said, 'Whence this sword?' I told him my captain had given it to me as a symbol of authority over the men. Then, very graciously he answered: 'My friend, you keep the sword, and you keep the company.' That is the way I got my commission. Now, the Secretary of War tells me he has a commission in store for any one of the boys who will go to France and try the same. So good luck to you. . . .

"And I must tell you a little story about two of my private soldiers—ordinary peasants—down in Lorraine. One day, I overheard one of them say to the other: 'They tell me that the Maid heard voices. Do you suppose it is true?' He shrugged his shoulders, turned to me, and said: 'What do you think, Lieutenant?' I answered: 'The Maid must have heard some sort of voice; for she had an inspiration to lead her country to victory and deliverance.' And then he asked: 'Do you think voices can still

[287]

be heard?' And before I could reply, the clear notes of an American bugle rang out over the valleys of Lorraine and I said: 'Listen! Voices can still be heard.'

" . . . So these boys go into the trenches for about a week or ten days, and then they go back to nice little villages where they may rest and come back to their work refreshed. But at the beginning of the war we were not so favoured, for we had to remain in the trenches three or four or five weeks at a time, as we were practically alone holding the entire Western Front. I remember remaining on the battlefield of Verdun for twenty-one days without ever getting a chance to wash. As I was saying this to a little boy in Oklahoma the other day, he looked at me smilingly and said, 'My, but weren't you lucky?' We were not lucky, for, if you have had any such experience you would know that if you stay away from water for that length of time you soon have about yourself a good deal more company than you would ever care for. So it happened to the most respectable of us in the French Army, and the government became very much alarmed about it, so they decided they would send the boys thus affected to a 'delousing hospital.' The first boys to be sent there came back with wonderful reports. Just imagine! They had slept in a bed! Of course, you all sleep in beds here, but not on the Western Front. I don't suppose I have slept in a bed more than forty times in the last three years. These boys had slept in a bed, had clean linen, good meals, and shelter, which is quite an asset to an infantryman. Then all the boys wanted to go to a delousing hospital, for it meant a week's vacation. But in order to go, you had to qualify, and there was an examination. The boys who couldn't qualify, those who didn't 'have them' would go about and ask their friends, 'Have you got any?' and if their friends said, 'Why, yes,' then the other boy would say, 'Now, won't you please give me a couple?' But the boys soon got very wise, and they would say, 'Oh, no, I am not giving them away any more. I am selling them.' So it is that we had to stop sending the boys to a delousing hospital. . . .

"Now, my friends, I could go on telling you a good many stories, but I have a more serious message for you, a message which I deliver with the keenest of pleasure. I bring to you the warmest greetings of the French Army. The French Army, that valorous body of officers and men who saved the liberties of the world at the Marne, at Ypres, and at Verdun. For three long years that army, although bleeding from a thousand wounds, having lost more than one million of its best children for the sake of democracy, was looking longingly at the manhood of this sister Republic across the seas, without uttering a word of complaint, but filled with a great fear, the fear that all these sacrifices might be in vain. But, behold, one beautiful morning a new flag appeared above the trenches. Its colours were well known to all. They were Red, White, and Blue. There were stars playing in its folds, a symbol of this nation's high purpose. Then a mighty voice arose, from the Adriatic to the Atlantic, and that voice spoke in all the known tongues of the world, 'Long live, long live the United States.' And that voice, do you know whose voice it was? My friends, it was the voice of heroes, heroes from every town and city of France,

[289]

every town and city of Italy, of England, of Scotland, of Ireland, of Canada, of Australia, of New Zealand—from every corner of the world in which there lives a liberty-loving nation came that mighty voice, speaking love and gratitude to you, the American people. It is an echo of that mighty voice, a humble echo, of course, that I bring you to-night. It was a happy day for me in which I saw over our trenches the Stars and Stripes. . . .

"Would you like to know what it is that, during this great struggle, has kept France so brave and strong? You might think it was her victories, for glorious they were. And please, please never speak to a British or a French soldier of German victories. There has never been during this war such a thing as a great German victory. Whenever the German Army has put up a clean, decent, honest, and manly fight, every time she has been defeated. Surely you, the strong and noble men of this nation, are not going to call a victory the crushing of Belgium; nor a victory the invasion of northern France through a door we had left open because we relied on the honesty of our neighbour; nor a victory the crushing of Serbia; nor the crushing of Rumania a victory; nor a victory the poisoning of the hearts and minds of the poor Russian people, great big children that they are. No, my friends, such are victories that no great nation, neither the United States, nor England, nor France, would ever want to see written in the annals of her people. But it is not the victories of France that have helped her most. Nor was it the fidelity of England, wonderful as it has been. Here, I must pay a tribute to England. You have not always been quite fair with England, and we have not always been friends with England. We have fought many a fight with her, but they were ever chivalrous fights, and an English king was able to say of France during one of our most bitter conflicts, 'our gentle enemy.' I know the wrongs of England, but to-day I am bound to confess that England, especially in the person of Lloyd George, stands, the friend, the knight, and the defender of liberty, and of liberty for all nations. . . . But it is not the fidelity of England that has helped France most. Nor was it the wonderful devotion of Italy, nor the thousand and one tributes of affection and gratitude that came to her from every corner of the civilized world.

"The sympathy of these United States has helped France much during this struggle. For, long before you came into this war officially, American boys, anxious to pay the old debt you so graciously mention, but of which France never speaks, came and volunteered in the most illustrious unit of the French Army, the Foreign Legion, and there they died the death of heroes. Others came into our aviation corps, and I assure you, my friends, they made their presence felt in the skies of Europe. Others came as nurses, doctors, and ambulance drivers, and they took care of our sick and our wounded with a devotion unequalled even by our own nurses and doctors. More than that, as soon as the women of America heard that there were orphans and widows in France, they not only volunteered their money, but they sent their very heart, their love, and they became mothers to these orphans and sisters to these widows, a wonderful charity that has enabled them to go through this terrible crisis. So that you may understand the better the impression that has been made by this form of charity upon the minds of the French people, just listen to this incident that happened to me in France but a short time ago. My regiment was going through the city of Toul in Lorraine, the place where the American boys now are. Whenever we go through a village or city, the little boys of the place follow the regiment, come up to us, and ask for the privilege of carrying our rifle or our sword. A little boy about eight years old came up to me and asked me for my sword, so I gave it to him, and we became very good friends. After a while, as every little boy will do to the first stranger he meets, he began telling me all about his family. He was very proud of his father, who had been a captain in the infantry and had been killed at the battle of the Marne. 'Since then,' he said, 'I have had a godmother.' That godmother to him was the most wonderful woman in the world, as she was from that mysterious and distant land across the sea. He said, 'Mother has told me I must love her because she has been very good to us.' I became more interested in the matter, and I told him I expected to go to America very soon. 'Oh,' said he, 'if you go to America you must look up my godmother. Her name is Miss McFadden and she lives in New York City. When you find her,' he said, 'you must kiss her for me,' and I had to promise. I have been in New York City and I have looked for Miss McFadden, but I have not found her yet. If this is the impression that has been made upon the minds of the children, you may imagine what it has meant to the mothers.

" . . . But, beautiful as these expressions of sympathy have been, they are still not the thing that has helped France most, not the thing that has brought her the most comfort. What, then, is it? One morning a mighty voice was heard coming from across the seas. That voice, as it passed over the waves, seemed to take with it some of the grandeur and solemnity of the ocean itself. It was restating in the most sublime pages, in immortal words, the rights of individuals and of nations. It was branding with an indelible mark the criminal aggressors of mankind. It was placing the ends and aims of this war on the highest moral level conceivable. It was endeavouring to make this world safe for democracy. It was the voice of a man whose patience and forbearance have never been seen in the head of a powerful nation. That voice was the voice of your illustrious President, Mr. Woodrow Wilson.

"I am not, as you well know, making a political speech, but you, the citizens of this great nation, must know, you are entitled to know, the love, the veneration, and the respect with which the name of your President is spoken to-day over the fields of Europe. And believe me, wherever it is not spoken with respect, it is pronounced with fear. . . .

"I am not saying all this, my friends, to beg love from you for France. France would not permit it. But, while I am not begging love for France, I must rise here against a campaign which has been waged in this country to undermine your confidence in that nation. I know, for example, you have been told that France was a faithless nation. Have you not? Yes, many a time. Well, you may believe what you have heard or read, but I must believe what I have seen. Throughout this war I have seen, in all their churches, that people praying as I have seldom seen anywhere any people praying. I have seen in the army, soldiers, officers, generals, the very highest amongst them, such men as Castelnau, Foch, and Pétain, beginning and ending their day with prayer. And I have seen more than that. I have seen young men, thousands of them, going 'over the top,' as you say, to an almost certain death, and doing it with divine simplicity, with a smile on their faces as though they already saw their coming Saviour through that curtain of fire. Is that a faithless nation?

"Let me tell you the story of my brigade. You all know what a brigade is. It is a unit made up of two regiments, nearly six thousand men. You no doubt remember that in July, 1916, the Crown Prince, that great Prince who, up to that time, had succeeded in taking nothing but portraits and furniture out of French homes and castles, decided one day to take a city so that his father could celebrate the fourteenth of July, our national day, in a city. Of course, the only thing he could think of taking was a French city. Very thoughtful of him. Of course, we were equally anxious to keep him out, so the general-in-chief called for the general commanding our brigade and told him, 'General, I am not able to have at Verdun reserves sufficient to support the attack of the Crown Prince.' Unfortunately, there was but a single road to Verdun and a single railroad, and these could be broken easily. That brigade of ours was made up of the Seventh and the Fourteenth Infantry. The general-in-chief said to the general commanding our brigade, 'I am going to ask your young brigade to go to the fort of Souville,' which was the last fort that remained between the German lines and the city of Verdun, 'and those boys must hold that fort for me to the last man until such time as the reserves can be brought.' The general commanding our brigade called for me and said, 'Lieutenant, you are for the boys both a chaplain and an officer, and I think you had better tell them plainly what it means. You understand what it means: it means the sacrifice of our brigade.' So we gathered the boys in an open field and we held a service there for the repose of the souls of those who had died in the previous battles. I spoke to the boys and I told them frankly, as a soldier must, what their mission was, told them of the trust and confidence that France was placing in them, and tried to make them realize that, although they were going up there six thousand strong, very likely only a few would return. I asked all of them who wanted to receive my blessing to kneel down, and the six thousand boys knelt down to receive the priest's blessing. I cannot begin to tell you how I felt as I was blessing those young boys, all of them between eighteen and twenty-four. Most of them were going to their graves, and I did not even know whether I should come back myself.

"At any rate, we all went up cheerfully to the fort of Souville. Three days before the attack the shelling began, such shelling as I have never seen before, such concentration of fire that the landscape which we knew the evening before, the next morning was so changed that we thought, during the night, in some mysterious manner, we had moved into another place. After the shelling came the gas, wave after wave, cloud upon cloud, so as to kill the boys that might have survived the shelling. On the morning of the thirteenth, in the most confident fashion, came up the first German unit, about a brigade. They came up the slopes of the fort, confident that no human being could have survived the shelling. We saw them coming, and when they reached the edge of the plateau we charged down and crushed them at the foot of the hill. About twelve o'clock a new unit came up and that unit met with the same fate. About three o'clock another German unit came up in the last effort, but the boys were so tired that an entire company of that German unit entered the fort. The general called for me and said to me, 'Lieutenant, what are we going to do? The Germans are in the fort and the reserves are not coming.' I said, 'General, come and see the boys. They are all willing to die. That is all France can expect of them, and they are begging to be given the chance to charge once more.' They did charge once more. They put their whole heart into it, and in a great effort they drove back that last unit and made prisoners the Germans that had entered the fort. About five o'clock the reserves came, and the city of Verdun was saved. The Crown Prince, who had his mail sent to Verdun, did not get it there. It had to be sent back to him with the notice, 'Has not yet arrived.'

"These boys had gone up to the fort six thousand strong. Fifteen hundred of them came back. When they came down, their first request was that we should hold a service of thanksgiving for the wonderful protection they had enjoyed. And yet people tell you that France is a faithless nation. . . .

"And do you know what it means to go 'over the top'? To go over the top means this: One day you receive the order of attack. You have to leave your trench, jump over barbed-wire entanglements under the terrible fire of machine guns, nice little weapons that fire about eight hundred shots a minute, and under the fire of heavy artillery, and then run through No Man's Land and jump into the enemy's trench.   The enemy is waiting for you there, rifle and bayonet in hand.   You have to overpower him, take his trench away from him, and then run to another trench, and so on, until you fall dead, wounded, or exhausted.   When I tell my boys, 'To-morrow we are going over the top,' I see these boys for a while lost in a dream. And what is the dream?   Why, the dream is of home, far away, and in that home a father, a mother, or a wife and children, their hopes, their loves, their ambitions.   I can see the heart of these boys clinging fondly to the things they love.   But after a while, looking into those eyes again, I can read grim determination, and I realize that victory has been won in the hearts of these boys.   Although they love the people and things they have left behind, still they love their country more.   And the next day, when I go over the top, I do not have to look back and see whether my boys are following me, because I had read it in their eyes the day before.

"In order to make that supreme sacrifice, there is one thing needed: These boys must feel that the whole nation is backing them.   Remember, to-morrow there will be thousands of your boys going over the top.   The whole nation is living in them and by them.   Of course, those boys will go over the top anyway, because they are brave boys, but if you at home do not appreciate the value and the grandeur of their sacrifice, they will go over the top with agony in their hearts and they will say, 'Here we are, giving up all, and the folks at home do not care.   They do not know.   They do not understand.'   I assure you, my friends, it is not pleasant to die for people who do not care.

"As to the boys you are sending over there, do not worry. Of course, they are going to suffer. Of course, some of them will die, but believe a soldier, it is sweet to suffer and it is easy to die when you suffer and die for a great cause. And if it be sweet to suffer and easy to die for the French flag, how much sweeter and easier it must be to suffer and die for your flag, the fairest of all the flags of all the nations. Do not worry about the reception your boys are getting yonder. I saw the first American boys arriving in Paris, and the reception extended to them was such as to make all the French mothers jealous, for we, the boys of France, have never been thus received in our own capital city.

"As to the boys who are going there to stay, for some will stay, please take this message home with you and give it to anybody within your reach: The number of American boys who are going there to sleep for ever will depend upon your loyalty and your support. To the mothers of those boys I wish you would say what I went the other day and said to the mother of the first American boy to fall on the fields of France when I brought her some flowers in the name of the French Army. Tell them that the mothers of France, with empty hearts now, will take their places by the graves of their children. I know that the little boys and the little girls of France will go and gather the fairest flowers of our land to place on these graves with their best prayer. And if you ever go to France after the war, you will see that France lovingly guards your sleeping boys. You will not be able to tell which is the grave of an American boy or of a French boy, for they will all be taken care of with the same love and the same gratitude."

[298]

This was the best speech I heard during the war except the President's War Address; and the little story about the "voices" was the prettiest story.

Several incidents happened on the trip which I cannot pass over. When we were travelling from Houston to Shreveport over the Houston, East and West Texas Railroad, through a section somewhat out of the beaten track, noticing that at the stations there were usually pretty fair size crowds, I said to Périgord: "These people probably have never seen a French uniform. Let's go out and let them have a look at one." He cheerfully acquiesced in my suggestion. At the next stop, we got out. The crowd showed much interest and gathered about the lieutenant. Looking around, I saw a man well past middle age. I suggested to the lieutenant that we go over and speak to him. We did so. The man did not seem to be especially cordial. In fact, he appeared to be embarrassed. After a few seconds, somebody touched me on the arm and motioned me aside. He said: "I am an officer of the Department of Justice. That man you are talking to is under a $10,000 bond for obstructing the draft. He is a violent pro-German." I thanked him, called Périgord aside and repeated what the officer had told me. He smiled and said: "Oh, well, who knows? We may have made a Christian out of him."

At Shreveport, as usual, Périgord told his little story about the French boy and his godmother, Miss McFadden, whom he charged Périgord to locate when he reached New York and to give his love and to kiss for him, if he found her. After the meeting, two very pretty girls dressed in their Red Cross uniforms, who had been sitting in a box with six or eight of their fellow workers, came on to the stage locked arm in arm and, approaching Périgord, saluted him as he looked at them, and said with a jaunty and daring air: "Lieutenant, we are Miss McFadden." Périgord was equal to the occasion. He paid them a fine compliment in the best French manner and said: "Oh! But I am only the Secretary's orderly. The honours must go to him."

At Jackson, Mississippi, much to my surprise, I found in the afternoon papers an attack on France, in which the French people were represented as being faithless and irreligious. I showed it to Périgord just before we went to our meeting. He looked grieved, but said nothing. During his speech which followed, without breaking the thread of his thought and without specific reference to the article, he told the story of his brigade at the siege of Verdun. When he finished, his audience was in tears.

On our way from Jacksonville to Columbia, the news reached us that the great German drive had broken the Fifth British Army. I was much worried, because I had been told repeatedly and had come to believe that, while the Allies might not break through the German line, there was no danger of the Germans making a dent in the Allied line. I felt that I should have very little heart in my appearance before the Columbia people that evening. I spoke to Périgord about the matter. He was serious but superbly confident. He said: "Don't you worry, my friend. They will not win. The brave American and English and French boys will beat them back. It may be the beginning of the end for the Germans."

CHAPTER XVIII

His Attack on German Morale—Undermining Confidence in the German Government—Cabinet Discussions of Foreign Policy —The Armistice

GENERALLY speaking, after we entered the war, there were few new matters of broad policy which had to be discussed in Cabinet meeting till the fall of 1918. Action was what was demanded, and action was the order of the day, rapid action, and everybody was working at top speed. Every department and every agency had its hands full trying to furnish the necessary support and supplies to the army and navy and to get men to France. There was endless consideration by every agency and department of measures which would further the military activities of the nation. It would be hopeless even to attempt to give a hint of what was thought and done.

In the meantime, the President was giving much attention to the psychology of the situation, to the possibility of influencing the minds of the people of the Central Empires and of causing a weakening of their will to continue fighting, by picturing the aims of their rulers and masters and contrasting those of this nation. The power which had brought war and destruction to the world was not, he assumed, the German people, but the ruthless masters of that people. There could be no peace with an

[301]

ambitious and intriguing government. We could not take the word of the present rulers of the German people as a guarantee of anything that is to endure, "unless explicitly supported by such conclusive evidence of the will and purpose of the German people themselves as other peoples of the world would be justified in accepting. . . . We must await some new evidence of the purposes of the great peoples of the Central Powers. We are not the enemies of the peoples of the Central Powers—they are not our enemies. They did not originate this war. We are vaguely conscious that we are fighting their cause as some day they will be. They are in the grip of a sinister power. The whole world is in the grip of that power. The military masters of Germany have never regarded nations as peoples—men, women, and children of like blood and frame as themselves, for whom governments exist and in whom governments have their life. But now those masters see very clearly to what point fate has brought them. If they fall back, their power will fall to pieces like a pack of cards. It is their power at home they are thinking about more than their power abroad. It is that power which is trembling. Deep fear has entered their hearts. If they fail, their people will thrust them aside. A government accountable to the people will be set up. If they succeed, they are safe, and Germany and the world are undone. America will fall within their menace. But they will make no headway. It rests with us to break through their hypocrisies. We have only one choice. We have made it. Woe be to the man or group of men that seeks to stand in our way in this day of high resolution when every principle we hold dearest is to be vindicated and made secure for the salvation of nations, including Germany herself.

[302]

Once more we shall make good with our lives and fortunes the great faith to which we were born, and a new glory shall shine in the face of our people. Germany has said once more that force and force alone shall decide whether Justice and Peace shall reign. There is but one response from us: 'Force, force to the uttermost, force without stint or limit, the righteous and triumphant force—which shall make Right the law of the world, and cast every selfish dominion down in the dust.'"

Brave words these for the dark days from June, 1917, to the middle of April, 1918, and a bold prophecy considering the collapse of Russia, the havoc of submarines, and the state of things on the Western Front! And much of the spirit and words of the men of the days of our Revolution and of those who humbled the Stuarts! Evidently there is something else in this man for those to study who thought they had much ground for criticism of him when he said: "There is such a thing as a man being too proud to fight. There is such a thing as a nation being so right that it does not need to convince others by force that it is right." Evidently there were more ways of interpreting these statements than one.

But he was ready "to discuss a fair and just and honest peace at any time that is sincerely purposed—a peace in which the strong and the weak shall fare alike." In spite of appearances, the President believed that that time was not far off. He apparently never let the thought enter his head that we should fail. Like Lincoln, he held firmly to his belief in the might of right, and he knew also the power of this nation and believed, I think, that, if necessary, it alone would overcome Germany. "As, God willing, it assuredly will be," and "the eyes of the people have been opened and they see," and "the hand of God is laid upon the nations," and "he will show them favour," were of the essence of his thinking and faith. But there was need of a look ahead, because of the possible effects, not only on the enemy, but also upon ourselves and the Allies. There must be a permanent peace and therefore a just peace. The minds of men must be influenced in right directions before the end was too clearly seen and uncontrolled ambitions were let loose. The war would be simple, pure tragedy and horror if passion prevailed and there was not permanent gain secured—if once more there was to be a mere carnival of looting and grabbing, a display of greedy national self-seeking. Therefore, the President bent much of his energy to the unfolding of worthy national aims and the terms of a just settlement and a secure peace. Time and again, he raised his voice and took Congress into his confidence, seeking its support. And already there were discordant voices, particularly in the Senate, partisan voices of men who apparently were thinking more of themselves and the fortunes of their party and of humbling Woodrow Wilson than they were of the vast issues involved. One of them in particular, occupying a position of peculiar strength, apparently cherished such personal hatred of the President that it would have been impossible for him to take a clear view of things, even if he had not been so constituted as to make it impossible for him to entertain a generous emotion or a constructive thought. The air was charged with misrepresentation; and especially from the first of March, 1918, a ceaseless campaign was waged in Congress and outside to inject poison into the public mind. This was obvious to those in Washington who were observant, but it was not patent to the great body of the American people of all shades of political opinion who were patriotically bent on winning the war. They did not perceive it, and they would not have credited it; but it was a fact and furnished some justification for the appeal which certain leaders urged the President to make for the return, in 1918, of a Congress which would support him and which he did finally make, to the dismay of many of his warmest supporters and to the irritation of many other high-minded men and women.

There are those who smiled at the President's assumption that the German rulers and not the German people were responsible for the war, at his attempt to fasten in their minds the fact that they were being led in false directions to their injury, and at his assertion that no peace would ever be made with them. Senator Lodge seemed to be one of these. As late as October 6, 1918, he regretted the President's discussion with the German Government and his inquiry whether Maximilian represented merely the constituted authorities, saying: "I do not understand what he can possibly represent except the constituted authorities, which represent the German Empire and people, unless a revolution has occurred of which the world has as yet no knowledge." We shall see. I shall be greatly surprised if the President's messages do not have a marked effect among the people of the Central Empires and on the course of the war.

The President's course in outlining terms of a just peace seems to be received with approval by the public, and his suggestion of a plan to underwrite future peace runs along the lines of the proposals of leaders such as Taft and Roosevelt; but there appears to be apprehension in certain quarters lest the President get too much glory from the war and still greater fame if peace comes. Partisanship is on guard to see that his achievements do not redound to his or to his party's advantage!!

On October 4th, Prince Maximilian had become Chancellor of Germany. He immediately asked the President "to take steps for the restoration of peace, to invite the Allied governments to send delegates to negotiate, and in order to avoid further bloodshed, to conclude an armistice." He accepted President Wilson's outlined terms. The latter asked for further light and added that he would propose an armistice only on condition that the Germans retire from Belgium and France. On October 12th, the Germans replied, saying that they would immediately evacuate occupied territory, and that they accepted the fourteen points with the understanding that only details would be negotiated. They added that the government was in agreement with the great majority of the Reichstag, and spoke in the name of the German people.

The President, in his reply of October 14th, was very specific on several points. The process of evacuation would be left to the Allied military advisers. There must be absolutely satisfactory safeguards and guarantees of the military supremacy of the armies of the United States and of the Allies in the field. The wanton and outrageous practices of German forces on land and sea must immediately cease. "It is necessary also, in order that there may be no possibility of a misunderstanding, that the President should very solemnly call the attention of the government of Germany to the language and plain intent of one of the terms of peace which the German Government has now accepted. It is contained in the address of the President delivered at Mount Vernon on the Fourth of July last. It is as follows:

"'The destruction of every arbitrary power anywhere that can separately, secretly, and of its single choice disturb the peace of the world; or, if it cannot be presently destroyed, at least its reduction to virtual impotency.'

"The power which has hitherto controlled the German nation is of the sort here described. It is within the choice of the German nation to alter it. The President's words, just quoted, naturally constitute a condition precedent to peace, if peace is to come by the action of the German people themselves. The President feels bound to say that the whole process of peace will, in his judgment, depend upon the definiteness and the satisfactory character of the guarantees which can be given in this fundamental matter. It is indispensable that the governments associated against Germany should know beyond a peradventure with whom they are dealing."

The German reply of October 20th said that, in accepting the proposal for evacuation, the government had started from the assumption that the procedure should be left to the judgment of military advisers. To the President's fundamental condition for peace, it said: "Hitherto, the representative of the people in the German Empire has not been endowed with an influence on the formation of the government.

"The Constitution did not provide for a concurrence of representation of the people in decisions of peace and war. These conditions have just now undergone a fundamental change. A new government has been formed in complete accord with the principle of the representa-

[307]

tion of the people, based on equal, universal, secret, and direct franchise.

"The leaders of the great parties of the Reichstag are members of this government. In the future, no government can take or continue in office without possessing the confidence of a majority of the Reichstag.

"The responsibility of the Chancellor of the Empire is being legally developed and safeguarded. The first act of the new government has been to lay before the Reichstag a bill to alter the constitution of the Empire so that the consent of the representative of the people is required for decisions on war and peace.

"The permanence of the new system is, however, guaranteed, not only by constitutional safeguards, but also by the unshakable determination of the German people, whose vast majority stands behind these reforms and demands their energetic continuance.

"The question of the President—with whom the governments associated against Germany are dealing—is therefore answered in a clear, unequivocal manner by the statement that the offer of peace and armistice has come from a government which is free from any arbitrary and irresponsible influence, is supported by the approval of an overwhelming majority of the German people."

At Cabinet meeting, Tuesday, October 22d, the German note which appeared in the papers on Monday was the main subject of discussion. It had come over the wireless. The President remarked that he had not seen the official copy—that it had not been received. Just then, Lansing came and told us that the message came to his office just as he was leaving.

The President said that he would like to have our reactions on the note. Nobody spoke for a few seconds. Then someone made a brief statement, asserting that everything depended upon the nature of Germany's intentions and the President's faith in them.

I asked why Germany had approached this country alone—why she did not approach the Allies as a whole, or France, or England—why she did not send the same message to each. Did she think she could produce friction? Did she think this country was a little less than neutral and not quite belligerent? Did she think she had fooled us for two years and might do so again? Did she think she could produce friction and impair our military effectiveness?

The President answered that it appeared to be technically sufficient that he had announced terms which Lloyd George and Allied sentiment indicated acceptance of, and that the Germans, knowing the facts, had addressed him as the author of the statement of terms. It was possible also that Germany regarded this nation as the only one which desired nothing except peace and justice and the one which would take a reasonable attitude.

I pointed out that the German suggestion that her military advisers agree with ours and those of the Allies as to evacuation, arrangement of forces, and indication of positions, was highly objectionable. This, I said, should not be entertained for a second. Our military chiefs should decide the terms, give them to the Germans, and demand their unconditional acceptance. These should include military guarantees, such as the surrender of arms, and the occupation by the Allies of such places as Metz, Cologne, and Strassburg, not only pending evacuation, but also through the peace negotiations and till the terms dictated to them were fulfilled.

I suggested that, while the political adjustments which had evidently been made were reassuring, they did not go far enough. Taking away from the military crowd the power of making or continuing war and making the ministry responsible to the Reichstag were not sufficient. The Reichstag had had little real power and had not been really representative of the German people. It was or had been three fourths Prussian. It represented the great land-owners and big business interests, and was conservative—Junkerish. There had been no redistricting since 1871, and the urban liberal elements had been largely shut out. Furthermore, the Bundesrath had too much influence over the Reichstag, and the Kaiser, or whoever exercised his power, could muster twenty-one votes in the Bundesrath and control that body and the lower house—could block any change. To make sure that the military lords were under control, it would be necessary, I thought, to know that the following things had been or would be done:

(1) That new districts were arranged honestly for the election of members to the Reichstag;

(2) That the Constitution and power of the Bundesrath be changed and its influence over the Reichstag be destroyed;

(3) That the Emperor's veto—the Executive veto power—be modified;

(4) That the three-class voting system for the Prussian Diet be changed and extended suffrage be adopted with a secret ballot;

(5) That the Prussian Upper House be reformed, and

(6) That a ministry in Prussia and in the Empire be created, responsible to the legislative bodies.

It was objected that this would be an unwarranted interference with the right of the German people to select their own government. I answered that they had never had that right, and that I wanted to confer it upon them, and, for that matter, that the President had already interfered, and properly, when he said in former notes that he would not deal with the Hohenzollerns or any others who had arbitrary power over the matter of peace and war. I added that, if Germany complied with the President's demands, she would have to do substantially what I suggested; and, furthermore, that we were treating with an untrustworthy enemy and had a right to dictate terms.

The President observed that it would carry us too much into technical detail to go fully into the matter in a note. I replied that I realized that; but that details were of the essence of the matter, and that I would make certain that Germany understood that rearrangements in detail in conformity with the assurance given would be insisted upon, and that we understood what they should be.

Burleson said that the Germans did not know the meaning of democracy, and that he would be satisfied with nothing short of abject surrender with absolute military guarantees. He would require the Germans everywhere to lay down their arms, and would not leave the terms to Foch, Haig, and Pershing. They might be too lenient. This brought a roar of laughter, but Burleson stuck to his guns.

The President said that he was not going to discuss terms with the Germans. He would simply give them his decision. He asked what impression we thought the note had made on the American people. What would their attitude be? Baker answered that the newspapers reflected the views of the people. I agreed that they did on the note, that the people were a unit, and would not be satisfied unless the terms were drastic, but that they would trust him and accept his lead.

The President remarked that doubtless the press reflected the views of the people of the East, but asked if it did those of the people of the West. "Yes," I answered. "I have recently been as far west as the Rockies. The people in the West want the war to end, but not till it ends right. They want the matter settled once and for all. They want no more menace from Germany. They would be willing to leave the matter of an armistice and its terms to Pershing, Haig, and Foch." I spoke of a man whom I had met in Cutbank, Montana, about fifty miles from the Rocky Mountains. I had gone there in connection with the work of lending money to the farmers in the drought-stricken area. I had found the country desolate. It was in the midst of its second year of drought. The country was brown and bare. The people had made little or nothing for two years. Some of the farmers were leaving their homes. Cutbank was dead. It was dusty and grimy. There was little or no business activity. As I was sitting in the lobby of the little hotel, people, as they passed by, would stop and gaze at me. Finally a small, dried-up, rather shabby elderly man came in and took a seat near me. I supposed he had a hard-luck story which he wanted to tell me or that he wanted some of the government's money. But nothing of the sort. He began to talk about the war. I soon found that I could tell him little or nothing new. He was familiar with its origin, understood its causes, and was acquainted with its progress. As I was getting ready to leave to take the train, he said:

"I have three sons in France at the front. They are all I have. I cannot reasonably expect to get them all back. I hope I may get two or one of them back, but whatever happens, they are my contribution to my country's cause and to the cause of civilization. What I ask is that they do not give themselves in vain. Let them stay till the war ends right, till the thing is settled once and for all, till a permanent peace can be made, and men may go about their business free from apprehension and disorder, till the nations can take steps to see that there shall never be another tragedy like this. See that they do not die for anything less worth while. Fix the matter so that neither Germany nor any other nation can ruin the world."

I added another little story which Lieutenant Périgord told me about a ranchman whom he met at Great Falls on a speaking trip after he left me. After his speech in Great Falls, he said, a tall, splendid specimen of a man, about fifty years old, dressed in plains' fashion, came up to him and said that he wanted to shake a Frenchman's, a French officer's, hand. "I expressed my gratitude to him," Périgord said, "and asked why he was so kind. 'I felt that I must see you,' the man replied. 'I have travelled fifty miles to see you and to hear you. Do you know this place?' he asked, showing me a card which had a picture of a little French cemetery near Vimy Ridge. 'I do not know the cemetery,' I said, 'but I know Vimy. I was wounded near there when the Germans made their gas attack. What is it?' 'They tell me,' the man answered, 'that my only son is buried there. After England declared war, he went to Canada and volunteered, and fought for many months, and then I received word that he was dead and had been buried near Vimy.' 'Well, my friend,' I said, 'you take it very bravely.' 'Oh, well!' replied the man, 'this is no time for weakness. But when the war is over and we have won the victory, I am going to France and find my boy's grave and lie down on it and have a good cry. What I want is assurance that his death will be justified in the issue. The war must not stop till the Germans are soundly whipped and things can be so arranged that the world will not have to go through this sort of thing again. Get the right sort of terms and get the nations to arrange guarantees that disputes can be settled without resort to war, and peace can be long continued. This is what my boy died for.'"

This, I said, was what I found everywhere.

Baker spoke of a soldier who had come back and said that the matter must be settled right and firmly this time, as he did not have time to go to Europe every ten or fifteen years to lick the Kaiser.

I gave another instance of the spirit found in Montana, which certainly was staggering under as heavy a load as any other state in the Union. On the train from Cutbank to Havre, as we were discussing the situation and the loans we were making, I noticed that two of the trainmen were listening and taking a deep interest in what we were saying. This was rather unusual for flagmen and brakemen.

Finally, one of them said: "We are farmers."

I answered: "You don't look like it. You look like trainmen."

"We are, temporarily," he replied, "but normally we are

farmers. We made nothing last year except a little wheat for seed, and we had to get jobs to help us support our families."

"Have you applied for a loan?" I asked.

"No," he answered, "I do not expect to. I can pull through. With what I am getting from the road, I can feed my family and stock. Next spring, the road will give me a vacation. I shall go home and work as long as I am needed. Then I will come back to the train. I can work it out in this way. If you have any money to lend, let the boys have it who cannot get away or get other jobs. It will save their farms for them. Don't bother about us. We have got to work together to lick the Kaiser and see this war through to the right end."

McAdoo thought that the President ought to take the matter up with the Allies, not with the Germans. "The President," he added, "ought not to have to consider such a matter as that before him in an atmosphere of passion; and the air about us seems to be charged with it." Funny to have McAdoo advising caution and moderation! "We had better be careful," he asserted, "how we decide matters at this juncture. There are more sides than one to this matter of prolonging the war, if we can end it and secure all that reason demands. We may as well face the fact that the Allies and even we may not be able to finance this war on its present scale—and it really means our financing it—for two years more. The expenditures are frightful, and I do not know where we can get the means without wrecking ourselves."

I remarked that there was another reason for not going too far with the business of insisting that Germany be absolutely crushed and that the armies go to Berlin. That might gratify us as a spectacle and satisfy our passions, but it might not be of any value from a military point of view and might involve vast additional expenditure and loss of life. "But the thing in my mind is that a situation might develop where the obstacle to a just peace would not come from Germany but rather from certain of the Allies. Human nature has not been fundamentally changed by the war. There have been other similar upheavals. Nations are not going to be angelic when peace comes. There will be much of the same old exhibition of national ambitions and national selfishness. I have seen many indications already since the Allies have recovered from their desperate situation last spring and have begun to realize that they will win, that there will be a resort on the part of some of them to the old mediæval European practices and struggles for advantage, under the guise, of course, of seeking national protection. The tigers will be let loose. I have already heard representatives of the Allies assert that much must be demanded from Germany which would certainly create conditions favourable to another hideous explosion. As the collapse of Germany becomes more certain, the demands of some of the Allies, particularly of France, will probably become unreasonable. This would be natural, but in the interest of world peace, they will have to be held in check."

The President said that only Lloyd George and the British Labour Party had expressed concurrence in the terms he had outlined, that Clemenceau had not as yet, and Italy had not. The English, he said, were giving trouble on the matter of the freedom of the seas, and were asking what he meant by it. He was not prepared to say more than that private property seized at sea must be paid for, and that there must be insistence on a few other points.

I added that what I had just said did not modify what I had before insisted upon, that we should take military guarantees which would give us an absolute hold on the Germans to force evacuation and compliance with all necessary conditions and promises.

The President said that he thought he understood the sense of the meeting, and that what he still wanted was a suggestion as to the procedure.

I said I would tell Germany that I would transmit her note to the Allies with the distinct statement that he would advise that nothing be done except under such guarantees as Pershing, Haig, and Foch would demand, and only if they advised that an armistice be arranged—that he could not trust people who had violated all their pledges.

I told the President that I would, of course, give Germany no hint of what I thought the Allies might or should do. The President said that he hoped we would exempt him from the necessity of taking up any other matter—that his mind was all on the note and that he had none to let on any other matter.

The President's reply appeared in the press Wednesday, October 23d. He could not decline, in view of the explicit assurances of Germany, to take up with the Allies the question of an armistice, but the only armistice he would submit for consideration would be one which would leave the Allies and the United States in a position to enforce any arrangements entered into and to make a renewal of hostilities by Germany impossible. He had transmitted to the Allies his correspondence with the suggestion that if they were disposed to effect peace *upon the terms and principles indicated,* their military advisers and those

[317]

of the United States be asked to submit to their governments the necessary terms of an armistice "provided they deem such an armistice possible from a military point of view."

The note further stated that the President felt bound to point out why "extraordinary safeguards" must be demanded. Significant as the constitutional changes seem to be, it said, "it does not appear that the principle of a government responsible to the German people has yet been fully worked out, or that any guarantees either exist or are in contemplation that the alterations of principle and of practice now partially agreed upon will be permanent. Moreover, it does not appear that the heart of the present difficulty has been reached. It may be that future wars have been brought under the control of the German people, but the present war has not been, and it is with the present war that we are now dealing. It is evident that the German people have no means of commanding the acquiescence of the military authorities of the Empire in the popular will; that the power of the King of Prussia to control the policy of the Empire is unimpaired; that the determining initiative still remains with those who have hitherto been the masters of Germany. Feeling that the whole peace of the world depends now on plain speaking and straightforward action, the President deems it his duty to say, without any attempt to soften what may seem harsh words, that the nations of the world do not and cannot trust the word of those who have hitherto been the masters of German policy, and to point out once more that in concluding peace and attempting to undo the infinite injuries and injustices of this war, the government of the United States cannot deal with any but veritable representatives of the German people who have been assured of a genuine constitutional standing, as the real rulers of Germany.

"If it must deal with the military masters and the monarchical autocrats of Germany now, or if it is likely to have to deal with them later, in regard to the international obligations of the German Empire, it must demand not peace negotiations, but surrender. Nothing can be gained by leaving this essential thing unsaid."

This note was entirely satisfactory and covered all the essential points emphasized at Cabinet meeting. It could not have covered or referred to the point that it was desirable to commit the Allies to the President's terms which the Germans accepted, but it is obvious that if the Allies assent to the Armistice they will be morally bound to conclude peace on the basis of those terms; and they will accept them. They are what we are fighting for and what they profess to be fighting for. If they do not accept them or if they now appear to accept them and later do not observe them, they will become obstacles to a peace of justice and will violate faith. The President referred to this phase of the matter in his discussion on Tuesday.

Germany replied that she was awaiting armistice proposals and added: "The peace negotiations are being conducted by a government of the people, in whose hands rests, both actually and constitutionally, the authority to make decisions. The military powers are also subject to this authority."

At Cabinet meeting Tuesday, the 29th of October, the President said that he wished to discuss the Austrian Note which appealed for an immediate armistice on all fronts.

The question was raised at once as to whether there was really an Austrian Government with which we could deal. Hungary had set up an independent establishment, as had the Slavs in the south. Poland was engaged in setting up a government and Czecho-Slovakia was represented in Paris by Masaryk. It was certain that all these factions except Austria and Hungary would seek to be represented at the Peace Conference. At least they would have to be considered and dealt with. An interesting letter from the new Premier of Austria was read. It represented that the new government of Germany was liberal and sincere and that it could be regarded as free from the control of the old military power and could be trusted. It urged that the German people be not humiliated as they had been after Tilsit.

A letter was read also from a socialist observer in Switzerland. He wrote that the German people trusted the President of the United States and would throw out the Hohenzollern crowd if he said the word. There was danger of chaos, he added, if Germany was pushed too far. Bolshevism was menacing, and the Russian Government was sending funds into Switzerland, Sweden, and other countries.

It was evident that Germany was going to pieces and that there would be an armistice in a very few days, if the Allied chiefs thought there should be one.

At Cabinet meeting, Tuesday, November 5th, the President came in looking well and happy. He acted as if a load had been taken off his mind. He appeared to be less hurried and less under a strain than I had seen him for years. He immediately announced that the terms of an armistice had been agreed upon in France, and that the Fourteen Points had been accepted with two interpretations, namely, that "Freedom of the Seas" would have to be exactly and satisfactorily defined, and that the restoration of Belgium was to be understood to include financial as well as political restoration. The President said that these two reservations were satisfactory to him.

Foch, the President said, was to dictate the terms of the Armistice to the Germans. This he heartily approved, just as he had agreed that it was essential that the Allied chiefs should determine whether there should be an armistice at all. He expressed the opinion that Germany would accept Foch's terms. Her morale, he was convinced, was gone. He based his view, not so much on what was said in Socialist papers as on the contents of the Pan-German papers.

All the Cabinet agreed that Germany would have to accept. I asked the Secretary of War if there was convincing evidence that the German Army had deteriorated. He replied that there was not, but that German shells appeared to be of inferior quality. I stated that I was satisfied that the army had deteriorated and was continuing on the down grade in point of morale, spirit, and supplies, and that I thought the spirit of the people back of the army was broken.

The President spoke at length of the possibility of revolutions in Europe under the stress of conditions and the influence of Bolshevist propaganda. He especially referred to the presence of conspirators in Switzerland and Sweden and to the report that the Russians had sent millions of francs into these countries. He asked what should be done. I immediately asserted that the Allies ought to ask the governments of these countries to impound the funds and expel the agents. The President said that Clemenceau was not afraid of revolution in France and that the Bolshevists themselves recognized that the French people and the French cantons of Switzerland would stand firm. Lloyd George, he added, thought that there would be a difficult faction in England and Scotland, but that the people as a whole would not be swept from their feet. The President attributed the French attitude to the wide diffusion of property. I added that they had also had their dose, their revolution, that it had been a severe surgical operation, and had laid foundations on which further progress could be made by evolutionary processes —by enlightened progressive measures. I pointed out that England had preceded France by a hundred and fifty years, and that, while she, too, had need of fundamental changes, she could work out a fuller measure of democracy, and a higher development of her people and of their economic and social well-being by the process of modification.

Of course, these countries have a long road to travel before they reach the point at which America now stands in the march to individual well-being and social and industrial democracy. Among other things, class distinction and privileges under law or custom must go, and adequate provision for the education of the masses of the people must be made; and in England, some solution of the ownership, by a very limited number, of the soil on which forty million people stand, must be found.

As for most of southern and eastern Europe, and, for that matter, all Asia, Africa, and part of South America, it may without extravagance be said that they are mediæval. They are in the raw. Illiteracy in them ranges from

[322]

30 per cent. to 93 per cent. and there has been, until recently, no sort of decent regard for the masses of the people
on the part of the ruling classes or the governments.
They have not recognized that the people are their greatest undeveloped resources and that, if they were developed, they would have to concern themselves little about
the development of their material resources. Nor have
they realized that their conditions will be menacing and
unstable till their people are developed and have higher
standards of living.

This war will set the cause of the people measurably
further forward. There will be a large liberal deposit and
substantial gains in all Europe and particularly in the
nations of southern and eastern Europe, including not
only Russia, Rumania, and Serbia, but also Italy and
Spain, in which the illiteracy ranges from 33 per cent. to
60 per cent. But progress will be slow, particularly in the
Eastern nations. Russia, in a hundred years, may possibly get in sight of where we started. People forget how
long it has taken nations to perform a surgical operation,
get back to convalescence, and straighten out on the
course of rapid progress. It took England twenty years
to get rid of the first Stuarts and the Cromwells, twenty-
eight more to get rid of the restored Stuarts, and fix the
lines for orderly institutional development, one hundred
and forty-four more years to reform the suffrage in part
and fix the forms of parliamentary government, and the
end is not yet. It took France six years to get rid of her
kings and discover Napoleon, nearly twenty years to get
rid of Napoleon, fifty-five more to settle down to a
somewhat unstable Republican foundation, and she is not
yet at the point which, in her enthusiasm, she thought

she had reached in 1790. Russia and Rumania and Serbia, and other countries, will move more slowly, because their people are less fitted for self-government and they have further to go.

It was said at the Cabinet meeting that many people in France were speaking of a revolution there as a matter of course. Many reasons were given, among them that the stay-at-homes had monopolized everything. Apprehension was expressed that force would have to be used to secure a redistribution. It was generally asserted that there would be financial collapse and economic ruin. The former, I said, was probable, but the latter was unlikely.

The President requested Lansing to talk confidentially with our representatives with a view to see if European governments would seize Bolshevist funds and expel agitators.

Nothing was said about the approaching election, partly because of the overshadowing importance of the international situation, and particularly of the imminence of the Armistice, and partly because no one had any uneasiness as to the outcome, notwithstanding the fact that it was obvious that certain Republican leaders, in spite of professions of non-partisanship, had been, both in Congress and on the outside, unceasingly playing politics and seeking to win Congress. The leaders had skillfully set out to poison the minds of the voters, playing upon the prejudices and passions engendered by war measures, and had actively and systematically organized every precinct, while the Democrats had done little or nothing.

When I reached my office the morning of November 11th, I received a message from the White House saying that the President would address Congress at one o'clock.

[324]

This left no doubt in my mind that the Armistice had been signed. I had been disturbed at five o'clock Monday morning by newsboys crying extras. I supposed that the extras meant the Armistice. The conditions in Germany and on the front, I believed, were such as to make it necessary for Germany to accept almost any terms.

I took steps to get a card of admission to the House for Mrs. Houston, and she and I met and walked to the Capitol. The people were crowding into the galleries when we entered the House, but the floor was rather empty, as many members of Congress had not returned from their electioneering trips. The diplomats were out in force.

When the President was announced there was great applause. He quickly took his place, greeting the Vice President and the Speaker, and then began his address. At first his voice was husky and much less distinct than usual. It seemed that the President either had a slight cold or that he was labouring under a strong emotion or partial exhaustion. He looked tired.

He had not read many lines of his message before it became evident that the Armistice terms were about as drastic as anybody had ventured to predict they would be, or as any reasonable person could have desired. What an answer to the silly creatures who were shouting that the President would fix the terms and that they would be very light on Germany!

The members of the Supreme Court were sitting immediately in front of the President, just as when the President read his war message. Whether they approved the verdict as they did the declaration in favour of war, I do not know.

"The war thus comes to an end," added the President,

[325]

after outlining the terms, meaning, of course, "The fighting thus comes to an end." The trouble with war is that it does not come to an end when the fighting ceases. The fighting ended as the President, from the moment we entered, thought it would end, and as I felt sure it would. The iron had entered the President's soul when he took up the sword. There was much of the Roundhead of the 17th Century in him. He would smite the enemy and have good execution of him, in the sight of the Lord, for the good of his soul. He felt, as I did, that the world was not going and would not go the Kaiser's way, but the way of righteousness and justice. I had been told that Foch had the same faith in an overruling Providence and could not imagine a German victory.

This armistice marks the turning point in one of the world's great epochs. It may be thought of in comparison with the turning back of the Persians, the Fall of Rome, the breaking up of the Feudal System, and the French Revolution.

Europe, in certain respects, is still mediæval in many parts, but this war, with its victory for the Allies, will bring great and beneficent changes. It will break the strangle hold of the privileged classes and mark the beginning of a real march toward democracy, liberty, and regard for the average man. These things will not appear in full measure in our day, but they will be set far forward. The people have seen a vision, and they will not lose it. The king business, the whole aristocracy business, will be less flourishing. Many kings and princes will be turned loose on the world. Some may return, but with impaired prestige and power. Those that remain will feel lonesome and will keep their eyes peeled and watch their step. It would not be surprising if England has the last king. It will be interesting when there is only one. He will be "all dressed up and nowhere to go."

The whole city, the whole nation is celebrating; and well it may. The horrible butchery of men and the criminal waste of wealth have ceased. The victory means many things. It means or may mean the end of menace from mediæval-minded, irresponsible despots; the return of Alsace-Lorraine to France; a number of new independent states, such as Poland and Czecho-Slovakia; the recovery by Italy of her natural boundaries; probably the Turk out of Europe; a measure of disarmament; and a scheme to settle disputes between nations without resort to war in so many instances. And so the world slowly and painfully progresses!

Speaking of new states, I saw Masaryk at the Capitol and congratulated him on the outcome and the fact that his country would be permitted to exist as a separate power. He showed much emotion, but expressed confidence that his people would exhibit reasonableness and ability to control their destinies. Masaryk will be a powerful force for good in Europe. I also saw Demowski, President of the Polish National Committee. I asked if he thought that his people would exhibit the requisite spirit of tolerance and teamwork. He replied that he thought they would. I expressed my doubts, saying that they had never done so. He replied that they would have a severe test, but that they ought to be warned by their former experiences. I added that, unless the new small nations controlled their spirit of nationalism, refrained from embarking on purely selfish particularistic policies, and worked out together some form of economic coöperation, they would commit economic suicide, impair their productive forces, and retard the recovery of Europe. He agreed. The danger is that they will not show the requisite wisdom and forbearance and prove a curse to themselves and to the world. It makes no difference how people are grouped, how small nations are, provided they work with other peoples in Christian and neighbourly fashion, with intercommunity adjustments, as do the peoples of the states of the United States. But it is going to be difficult for the new nations to restrain themselves and to coöperate effectively with one another and with oldern nations; and they may become political and economic nuisances.

CHAPTER XIX

AGRICULTURE IN THE WAR

Division of Work Between the Department and Food Adminis-
tration—Results of the Food Production Act—Agricultural Ad-
visory Committee

THE part which the millions of men, women,
boys, and girls on the farms and the organized
agricultural agencies assisting them, including
the Federal Department of Agriculture, the state
colleges and departments of agriculture, and farmers' organizations, played during the war in sustaining this nation and those with which we were associated, is striking,
but altogether too little known and appreciated.   On them
rested the responsibility for maintaining and increasing
food production and for assisting in securing fuller conservation of food and feedstuffs.   The satisfactory execution of their task was of supreme importance and difficulty.

The conservation of available foods is one thing; the
increase of production along economic lines is quite a
different thing.   It is prerequisite and fundamental.   It
is one thing to ask a man to save; it is another to ask him,
confronted as he is by the chances of the market and the
risk of loss from disease, flood, and drought, to put his
labour and capital into the production of food, feeds, and
the raw material for clothing.

The work of the agricultural agencies is not much in the
public eye.   There is little of the dramatic about it.   The

millions of people in the rural districts are directly affected by it and are in more or less intimate touch with it, but to the great urban population it is comparatively unknown. Usually people in cities devote very little thought to the rural districts; and few of them, fortunately, in normal times, have to concern themselves about the food supply and its sources. The daily press occupies itself largely with the news of the hour, and the magazines have their attention centred chiefly on other activities. Consequently, the people in large centres have slight opportunity to acquaint themselves with rural problems and agencies. Although the nation has, in its Federal Department and the state colleges and departments, agricultural agencies for the improvement of farming which, in point of personnel, financial support, and effectiveness, excel those of any other three nations combined, very many urban people, when we went to war, were unaware of the existence of such institutions, and not a few representations were made to the effect that an agency ought to be created to secure an increase of production. These people saw the windows of cities placarded and papers filled with pleas for conservation, for investment in bonds, and for subscriptions to the Red Cross. They wondered why they did not see similar evidence of activity in the field of agriculture. They did not know of the thousands of men and women quietly working in every rural community of the nation and of the millions of bulletins and circulars dealing with the problems from many angles. They overlooked the fact that the field of these workers lies outside of the city, and did not recognize that both the problem and the methods were different.

On April 18th, I transmitted to the Senate certain proposals for increasing the production, improving the distribution, and promoting the conservation of farm products and foods. The suggestions were based in large measure upon the programme adopted at the St. Louis and Berkeley conferences. The Committee on Agriculture in each House soon afterward took the matter in hand, held extensive hearings, and finally formulated two measures. In the preparation of these, there were two leading thoughts in mind. One was to speed up and add to the activities of the Federal Department of Agriculture and its coöperating forces. The other was to vest in the President regulatory powers, in considerable part of a commercial nature, to be exercised through an emergency agency rather than through any existing department, to deal with special and urgent national and international food problems growing out of the war. After an extended debate the two bills—the Food Production and the Food Control—were passed by Congress and approved by the President on August 10th.

The Food Production Act—"an act to provide further for the national security and defence by stimulating agriculture and facilitating the distribution of agricultural products"—to be administered by the Department of Agriculture, carried an appropriation of $11,346,400 for the following purposes:

The prevention, control, and eradication of the diseases and pests of live stock; the enlargement of live-stock production, and the conservation and utilization of meat, poultry, dairy, and other animal products; procuring, storing, and furnishing seeds for cash at cost to farmers in restricted areas where emergency conditions prevailed; the prevention, control, and eradication of insects and plant diseases injurious to agriculture, and the conservation and utilization of plant products; the further development of the coöperative agricultural extension service; surveys of the food supply of the United States; gathering and disseminating information concerning farm products; extending and enlarging the market-news service; preventing waste of food in storage, in transit, or held for sale; giving advice concerning the market movement or distribution of perishable products; investigating and certifying to shippers the condition as to the soundness of fruits, vegetables, and other food products received at important central markets; the development of the information work of the Department; enlarging the facilities for dealing with the farm-labour problem; and extending the work of the bureaus of Crop Estimates and Chemistry, $650,000.

While the Food Production bill was pending in Congress, detailed plans were formulated for carrying out its provisions as soon as it should become law. The Department therefore was ready to proceed promptly and effectively with their execution.

It was apparent that the Food Production and the Food Control acts dealt with very closely related matters, that effective coöperation between the Department of Agriculture and the Food Administration was essential, and that needless duplication of effort should be avoided. It was recognized that the relation between the two agencies was intimate and fundamental; that it was impossible completely to disassociate them, and undesirable to do so. After a full conference, a satisfactory working agreement was reached.

In a broad way, the Food Administration had as its

prime functions the control and regulation of the commercial distribution of foods and feedstuffs, that is, of products which had reached the markets and were in the channels of distribution or in the hands of consumers, their conservation by consumers, and the elimination of waste, through the employment of regular official as well as volunteer agencies.

The Department of Agriculture continued to administer the usual laws placed under its jurisdiction and assumed the direction of the increased and varied activities provided for by the Emergency Food Production Act.

It early became apparent that there would be no little delay in framing and passing the necessary legislation. Time was the essence of the situation. Prompt action was necessary. It was essential that many of the recommendations included in the St. Louis programme should be put into effect. Farmers already were in the field or had made their plans for the season. The Department and the state agencies therefore speeded up their work along the most promising lines with the forces and funds at their command. Projects not having an immediate bearing on the emergency were set aside in order that the energies of the workers might be concentrated on the main problems.

Assuming that Congress would enact, in part, at least, the legislation desired to stimulate production and to promote conservation, the Department of Agriculture, in coöperation with the Land-Grant colleges, undertook the preliminary work of developing additional machinery and agencies; and, in a number of states, these additional agencies, including especially an extension of the farm demonstration force, actually were put into operation.

[333]

It was recognized that the Coöperative Extension System, with its combination of Federal and state administrative officers and specialists, county agents, home-demonstration agents, farm bureaus, and other local organizations, furnished a ready and effective means for the nation-wide dissemination of the needed facts, as well as for practical demonstrations of the best methods of increasing agricultural production and securing the most economical utilization of the products of the farm. With remarkable promptness and unanimity, these agencies addressed themselves to the important problems of increasing and conserving the food supply and cordially furthered the Department's efforts in this direction.

It would require a volume even to outline all the things which were done by the Department of Agriculture. It stimulated production, increasingly controlled plant and animal diseases, reducing losses from the cattle tick, hog cholera, tuberculosis, predatory animals, and crop pests, and, in conjunction with the Department of Labour, rendered assistance to the farmers in securing labour. It safeguarded seed stocks and secured and distributed good seeds to farmers for cash at cost; acted jointly with the Treasury Department in making loans from the President's special fund to distressed farmers in drought-stricken sections; aided in transporting stock from the drought areas; greatly assisted in the marketing of farm products, and, under enormous difficulties, helped the farmers to secure a larger supply of fertilizers. At the direction of the President, it administered under license the control of the stockyards and of the ammonia, fertilizer, and farm-equipment industries.

The Department maintained intimate touch with the War and Navy departments, the War Industries, War Trade, and Shipping boards, and the Fuel and Food administrations. Through the Bureau of Animal Industry, it not only continued to safeguard the meat supply for the civilian population, but it also inspected the meats used at the various cantonments, training camps, forts, posts, and naval stations, and aided in the organization of the veterinary corps. Through the Forest Service, it rendered valuable assistance to practically all branches of the government having to do with the purchase or use of forest products and to many industries which supply war material to the government, made a thorough study of the lumber situation, aided in many directions the Bureau of Aircraft Production and the Navy Department in the execution of their aëroplane programmes, conducted coöperative tests on a large scale at the Forest Products Laboratory, and collaborated in the organization of the forestry regiments. Its Bureau of Markets handled the distribution of nitrate of soda to farmers for cash at cost, coöperated with the War Industries Board in broadening the channels of distribution and in stimulating the use of stocks of low-grade cotton, and worked with the Food Administration in the handling of grains and in other of its activities. Its Bureau of Chemistry assisted other departments in preparing specifications for articles needed by them, aided the War Department in the organization of its chemical research work and in making tests of fabrics and supplies, worked out formulas for waterproofing leather, and maintained intimate touch with the related services of the Food Administration. The Department collaborated with the War Department in its handling of the draft, aiding it particularly in passing upon the exemption of agricultural labourers.

An appropriation of $4,348,400 was made by the Food Production Act for the further development of the Extension Service. By the end of October, more than sixteen hundred emergency demonstration agents, men and women, had been appointed, making a total of approximately five thousand coöperative extension workers, including the specialists performing extension work, employed through both state and Federal regular and emergency funds. This number was further increased as soon as men and women with the requisite training and experience could be secured. Nearly seven hundred and fifty additional counties coöperated with the Department under the Food Production Act in employing country agents. The total number of men in the service acting as country agents was about two thousand and many district agents were designated to supervise their activities. About thirteen hundred state, district, county, and urban women home-demonstration agents were set to work. Of the 600 women employed as emergency agents, 500 worked in counties, principally among farm women, and 100 were assigned exclusively to urban communities. More than one hundred additional assistants in boys' and girls' club work were placed in the field.

It would be almost easier to tell what these men and women did not do than to indicate the variety and extent of their operations. They constituted the only Federal machinery in intimate touch with the millions of people in the farming districts. They were, therefore, able to render great service to other branches of the government, such as the Treasury in its Liberty Loan campaigns, the

Red Cross, the Young Men's Christian Association, and other organizations in their war activities, and the Food Administration in its special tasks.

Conditions growing out of the war gave added impetus to the already well-established policy of extending and promoting local organizations to support, aid, and extend the influence of the county-agent work. The number of such organizations was rapidly increased throughout the country. In the fifteen Southern states the number of community organizations of farmers formed to aid the county agents increased from 1,654, with a membership of 44,548, to 2,508, with a membership of 78,660. As in the South, so in the North and West, impetus was given to the organization movement already under way, and there was an emphatic demonstration of the increased usefulness of the county agent when backed by a supporting local organization. In the thirty-three Northern and Western states, the number of farm bureaus and similar local organizations was increased to 374, with a membership of 98,654. The number of community clubs organized among rural women in the South increased from 250 to 1,042, and 1,635,000 women and girls actually participated in some form of emergency work.

The enrollment in the regular boys' clubs in the South was largely increased, and the total membership was approximately 100,000. In addition, 20,000 boys were enrolled to assist in war emergency activities. The boys' and girls' clubs in the Northern and Western states had a regular membership of 406,000 and an additional emergency enrollment of 400,000. These clubs in all sections of the nation were efficient agencies in the campaigns for promoting food production and conservation.

[337]

The passage of the Food Production Act made possible a marked expansion of the machinery of the Bureau of Markets. An appropriation of $2,522,000 was provided for this purpose.

Realizing the importance of continued efforts to promote the production of staple commodities and of making plans promptly for the immediate future, in June I appointed a committee of experts of the Department to make suggestions for future action, especially with reference to winter-wheat planting. The Committee considered the problem from every angle and reached the conclusion that a strenuous effort should be made to secure the planting of an area that would, under favourable conditions, produce a billion bushels of wheat in 1918. The Committee also recommended that steps be taken to encourage the production of more than 83,000,000 bushels of rye, and that the production of winter oats in the South should be increased to the extent that seed was available. This programme called for the planting of 44,634,000 acres of winter wheat and 5,522,000 acres of rye, and was submitted by telegraph to the leading agricultural authorities of various states concerned. As a result of their suggestions, it was finally determined to propose the planting of 47,337,000 acres of winter wheat and 5,131,000 acres of rye.

Through a number of channels, the Department proceeded to bring the programme to the attention of the grain farmers of the country and to seek their coöperation in making the recommendations effective. It was published as a circular and also was given wide distribution through the press and the *Weekly News Letter;* and a series of conferences immediately was held by representatives of the Department in each of the great grain-growing sections of the country.

Following the publication of the programme and the holding of the conferences, the Department carried on an intensive campaign to emphasize the need for an increased production of grain and the best methods to be employed in obtaining the increases suggested.

The task of increasing the meat supply, necessarily a slow one, was particularly difficult. Hogs and poultry yield the quickest returns, and therefore urgent efforts were made to increase their production. Special campaigns were conducted by the specialists in animal husbandry. At the same time, active steps were taken to stimulate the production of beef and dairy cattle, and specialists in sheep husbandry were assigned to duty in the Eastern states to encourage the production of sheep on farms.

A very material increase was brought about in the production of meat and wool on the forest ranges. In two years, there were placed on the forests approximately 1,000,000 additional head of live stock, representing about 25,000,000 pounds of beef, 16,000,000 of mutton, and 4,000,000 of wool.

It was early apparent that in certain sections of the country, particularly near the great industrial centres in the North and Northeast and especially in the vicinity of plants undertaking large war contracts for the government, there would be a marked shortage of farm labour. It was obvious, too, that, on account of the abstraction of labour through enlistments in the regular army and through the operation of the draft law, difficulties would be experienced in many sections of the Union. The situation called for constructive action. A large army cannot be constituted without causing inconvenience in many directions. It was clearly impossible to make exemptions by classes and to admit no farmers to the army. Still, it was highly important that agricultural production be increased. Military failure could arise no less from shortage of foodstuffs than from shortage of ammunition or man power. The task was presented of making the labour remaining on farms more effective, of securing fuller coöperation among farmers, and of utilizing on the farms urban and rural labour not heretofore fully or regularly employed. Past experience made it clear that labour might be transferred from certain communities where the seasonal pressure had passed to others and where the need was immediate. It was known, too, that there were hundreds of thousands of boys in rural districts and villages who might render useful service, and that the army of boys and girls organized in agricultural clubs might be enlarged and its members employed in additional directions. It was assumed that there were more than two million boys between the ages of fifteen and nineteen years in the cities and towns who were not engaged in productive work vital to the nation, that many of these had had contact with rural life, and that their services might be utilized on the farms, especially in the harvest season.

The Departments of Agriculture and Labour and other agencies immediately after the outbreak of the war undertook to furnish assistance. The War Department itself held definitely in mind the thought of lightening the burden as far as possible by not calling to the colours those essential for leadership and direction. Under the pressure of the first draft, it was difficult to work out satisfactorily the underlying principle of selection. For the future, a system of classification was adopted. The selectives were classified into five groups, indicating the order in which they would be called to service. Skilled farm labour was in Class 2, highly specialized agricultural experts in agencies of the state or nation in Class 3, and heads of necessary agricultural enterprises in Class 4. The operation of this new arrangement removed many of the difficulties previously encountered and, in reasonable measure, met the demands of the situation.

It was realized that, after all was done, there would be need of additional labour in many sections. The Department of Labour therefore undertook to study the available supplies in towns and cities and developed its system of employment agencies for this purpose. One object was to secure information, which could be conveyed to the Department of Agriculture and to state agencies, as to available labour in urban centres and to have it drawn upon for aid in farming operations in near-by communities. The Department of Agriculture assumed the task of studying the supplies and needs in rural districts. It arranged to place a man in each state in touch with the State Council of Safety with the special duty of assisting in the mobilization and organization of rural labour. Under the provisions of the Food Production Act, thirty-eight farm-labour agents were appointed and devoted their entire energies to the problem.

There was an unusually large demand for the publications of the Department. More than 22,000,000 farmers' bulletins, circulars, leaflets, posters, dealing with emergency problems of production and conservation and an equal number of publications covering the regular activi-

[341]

ties of the Department making a total of approximately forty-four million were published between April 1st and the end of October. The special circulars and posters were distributed largely through the county agents and other coöperating agencies. Copies also were supplied to official organizations, war committees, civic associations, and patriotic clubs throughout the United States.

At the request of the Secretary of War and the Secretary of the Navy, the Department participated in protecting our military and naval forces against unwholesome foods. The Federal meat inspection service, which for years has safeguarded the civil population of the United States from bad meat in interstate commerce, was extended to include the special supervision of the meat supply of the American Army and Navy. The examination, selection, and handling of meats and fats were in expert hands from the time the live animals were driven to slaughter until the finished product was delivered in good condition to the mess cooks. Inspectors were assigned to the various cantonments, training camps, forts, posts, and other places in the United States, where large numbers of troops were assembled

In all the undertakings during 1917 and 1918 to increase the nation's food supplies, the Department and the state colleges and commissioners of agriculture worked in cordial coöperation. The authorities and staffs of the agricultural colleges in every state of the Union placed their facilities at the disposal of the Department, supported its efforts and plans with the utmost zeal, and omitted no opportunity, on their own initiative, to adopt and prosecute helpful measures, and to urge the best agricultural practice suited to their localities. They not only responded promptly to every request made on them to coöperate in the execution of plans, but also liberally made available to the Department the services of many of their most efficient officers. Equally generous was the support of the great agricultural journals of the Union.

Very much assistance also was rendered by the National Agricultural Advisory Committee, created jointly by the Secretary of Agriculture and the Food Administrator for the purpose of securing the views of farmers and farm organizations, and of seeing that nothing was omitted to safeguard all legitimate interests. This body, as a whole and also through its subcommittees, studied the larger and more critical agricultural problems confronting the government, gave many valuable criticisms and highly useful suggestions, and assisted in the several communities in making known the plans and purposes of the Department. The Committee included, in addition to representative farmers, the heads of a number of the leading farm organizations. It was composed of former Governor Henry C. Stuart, of Virginia, a farmer and cattleman and member of the price-fixing committee of the War Industries Board; Oliver Wilson, of Illinois, farmer and master of the National Grange; C. S. Barrett, of Georgia, president of the Farmers' Educational and Coöperative Union; D. O. Mahoney, of Wisconsin, farmer and president of the American Society of Equity; Milo D. Campbell, of Michigan, president of the National Milk Producers' Federation; Eugene D. Funk, of Illinois, ex-president of the National Grain Association and president of the National Corn Association; N. H. Gentry, of Missouri, vice-president of the American Berkshire Association; Frank J. Hagenbarth, of Idaho, president of the National Wool

Growers' Association; Elbert S. Brigham, of Vermont, dairyman and Commissioner of Agriculture; W. L. Brown, of Kansas, wheat grower and member of the State Board of Agriculture; David R. Coker, of South Carolina, chairman of the State Council of Defence, producer of improved types of cotton; W. R. Dodson, of Louisiana, farmer and dean of the Louisiana College of Agriculture; Wesley G. Gordon, of Tennessee, demonstrator of better farming; John Grattan, of Colorado, agricultural editor and cattle feeder; J. N. Hagan, of North Dakota, general farmer and Commissioner of Agriculture and Labour; W. W. Harrah, of Oregon, wheat grower and director of the Farmers' Union Grain Agency of Pendleton; C. W. Hunt, of Iowa, general farmer; H. W. Jeffers, of New Jersey, dairyman, president of the Walker-Gordon Laboratory Co., and member of the State Board of Agriculture; Isaac Lincoln, of South Dakota, banker and farmer; David M. Massie, of Ohio, general farmer and successful business man; William F. Pratt, of New York, general farmer, agricultural representative on the Board of Trustees of Cornell University, and member of the State Farm and Markets Council; George C. Roeding, of California, fruit grower, nurseryman, and irrigation farmer, and president of the State Agricultural Society; Marion Sansom, of Texas, cattleman, live-stock merchant, and director of the Federal Reserve Bank at Dallas; and C. J. Tyson, of Pennsylvania, general farmer and former president of the Pennsylvania State Horticultural Association.

The efforts put forth by the farmers to secure increased production of plant foods can best be indicated in terms of planting operations. The size of the harvest may not be a measure of the labours of the farmers. Adverse weather conditions and unusual ravages of insects and plant diseases may partly overcome and neutralize the most exceptional exertions. The farmer is in no small measure the slave of the elements.

The first year of our participation in the war witnessed the nation's record for acreage planted in the leading cereals and potatoes, 237,000,000 as compared with 210,000,000 in 1914, and for the five-year average, 1910–1914, an increase of 27,000,000 acres. It was 18,000,000 acres greater than that for 1916, by which time the stimulus of high prices had powerfully operated to bring about unusual exertions. In 1918, the acreage was further increased by a half million; and yet, by this time, hundreds of thousands of farm boys had been taken by the army and navy. In fact, when the draft began to operate, delegations of farmers came to see me to tell me that they were willing to respond to our requests for increased planting and to do anything they could to help win the war, but that they did not see how they could do so if their young men were taken into the army. They asked that I see General Crowder and beg him to let their boys stay at home. Of course, I declined. I told the delegations that General Crowder would not and should not do what they asked; that their boys would not be willing to have me do what was suggested; that they would not want it said that only the town and city boys were doing the fighting; that they themselves really did not want what they had come to ask; and that I was confident that they would go home, take up the slack, and do more than they were asked to do. I added that everybody would turn in and help them at critical times, and that we would organize men and women and boys and girls especially to aid them during the planting and harvest seasons. They made no reply. They went home and did the job.

In spite of the fact that the climatic conditions were adverse in 1917, especially for wheat, and in 1918 for corn, the aggregate yield of leading cereals was larger in each year than in any preceding year in our history except 1915. It exceeded in 1917 the pre-war five-year average by 870,000,000 bushels and, in 1918, by 610,000,000.

Equally successful were the efforts to secure a larger number of meat animals and an ampler supply of dairy products and fats. The number of milch cows and other cattle and hogs in 1918 was 138,400,000 as compared with 115,000,000 in 1914, an increase of 23,400,000; and the increase over the pre-war five-year average was 18,400,000. The increase in the number of pounds of beef, pork, and mutton in 1918 over 1914 was 4,000,000,000 and, in the number of gallons of milk, 922,000,000. The total value of all crops in 1918 was $14,222,000,000 as against $6,112,000,000 for 1914 and $5,827,000,000 for the five-year average, 1910–1914; and the value of live stock on the farms was $8,284,000,000 as compared with $5,890,000,000 and $5,318,000,000. Armies, they say, fight on their stomachs. Our forces had no reason to fear that theirs would be empty.

CHAPTER XX

The President Addresses Congress—Leaves for France—Taft's, Roosevelt's, and Lodge's Opinions on the League—The President's Manchester Speech

THE Cabinet met at the usual time, Tuesday, November 12th. It was the first meeting after the election, but there was no reference to the election. We had more momentous things to think about. There was much discussion of readjustment and its necessities and processes and of the course of change to a peace basis. The President read a document from a correspondent in Switzerland about conditions in Berlin. It stated that Bernstorff was back in Berlin, and also Ludendorff, that the latter looked very dejected, that he was on foot, as his automobile had been taken from him, and that he was apprehensive that he would be murdered, as many other German officers had been shot.

Two evenings later, I dined at the Argentine Ambassador's and saw the Swiss Minister and his wife. The latter had much to say to me about Bolshevist propaganda in Switzerland, its responsibility for the Swiss strike, and its dangers. I told her that I did not believe such crazy creatures could do much harm in Switzerland, that I had too much faith in the Swiss people and in Swiss democracy, and that Switzerland was farther along on the path of political and economic well-being than Russia would be in generations or than the Bolsheviki could conceive. I added that one might legitimately be a Bolshevik or anything else in Russia and some other places and still be a reactionary in Switzerland and America, with their progressive spirit, beneficent institutions, and general well-being. The Swiss Minister was called out of the room to answer the telephone. When he returned, he announced that the Socialist leaders had surrendered to the government. It appeared that the peasants, weary of the folly of the extremists, had come to the assistance of the authorities and had helped to make a quick end of the matter.

The Argentine Ambassador and the Swiss Minister discussed the Peace Conference with me after dinner. They expressed an earnest hope that the President would attend the Conference and that his views would prevail. They thought that he only could exercise the necessary restraining influence and get a peace which would last. They further expressed the hope that neutral nations which had all been seriously affected by the war might be called in, especially when the time came for discussing plans to prevent a recurrence of war.

Before the Cabinet meeting Tuesday, the nineteenth there had been much discussion in the press and in Washington as to the composition of the Peace Commission. I felt confident that House and Lansing would be on the body.

On Monday, the twenty-fifth, I was told that Mr. Henry White was going as the Republican member. This, I thought, would be a political blunder, because his appointment would probably not satisfy the regular Republicans in the Senate or elsewhere. It would not add the sort of strength to the Commission which the political situation demanded. His diplomatic knowledge and services could have been commanded in some other capacity. I understood that his name was suggested and urged by Lansing.

It is evident that the President is bent on being the Commission, just as he is his own Secretary for Foreign Affairs, but, even so, he ought to have at his side the strongest, most influential, and best-informed men from both parties. Such men would render him great service in Paris and at home after the completion of the Treaty.

At Cabinet meeting on Tuesday, the twenty-sixth, the President spoke of his intention to go to Paris. This was his first mention of the matter to us. He said he thought he ought to go to see that the negotiations took the right direction, and that leaders in certain European countries were urging him to attend the Conference. He added that he was satisfied that everything would go well at home and that, as he understood us and we him, he could send brief messages when necessary with the assurance that we could easily interpret them. On the other hand, he observed that, if he remained in Washington, those who were sent to Paris might not get his thought and that, in any event, things would move so rapidly in Paris and be so tangled that he might not be able to keep track of them at a distance.

He remarked that he would have to return by March and that, in the meantime, he could consider and dispose of any measures passed by Congress, including any he might have to veto, as he would have ten days after such measures reached him abroad. He asked us to continue Cabinet meetings and inquired if it would be agreeable to us to have the Vice President preside. We immediately responded that it would be a very acceptable arrangement. The President stated that it had not been settled how many delegates there would be or when the Conference would begin. He said nothing about the membership of the Commission.

On Saturday, November 30th, the papers contained an announcement of the list of delegates. I do not regard the Commission as a particularly strong or satisfactory one. It means that the President is going to Paris to stay, which I think is a mistake. He ought to go to Europe, talk with the leaders, visit France, Belgium, England, and Italy, make addresses in each country, canvass matters fully with his delegates, and then come home. The President would be stronger if he stayed at home and passed upon the essential matters referred to him than he will be if he goes to Europe and engages in the daily wrangling. The very fact of nearness to the scene of action may be a disadvantage to the President. He is now all that he is plus something else, and his voice would be mightier going across the ocean. Furthermore, if he stayed here, he would have an opportunity to keep track of the development of public sentiment and to confer with leaders of both parties.

On December 2d, the President again addressed Congress. When I got to the Capitol before 12:30 there were great crowds about the building and on the inside, as big as any I had seen since the night of the war message. Every seat on the floor of the House was occupied except one reserved for the Chief Justice in front of the President. All the diplomats were sitting in the body of the House back of the Cabinet.

The President, when he began to speak, again seemed to

[350]

be hoarse and to be bothered by something. He first dwelt on the closing of the war and the part played by the different classes in the nation; and then he turned to the processes of reconstruction. Incidentally, he endorsed Secretary Lane's hastily evolved soldier settlement scheme —a scheme which I had turned down, which Lane had not canvassed with me, and which was disapproved by most agricultural leaders of authority in the nation. His plan was not novel; in fact, it was as old as the Gracchi and older. The Gracchi had a plan to enlarge the public domain by limiting the amount of land private owners could retain, adding the aggregate excess to the public land, and dividing the increased acreage among the returned soldiers. As this would, they assumed, benefit the rural districts, they planned to compensate urban dwellers by developing a grandiose system of public highways so that agricultural products could be transported to the cities, and by fixing the price of grain and selling it to urban dwellers below the market. There are very few things which have not been tried by somebody, somewhere, at some time in the world.

The scheme had many defects, not the least of which were that it contemplated developing desert, swamp, and cut-over lands in remote sections, taking soldiers away from their homes and friends at a time when there were available near-by lands which could be secured. The nation has not reached the stage in its agricultural development when it would pay it on a large scale to put water on land in many arid sections or to drain the difficult swampy places, and it is not now suffering from a lack of farmers and underproduction of farm products.

Finally, the President announced that he intended to

[351]

go to Paris to join the representatives of the Allied governments. He gave as his reasons that the Allies had accepted as the basis of peace what he had outlined on January 8, 1918, as had Germany and her associates; that they reasonably desired his presence to interpret and apply his conditions; that there was no other business of such transcending importance; that our soldiers had fought for ideas which he had sought to express; that they had accepted his views as the substance of their own thought; and that he owed it to them to see that there was no false interpretation of our ideals and purposes, and to omit nothing to see that they were realized.

"It is now my duty to play my full part in making good what they offered their lives to obtain. I can think of no call to service which could transcend this. . . .

"May I not hope, Gentlemen of the Congress, that in the delicate tasks I shall have to perform on the other side of the seas, in my efforts truly and faithfully to interpret the principles and purposes of the country we love, I may have the encouragement and the added strength of your united support? I realize the magnitude and difficulty of the duty I am undertaking; I am poignantly aware of its grave responsibilities. I am the servant of the nation. I can have no private thought or purpose of my own in performing such an errand. I go to give the best that is in me to the common settlements which I must now assist in arriving at in conference with the other working heads of the associated governments. I shall count upon your friendly countenance and encouragement. I shall not be inaccessible. The cables and the wireless will render me availabe for any counsel or service you may desire of me, and I shall be happy in the thought that I am constantly in touch with the weighty matters of domestic policy with which we shall have to deal. I shall make my absence as brief as possible and shall hope to return with the happy assurance that it has been possible to translate into action the great ideals for which America has striven."

When the President ended this appeal, many Re publicans and some Democrats sat and looked sullen and as stolid as wooden men. I wondered how, even though they disapproved the President's plan to go, they could have so little magnanimity and feeling. The partisan spirit which had been so much in evidence since March, 1918, and which had been so greatly stimulated during the Congressional campaign is much in evidence. It is menacing. I wondered if the President sensed it while he was speaking, and if it would pursue him to Europe. It is the obvious duty of every American to back him to the limit while he struggles in Paris against the violent and selfish forces of Europe. He has the future welfare of the world in his hands, if he is given loyal support at home. He has the people of the world, if not the leaders, with him, and he has no personal ends to serve. The people have caught his vision, and they are ready for great things if their leaders are equal to their responsibilities and do not fail them.

The President sailed for France December 5th, three days after his appearance before the Congress. His attitude as to his leaving this country was still one of reluctance, but, nevertheless, he went with high hopes and a great purpose. His main thought was to secure a just peace. He knew that this would be difficult. He was keenly aware of the fact that the pent-up passions of the peoples of many nations would be released and that, as a

Frenchman expressed it, "the tigers would be loose in Europe." He felt confident, however, that with the united backing of this nation, with the economic position which it had attained, which backing he had every right to expect, he could accomplish a great deal. He was all the more optimistic because the leading nations, including Germany, had already accepted the bases of peace which he had repeatedly outlined. In fact, his Fourteen Points had been accepted as the foundation of the Armistice.

He was bent on securing a just peace and, therefore, a reasonably permanent peace. He knew that no peace could be permanent which was not measurably just. He was not blind enough to believe that ideal justice could be attained at the time and, therefore, he was eager to see a league created and made a part of the Treaty which would aid in effecting readjustments after passion had cooled and a clearer sense of direction had been reached. In short, he had gradually come to the conclusion that a league of nations would be an essential part of any arrangement arrived at by the Peace Conference.

He, himself, had slowly arrived at a conclusion that it would be necessary for the United States to participate in an effective agency of this sort. This was evidenced first by his reluctance to identify himself with the League to Enforce Peace, which had been organized under the direction of distinguished American leaders, a number of whom were foremost in the ranks of the Republicans. He did finally accept an invitation to address the first assembly of the League to Enforce Peace, which was held in Washington, May 27, 1916. At this meeting, he dwelt on the fact that the nations of the world had become neighbours, that it was necessary that they should agree to coöperate in the common cause, and that they should act on the basis of even-handed and impartial justice. He emphasized three fundamental things: first, that every people has a right to choose the sovereignty under which it shall live; second, that small states should enjoy the same respect for their sovereignty and their territorial integrity that big nations insist upon; and third, that the world has a right to be free from every disturbance of its peace which has its origin in aggression and disregard of the rights of peoples and nations. He believed that he spoke the mind of America when he said that the United States was willing "to become a partner in any feasible association of nations formed in order to realize these objects and make them secure against violation"; or, as he again stated it, "an universal association of the nations to maintain the inviolate security of the highway of the seas for the common and unhindered use of all the nations of the world, and to prevent any war begun either contrary to treaty covenants or without warning and full submission of the causes to the opinion of the world—a virtual guarantee of territorial integrity and political independence."

There were present at this meeting such leaders as Lodge and ex-President Taft.

The President had a right to feel great confidence that his position, especially with reference to a league, would be endorsed by the leaders of the League to Enforce Peace, and by others, especially Republicans, who had been promoting this idea effectively for some time. He had a right to expect support particularly from the two men who afterward became his bitterest critics—Lodge and Roosevelt. In his Nobel Prize thesis, Roosevelt had said:

"The one permanent move for obtaining peace which has

[355]

yet been suggested with any reasonable chance of obtaining its object is by an agreement among the great powers, in which each should pledge itself, not only to abide by the decisions of a common tribunal, but to back with force the decision of that common tribunal. The great civilized nations of the world which do not possess force, actual or immediately potential, should combine by solemn agreement in a great world league for the peace of righteousness. . . . The nations should agree on certain rights that should not be questioned, such as territorial integrity, their right to deal with their domestic affairs, and with such matters as whom they should admit to citizenship. All such guarantee each of their number in possession of these rights."

Four years later, in his address on "International Peace" before the Nobel Prize Committee at Christiania, Norway, May 5, 1910, Roosevelt said that advance in the direction of world peace could be made along several lines: First, by treaties of arbitration; second, by further development of the Hague Tribunal; third, by checking the growth of armament; and—

"Finally, it would be a master stroke if those great powers honestly bent on peace would form a league of peace, not only to keep the peace among themselves, but to prevent, by force if necessary, it being broken by others. The supreme difficulty in connection with developing the peace work of The Hague arises from the lack of any executive power, of any police power, to enforce the decrees of the court. In any community of any size, the authority of the courts rests upon actual or potential force, on the existence of a police, or on the knowledge that the able-bodied men of the country are both ready and willing to see that the decrees of judicial and legislative bodies are put into effect.   In new and wild communities where there is violence, an honest man must protect himself, and, until other means of securing his safety are devised, it is both foolish and wicked to persuade him to surrender his arms while the men who are dangerous to the community retain theirs.   He should not renounce the right to protect himself by his own efforts until the community is so organized that it can effectively relieve the individual of the duty of putting down violence.   So it is with nations. Each nation must keep well prepared to defend itself until the establishment of some form of international police power, competent and willing to prevent violence as between nations.   As things are now, such power to command peace throughout the world could best be assured by some combination between those great nations which sincerely desire peace and have no thought themselves of committing aggressions.   The combination might at first be only to secure peace within certain definite limits and certain definite conditions; but the ruler or statesman who should bring about such a combination would have earned his place in history for all time and his title to the gratitude of all mankind."

On May 27, 1916, at the same dinner at which the President spoke, Lodge said this:

"I know, and no one, I think, can know better than one who has served long in the Senate, which is charged with an important share of the ratification and confirmation of all treaties; no one can, I think, feel more deeply than I do the difficulties which confront us in the work which this league—that is, the great association extending throughout the country, known as the League to Enforce

Peace—undertakes, but the difficulties cannot be overcome unless we try to overcome them. I believe much can be done. Probably, it will be impossible to stop all wars, but it certainly will be possible to stop some wars, and thus diminish their number. The way in which this problem must be worked out must be left to this league and to those who are giving this great subject the study which it deserves. I know the obstacles. I know how quickly we shall be met with the statement that this is a dangerous question which you are putting into your argument, that no nation can submit to the judgment of other nations, and we must be careful at the beginning not to attempt too much. I know the difficulties which arise when we speak of anything which seems to involve an alliance, but I do not believe that when Washington warned us against entangling alliances he meant for one moment that we should not join with the other civilized nations of the world if a method could be found to diminish war and encourage peace.

"It was a year ago, in delivering the chancellor's address at Union College, I made an argument on this theory, that if we were to promote international peace at the close of the present terrible war, if we were to restore international law as it must be restored, we must find some way in which the united forces of the nations could be put behind the cause of peace and law. I said then that my hearers might think that I was picturing a Utopia, but it is in the search of Utopias that great discoveries are made. Not failure, but low aim, is the crime. This league certainly has the highest of all aims for the benefits of humanity, and because the pathway is sown with difficulties is no reason that we should turn from it."

It is particularly interesting to note that Senator Lodge, adverting to Washington's warning against entangling alliances, expressed the belief that Washington did not for one moment intimate that we should not join "with the other civilized nations of the world if a method could be found to diminish war and encourage peace."

It may be worth while recalling that the President had repeatedly, both before the Senate and in other public ways, not only indicated the fundamental conditions of peace, but his belief that we should combine with other nations to maintain peace. And at no time was there uttered any warning by leaders on either side.

And yet, even before the President sailed, certain Republicans began to issue warnings and to utter threats. They recalled that the Republicans had won the Congressional elections of 1918, insisting that this was a vote of lack of confidence in the President, and that Europe should bear in mind that he could not properly speak for the people of the United States. On November 27th, Roosevelt made a statement which, of course, immediately found its way to the capitals of Europe. He said:

"Our allies and our enemies and Mr. Wilson himself should all understand that Mr. Wilson has no authority whatever to speak for the American people at this time. His leadership has just been emphatically repudiated by them. The newly elected Congress comes far nearer than Mr. Wilson to having a right to speak the purposes of the American people at this moment. Mr. Wilson and his Fourteen Points and his four supplementary points and his five complementary points and all his utterances every which way have ceased to have any shadow of right to be accepted as expressive of the will of the American people.

"He is President of the United States. He is a part of the treaty-making power; but he is only a part. If he acts in good faith to the American people, he will not claim on the other side of the water any representative capacity in himself to speak for the American people. He will say frankly that his personal leadership has been repudiated, and that he now has merely the divided official leadership which he shares with the Senate."

This was characteristic of Roosevelt. It was absurd in theory and it was highly objectionable coming from an American, and particularly from one who had been President of the United States. Only a man of Roosevelt's type, animated by bitter personal and political hatred, could have been guilty of such a grave error.

The President arrived at Paris on December 14th. Almost immediately, he became absorbed in the ceremonies incident to his reception, and from December 21st through January 6th he was visiting the principal nations with whom we were associated, and making addresses for which the situation imperatively called. It was singularly fortunate that for such purposes this country was represented by a man who not only knew history and government, but also the higher things in the civilizations of the countries he visited, and could touch with great skill and confidence upon a great variety of problems. In France, he spoke to the University of Paris, to the soldiers of the United States at Humes, and at a reception given by one of the French generals at Chaumont. In England, he spoke at Dover, at Buckingham Palace, to a committee of the National Church Council at London, to the League of Nations Union, at the American Embassy in London, at the Guild Hall, at the Mansion House, at a luncheon in

Manchester, and at the Free Trade Hall in Manchester. In Italy, he made three addresses in Rome on January 3d —at the Quirinal, at the Capitol, and to the Italian Parliament. On January 4th he spoke to the Academy of the Lencei and to the press representatives. On January 5th he spoke in Genoa and made five brief addresses at Milan, including an address to the League of Mothers and Widows, and the Municipalité. In Turin, on January 6th, he made three addresses, including addresses to the Municipalité and to the University of Turin. Returning to Paris, he again was called upon to make many addresses including the one at the opening of the Peace Conference on January 18th, one at the French Senate on January 20th, another at the Peace Conference on January 25th, one to the delegation of the working women of France the same day, one to the League for the Rights of Man on January 28th, one to the delegation from the French Society of Nations on February 12th, and another at the Peace Conference on February 14th. Throughout this entire period, of course, his thoughts were occupied with the immediate problem ahead of him, involving interminable conferences.

Perhaps the most dramatic, in a way, of his general addresses during this period was that at the Free Trade Hall, Manchester, on December 30th. Here, because of his knowledge of the economic forces that had operated here for liberalism in England, he felt particularly at home, and touched upon Manchester's leadership in very graceful terms. But the thing uppermost in his mind was the utterance just made by Clemenceau who, in a sense, had challenged him, by making a plea before the Chamber of Deputies in favour of maintaining the old doctrine of the

[361]

Balance of Power.   Mr. Wilson accepted the challenge in these words:

"You know that the United States has always felt from the very beginning of her history that she must keep herself separate from any kind of connection with European politics, and I want to say very frankly to you that she is not now interested in European politics.   But she is interested in the partnership of right between America and Europe.   If the future had nothing for us but a new attempt to keep the world at a right poise by a balance of power, the United States would take no interest, because she will join no combination of power which is not the combination of all of us.   She is not interested merely in the peace of Europe, but in the peace of the world.   Therefore, it seems to me that, in the settlement that is just ahead of us, something more delicate and difficult than was ever attempted before is to be accomplished, a genuine concert of mind and of purpose.   But while it is difficult, there is an element present that makes it easy.   Never before in the history of the world, I believe, has there been such a keen international consciousness as there is now.   Men all over the world know that they have been embarrassed by national antagonisms and that the interest of each is the interest of all, and that men as men are the objects of government and international arrangements.   There is a great voice of humanity abroad in the world just now which he who cannot hear is deaf.   There is a great compulsion of the common conscience now in existence which, if any statesman resist, he has gained the most unenviable eminence in history.   We are not obeying the mandates of parties or of politics.   We are obeying the mandates of humanity.   That is the reason why it seems to me that the things that are most often in our minds are the least significant. I am not hopeful that the individual items of the settlements which we are about to attempt will be altogether satisfactory. One has but to apply his mind to any one of the questions of boundary and of altered sovereignty and of racial aspiration, to do something more than conjecture that there is no man and no body of men who know just how it ought to be settled. Yet, if we are to make unsatisfactory settlements, we must see to it that they are rendered more and more satisfactory by the subsequent adjustments which are made possible.

"So that we must provide a machinery of readjustment in order that we may have a machinery of good-will and of friendship. Friendship must have a machinery."

Immediately after his return to Paris from Italy, the President entered actively into the work of formulation of the Treaty including the Covenant of the League of Nations. On January 25th, he was accorded the privilege and assumed the task of opening the discussion on the League. He said, in part:

"I consider it a distinguished privilege to be permitted to open the discussion in this conference on the League of Nations. We have asembled for two purposes, to make the present settlements which have been rendered necessary by this war, and also to secure the peace of the world, not only by the present settlements but by the arrangements we shall make at this conference for its maintenance. The League of Nations seems to me to be necessary for both of these purposes. There are many complicated questions connected with the present settlements which perhaps cannot be successfully worked out to an ultimate issue by the decisions we shall arrive at

[363]

here. I can easily conceive that many of these settlements will need subsequent reconsideration, that many of the decisions we make shall need subsequent alteration in some degree; for, if I may judge by my own study of some of these questions, they are not susceptible of confident judgments at present.

"It is, therefore, necessary that we should set up some machinery by which the work of this conference should be rendered complete. We have assembled here for the purpose of doing very much more than making the present settlements. We are assembled under very peculiar conditions of world opinion. I may say without straining the point that we are not representatives of governments, but representatives of peoples. It will not suffice to satisfy governmental circles anywhere. It is necessary that we should satisfy the opinion of mankind. The burdens of this war have fallen in an unusual degree upon the whole population of the countries involved. I do not need to draw for you the picture of how the burden has been thrown back from the front upon the older men, upon the women, upon the children, upon the homes of the civilized world, and how the real strain of the war has come where the eye of government could not reach, but where the heart of humanity beats. We are bidden by these people to make a peace which will make them secure. We are bidden by these people to see to it that this strain does not come upon them again, and I venture to say that it has been possible for them to bear this strain because they hoped that those who represented them could get together after this war and make such another sacrifice unnecessary.

"It is a solemn obligation on our part, therefore, to make

[364]

permanent arrangements that justice shall be rendered and peace maintained. This is the central object of our meeting. Settlements may be temporary, but the action of the nations in the interest of peace and justice must be permanent. We can set up permanent processes. We may not be able to set up permanent decisions. . . .

"In a sense, the United States is less interested in this subject than the other nations here assembled. With her great territory and her extensive sea borders, it is less likely that the United States should suffer from the attack of enemies than that many of the other nations here should suffer; and the ardour of the United States—for it is a very deep and genuine ardour—for the society of nations is not an ardour springing out of fear or apprehension, but an ardour springing out of the ideals which have come to consciousness in this war. In coming into this war, the United States never for a moment thought that she was intervening in the politics of Europe or the politics of Asia or the politics of any part of the world. Her thought was that all the world had now become conscious that there was a single cause which turned upon the issues of this war. That was the cause of justice and of liberty for men of every kind and place. Therefore, the United States should feel that its part in this war had been played in vain if there ensued upon it merely a body of European settlements. It would feel that it could not take part in guaranteeing those European settlements unless that guaranty involved the continuous superintendence of the peace of the world by the associated nations of the world.

"Therefore, it seems to me that we must concert our best judgment in order to make this League of Nations a vital thing—not merely a formal thing, not an occasional thing, not a thing sometimes called into life to meet an exigency, but always functioning in watchful attendance upon the interests of the nations—and that its continuity should be a vital continuity; that it should have functions that are continuing functions and that do not permit an intermission of its watchfulness and of its labour; that it should be the eye of the nations to keep watch upon the common interest, an eye that does not slumber, an eye that is everywhere watchful and attentive.

"And if we do not make it vital, what shall we do? We shall disappoint the expectations of the peoples. This is what their thought centres upon. . . . The fortunes of mankind are now in the hands of the plain people of the whole world. Satisfy them, and you have justified their confidence not only, but established peace. Fail to satisfy them, and no arrangement that you can make will either set up or steady the peace of the world.

"You can imagine, gentlemen, I dare say, the sentiments and the purpose with which representatives of the United States support this great project for a league of nations. We regard it as the keystone of the whole programme which expressed our purposes and ideals in this war and which the associated nations have accepted as the basis of the settlement. If we returned to the United States without having made every effort in our power to realize this programme, we should return to meet the merited scorn of our fellow citizens. For they are a body that constitutes a great democracy. They expect their leaders to speak their thoughts, and no private purpose of their own. They expect their representatives to be their servants. We have no choice but to obey their mandate. But it is with the greatest enthusiasm and pleasure that

[366]

we accept that mandate; and because this is the keystone of the whole fabric, we have pledged our every purpose to it, as we have to every item of the fabric. We would not dare abate a single part of the programme which constitutes our instruction. We would not dare compromise upon any matter as the champion of this thing—this peace of the world, this attitude of justice, this principle that we are the masters of no people but are here to see that every people in the world shall choose its own masters and govern its own destinies, not as we wish, but as it wishes. We are here to see, in short, that the very foundations of this war are swept away. . . .

"I hope, Mr. Chairman, that when it is known, as I feel confident it will be known, that we have adopted the principle of the League of Nations and mean to work out that principle in effective action, we shall, by that single thing, have lifted a great part of the load of anxiety from the hearts of men everywhere. We stand in a peculiar case. As I go about the streets here I see everywhere the American uniform. Those men came into the war after we had uttered our purposes. They came as crusaders, not merely to win a war, but to win a cause; and I am responsible to them, for it fell to me to formulate the purposes for which I asked them to fight, and I, like them, must be a crusader for these things, whatever it costs and whatever it may be necessary to do, in honour, to accomplish the object for which they fought. I have been glad to find from day to day that there is no question of our standing alone in this matter, for there are champions of this cause upon every hand. . . ."[2]

On February 14, 1919, at three o'clock in the afternoon, at the French Foreign Office, Quai d'Orsay, the President, in the name of the commission constituted by the Peace Conference, presented the report on a plan for the League of Nations unanimously adopted by the representatives of fourteen nations. This plan, of course, was the preliminary draft and was before the Conference for considerations. Immediately after the presentation of this report, the President left Paris for the United States, as he had originally planned, to be present during the closing days of the Congress in order to consider and sign or reject legislative matters which demanded his attention.

Immediately after the terms of the preliminary draft became known in this country, Senators began their attack on it. They did not wait for the negotiations to be concluded, which, under the Constitution so far as we were concerned, were in the hands of the President. They did not delay in order to get such explanations as the President might see fit to make. On February 19th, Senator Poindexter launched his attack. On the 22d, Senator Reed made an assault on it. Four days after the President landed in Boston, that is, on February 28th, Senator Lodge delivered a speech against the plan.

As soon as possible after his arrival in Washington, the President took steps to secure the views of such Republican leaders in private life as Mr. Root and Mr. Taft on the draft of the Covenant. And when he received their criticisms, he gave assurance that their proposed changes would be presented upon his return to Paris and would be adopted. He also took pains to ask for a conference with the Senate and House members of the committees on Foreign Relations. He laid the Covenant before them and asked for their criticisms. A number of the Republican senators, not including Lodge, who refused to state his objections, pointed out what they regarded as defects, including the omission of express recognition of the Monroe Doctrine, the failure to provide specifically that the League should not act on domestic matters, that there was no expressed statement of the right of a nation to withdraw, and that the right of Congress to determine peace and war was not sufficiently safeguarded. The President listened patiently to these expressions and gave assurance that their views would be met.

END OF VOLUME I